MANAGERIAL BEHAVIOR

MANAGERIAL BEHAVIOR

*Administration
in Complex
Organizations*

Leonard R. Sayles

Professor
Graduate School of Business
Columbia University

*McGraw-Hill
Book Company*

New York
San Francisco
Toronto
London

6789101112131415 VBVB 7543210698

Managerial Behavior

Library of Congress Catalog Card Number 63–22424

To Risha

Preface

This is a book about administrative skill and action. It concerns solely the directly managerial component of executive work: dealing with people. It is not concerned with policy making, with risk taking and entrepreneurship, with techniques for optimizing combinations of materials, people, and time (the proper subjects of managerial economics and of the new, so-called management sciences). Thus the coverage is from one limited point of view, but we would argue that it embraces the executive's most distinctly managerial task and the one most subject to misunderstanding on the one hand or trivial exposition on the other.

Our analysis is a result of several years' research in one division of a large American corporation that develops and manufactures technically sophisticated capital equipment. The generous cooperation of the management of this division enabled us to observe, interview, and feed back the research findings to approximately 75 lower- and middle-level managers. The field work was conducted by techniques of anthropological studies: The researcher endeavors by living within a culture for extended periods of time to comprehend significant relationships and attitudes—even those which may depart from his predispositions and expectations.

The field experience has been supplemented by two other types of data. We reviewed a good share of the literature that describes actual executive behavior, as distinct from normative reports which tell managers what they should do and attitudinal surveys which summarize feelings and expectations. In addition we presented our research findings to executives in the com-

pany studied and to groups of managers brought together
for extended training in executive development programs in the
United States, Canada, and Great Britain; their reactions, criticisms, and case examples have been incorporated in the text.

We make no pretense of having conducted a scientific experi-
ment, so we are not proposing scientific hypotheses backed by
systematically collected validating data. Rather, we have looked
and pondered for a long time and then developed a scheme of
analysis, by which we mean simply that minimum number of
concepts which would "explain" what was happening. Thus our
study goes beyond mere description. The objective is not just to
set forth what occurred at the executive level within a large
organization. Instead the study seeks to explain, and so make
it possible to predict, the recurring patterns or uniformities of
human behavior there.

Another way of understanding this is to recall that a basic
problem in all social science is to identify meaningful units of
measurement. Large-scale organizations and their patterns of
administration have not been subject to significant numbers of
empirical studies because rather little attention has been paid
to *what* should be looked at. For the most part very elusive and
ambiguous variables, such as "morale" and "perceived leadership style," have been selected. We have sought to develop a
series of concepts that relate more directly to the operation of
organizations *qua* organizations and that are observable and,
hopefully, measurable.

It has been gratifying to note the reactions of managers to
this scheme of analysis. Most felt that the model of administrative action not only was consistent with their experience but
also, more importantly, enabled them to comprehend the world
about them, the maze that had to be traversed in "playing the
organization." Some went so far as to say that for the first time
they knew what had been happening to them.

No one would assert that such responses validate the model,
but we would contend that our view of administration does
provide a way of organizing experience that can add to understanding the relationship between individual managerial jobs

and the organizational environment, of the relationship between structure and behavior. We should also argue that it is more operational than many of the concepts traditionally part of classical management and classical "human relations." These are often abstruse with no obvious or definable referent in human behavior.

If the limitations noted have made us unable to develop more than the rudiments of a theory of administration, it should be emphasized that the conclusions apply most fully to large organizations with a substantial division of labor at the executive level. The administrative patterns presented are for the most part those of middle managers—here defined as those with managerial subordinates who are not primarily concerned with the major policy decisions that direct the enterprise.

We hope at least to have stimulated more systematic inquiries into managerial behavior, a neglected, much maligned, and poorly understood area of human activity.

Although these few words cannot fulfill their objective, I should like to thank several contributors to this research and writing project. The Ford Foundation's Program in Economic Development and Administration gave me a most helpful faculty fellowship during the early conceptual stage of the work. The faculty research funds of the Graduate School of Business at Columbia provided summer assistance and some typing. A number of executives had faith enough in these activities to support field work. Further, many devoted countless hours to answering what must have seemed like endless questions and permitted themselves to be tracked and watched for weeks on end. My good friends, Professors Ivar Berg and William Whyte, of Columbia and Cornell, respectively, made a number of helpful suggestions concerning the manuscript; many of which, it must be admitted, I was not perceptive enough to incorporate in the final draft. Ross Webber, one of our doctoral candidates, allowed me the privilege of reanalyzing his excellent case materials that comprise Chapter 13.

Leonard R. Sayles

Contents

Contents

The Prospects for a
Science of Administration

What does a manager do? Ask a simple question and you get a simple answer. He manages. In this age of organization in which most of us spend some time in business, educational, philanthropic, or governmental organizations, it is assumed that their management is not only crucial but well understood. It is taken for granted, like the job description of a doctor; he helps the ill, and the manager manages. This confidence is bolstered by our rich heritage of books and courses on the art, science, technique, and *problems* of management.

Yet, once past simple definitions such as "a manager is someone who gets work done through other people," there is mounting evidence that the job of manager in any type of organization is not understood or is badly misunderstood. (And is the manager's job the same in a department store, an engineering laboratory, a hospital, and a government agency?) How does one manage? How do executives spend their time and why? Is administration art or science?

CHANGING CONCEPTS OF THE MANAGER'S JOB

As recognition of the importance of business in the contemporary world becomes widespread, there is increasing interest in the manager's job. In many ways, one can draw an analogy to the realm of politics. For obvious reasons, the scholar and the man of affairs were interested in political science, politics, and politicians long before the subject of business became respectable. Political institutions came of age many centuries before business. Until relatively recently, business was a second-class activity beneath the dignity of the university or the individual who could choose law, the military, medicine, or government as a field of study or practice. For the economist, the entrepreneur had status, but the manager rarely achieved comparable recognition.

Now that the role of business is both assured and recognized, its contribution to the dynamics of any economy, either developed or developing, is well documented; the importance of the management function is highlighted.[1] The manager is the most notable representative of the institution of business, as the politician is of the institution of government, and the one whose job is most worthy of attention.

Management as a Profession

Efforts to describe and analyze the manager's job suffer from the same difficulties encountered in dealing with the role of the politician. On the one hand, there is the desire to treat this activity like other professional positions involving study, a lengthy learning period, technical knowledge, and, hopefully, a code of ethics, such as medicine, the law, and engineering. Both the scholar of the field and the practitioner, for the sake of prestige, identification, and self-justification, want to consider management a *profession*—hardly an inappropriate objective. Yet there

[1] See Frederick Harbison and Charles Myers, *Management in the Industrial World*, McGraw-Hill Book Company, Inc., New York, 1959.

always lurks in the background the fact that knowledge is but one small part of the job. Just as the politician must know a good deal about the day-to-day functioning of governmental machinery and the composition of the electorate, communities, and regions he serves, the business manager must be informed on accounting procedures, marketing channels, supply sources, business law, etc. The real test of both, however, is the ability to operate effectively within and between organizations—to deal with people.

The Critics of Administration

The necessity of dealing with people reemphasizes the so-called personal-skill aspects of the managerial position, but the tendency is to treat these as a totally separate part of the job, distinct from its *professional* aspects. Skill, after all, implies intuition, sensitivity, a "feeling" for the situation, inborn traits, even an art—not professional training. Just as the political scientist admits that there is a big gap between "knowing" and "doing," between a knowledge of political theory and institutions and effective "politicking," so the student of business draws a sharp line between the more professional aspects of management and its "skill" aspects. It is easier to conceive of a profession in terms of knowledge than of human behavior.

This point of view was advanced by a new, highly respected analysis of the philosophy of the large corporation, according to which the demands of intraorganizational life are "frictions" that interrupt the main and important job of the executive.[2] What are regarded as the unpleasant necessities of dealing with people mean that the operational tasks, which presumably are the major assignment of an executive, must be delayed in favor of the less important pressures emanating from fellow workers. While the analogy may not be appropriate, one is reminded of the now defunct economic theory that distinguished between

[2] Richard Eells, *The Meaning of Modern Business,* Columbia University Press, New York, 1960, pp. 147–148.

goods and services. The former were tangible and valued highly; the latter were transitory and less worthy. In everyday experience, this point of view is mirrored in the comments of the engineer, physician, or attorney who refuses an administrative post that would require neglecting his "real work" for the "petty personality problems and politicking" of the managerial job.

In our time, Admiral Rickover has become a highly vocal and eminently vigorous spokesman for the thesis that administration is the bane of the existence of scientists, engineers, and professional soldiers. "Red tape," that traditional symbol of bureaucracy, and the foolish foibles of the noncreative office personnel with their penchant for forms, procedures, and planning, are a drag on the efforts of those who have a real job to do in preparing the defense of our country. He argues cogently that if, by some miracle, the administrators could be banished (or at least restrained from playing their feeble role), productivity and morale would jointly soar in the government.[3]

While Parkinson also utilized examples drawn from government service (but with the more deft and dispassionate touch of the academic who does not suffer directly), he clearly suggests that business is not immune to the "disease" that bears his name.[4] To Parkinson, administration is also largely unproductive gamesmanship much like that practiced in the poor English town in which the economy is maintained only because the citizenry take in one another's laundry. Administrators' major preoccupations are with making work for one another and creating full employment (not products or services), and presumably no one is the wiser—although someone must be the poorer.

Even the mass media have joined the attack. A rather sharp editorial in *Life Magazine* refers to "management featherbedding."[5] The staid *New York Times* was hardly more complimentary when it described a controversy over one of President Kennedy's senior appointees:

---

[3] See the many speeches by Admiral Rickover in the period 1959–1960.
[4] See C. Northcote Parkinson, *Parkinson's Law,* Houghton Mifflin Company, Boston, 1957.
[5] *Life Magazine,* June 13, 1960, p. 41.

Some [of the supporters] of Chester Bowles said today that he had not been permitted to do the job he was hired for. When he was appointed Under Secretary, they said, he was supposed to be one of the principal makers of policy and an "idea man" for the department, *not an administrative hack*.[6]

Finally, the statisticians have endeavored to prove that the wartime innovations in mathematical statistics now encapsulated in the magical phrase "operations research" represent the true science of management. By conceiving of a "theory of the case," building a model, and solving the equations, the executive can solve all, or nearly all, his management problems. Mathematics, the open sesame to cost functions, production schedules, and warehouse locations, will eliminate the "haggling"; executives (or better yet, computers) will solve equations and no longer have to concern themselves with the inconstancy of the human element, or so it might appear.[7] Technical knowledge and decision making will be the supreme tests of managerial talent, since managerial activity is largely or most importantly intellectual: analysis, planning, decision making.

The Status of Administrative Work

In a sense, the administrative-skill part of the manager's job has now come full circle. It seems only yesterday that managers were berated for failing to emphasize the human-relations-skill component of their job. This was considered the *managerial* aspect of their work, to be distinguished from its technical components (which were really the province of the engineer or the accountant). What has happened to the status of administrative work as such? How did management return to emphasizing the non-human dimensions of the job?

The community places a high value on managerial activities, in terms of both salary and recognition. Executives are not only among the highest paid members of American society; they are

6 *The New York Times,* July 18, 1961, p. 10. (Italics are the author's.)
7 See Harold Leavitt and Thomas Whisler, "Management in the 1980's," *Harvard Business Review,* November-December, 1958, pp. 41–48.

highly regarded and respected, if the status-ranking surveys are to be believed. Our point is that the uniquely *managerial* element of the executive's job, namely, administrative activities themselves, has lost prestige in recent years. There is a trend to downgrade or exclude them, perhaps because they interfere with the professionalization of management.

One reason has already been noted. The dealing-with-people aspect of the managerial job appears to represent functions that are not as clear cut and definable as the manager's technical functions. It involves consideration of the "softer" fields of knowledge (the social sciences) as distinct from the more self-assured and reliable natural sciences and their derivations, e.g., mechanical engineering, industrial engineering, the mathematics of finance, etc.

Secondly, there have been a number of noteworthy failures in the efforts to define the skill aspect of the manager's job.

CONFLICTING DEFINITIONS OF THE MANAGER'S JOB

At least one contributing cause for the denigration of administration is the pendulumlike swings in the concepts of management itself. As we shall see, some of the variation can be explained by changes in the nature of organizations and technology.

Management as a Paternal, Moral Problem

In an age when technology was simple and most organizations relatively small, the manager was envisioned as occupying a position analogous to a father. Employees were dependent children. They had to be watched, and when deviant behavior was observed, they had to be punished. In turn, the manager—at least the good manager—had responsibilities for his charges. This was, in general, a period in which trade unions and governments were not involved or were only minimally effective in protecting and furthering the interests of employees. The burden of responsibility (and the opportunity for irresponsibility) was entirely in the hands of the manager.

The imposing status distinction between the manager and the managed reinforced this paternalistic relationship. The workers, who filled relatively simple jobs (for which watching, punishing, and rewarding were the requisite managerial actions), were drawn from the lower social classes in the community. They were considered unskilled, easily replaceable, and thus expendable. In contrast, the managers came from higher social classes.[8]

During this period workers were gaining some of the same rights that managers had won in an earlier mercantile era. Now it was the employees' turn to demand protection from arbitrary interference with some of their "rights" of decision making, not by government or kings but by authoritarian managers.

Given this structure of jobs and extreme status distinctions, it is not difficult to understand the types of management "problems" that arose:

1. Legally and morally, how can a manager justify absolute authority over his employees? What are the sources by which managerial authority can be legitimatized? (Some of the possible answers or rationalizations were these: The manager has a fiduciary responsibility to the owners or has unique knowledge and contributes unique benefits to the community, or, historically, there has always been such a division between the leader and the led, the skilled and the unskilled.)

2. By what methods can the imbalance in power between management and employees be rectified? (Answers were and still are given in terms of government action, trade unions, employee representation plans, etc.)

3. What is the meaning of the employment contract, i.e., how much loyalty, how much effort, how much of himself does the employee "owe" to the manager and what benefits and protection can the employee expect and demand in return? (In a sense, this is a type of "social contract" issue.)

8 See Harbison and Myers, *op. cit.*, p. 125. See also George Strauss and Leonard R. Sayles, *Personnel: The Human Problems of Management*, Prentice-Hall, Inc., Englewood Cliffs, N.J., 1960, pp. 723–724. Overseas, this definition of the managerial position persists.

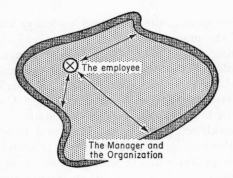

Stage 1 in the Development of Administration
The manager's job: relating the individual to the organization

4. Which is more effective as an administrative "tool," rewards (e.g., incentives) or punishments; what is the impact of paternalism on employee motivation and tenure?

All these questions involve the *overall* relationship of the individual to the organization. The manager personified the organization, and there was no differentiation among types of employees and types of positions.

This, then, was the first period in the evolution of systematic interest in managerial problems. The sociologist would say that the focus of interest was on the hierarchy. This meant a concern with the private (as distinct from governmental) power that men would wield over other men by virtue of their economic status within an organization. These were interests in the nature of private authority and the relationship of the individual to the organization upon which he was dependent for a livelihood. All represented imposing philosophic and legal questions because they were concerned with the root of a private-enterprise economy where individuals were dependent upon finding and maintaining a job—*working for others*—for their standard of living. There was a modest beginning of contemporary management "interests" insofar as the differential impact of rewards, threats of punishments, and paternalism was debated.

Such global, philosophic issues were challenging, and surely important, *but* they were essentially not researchable. They did not really involve the manager as an operating figure in the organization. Aspects of these questions are still debated, as well they should be. Many of our present concerns in the personnel administration field are related to these questions.

Management as a Training, Conditioning, Learning Problem

Scientific management grew along with an improvement in factory technology. It meant new and more complex tools for the employee and a growing differentiation in jobs at both the manual and the managerial level. This was the period of specialization, of rational division of labor, and also of more complex wage-payment plans calculated to motivate increased effort.

Now the managerial challenge was conceived in terms of training (teaching and grading). Jobs were analyzed meticulously to find the right combination of inanimate tools and animate motions. The manager taught the routines; constant repetition with sound training methods and under good learning conditions produced habitual, conditioned responses. These could be further reinforced by carefully designed payment-by-result plans, the "grading" or scoring element.

This was the high-water mark of *learning theory* as the foundation for managerial action, although it was rarely put in those words. Even the sociologists, with their Weberian concept of bureaucracy, emphasized learning and teaching. To Weber and his disciples, the dynamic of the modern rational organization (they called it bureaucracy) that distinguished it from earlier familial and monarchical institutions was just this teaching, learning, and grading. The manager selected people, not on the basis of ancestry, personal loyalty, or other "irrational" characteristics but on this potential to *learn* particular jobs. These jobs, in turn, could be arranged in ascending order of difficulty (always good classroom technique). Employees were retained and advanced on the basis of their ability to learn to perform the job according to prescribed patterns. Those who "passed the course" were assured of tenure. Thus Weber and the sociologists foresaw the application of scientific management "principles" to professional, technical, clerical, and even managerial positions, just as Taylor and his disciples dealt with manual employees. For both, the manager's task was easy to define:

1. Analyze the work to be performed.
2. Develop from this a series of job descriptions incorporating an appropriate degree of specialization so that the requisite tools could be provided and employees with adequate abilities could be recruited and trained for the positions.[9]
3. Appraise the performance of employees, their ability to follow the content and motions of the job descriptions and the rules of the organization. Those who succeeded should be given increased remuneration, responsibility, and assurance of tenure.

For this reason, we have said that the manager was conceived in pedagogical terms. He was primarily concerned with relating the individual employee to a well-defined course of study (the job or task or position). With training and conditioning (the right rewards at the right time), the human relations problems of the organization could be solved. These efforts fitted well the complementary trend toward more individually operated machines, more careful layout, materials handling, and the growth of management specialists in engineering, quality control, marketing, etc.

There is another theory implicit in this view of the manager's job. Taylor and his associates leaned heavily on the physiological structure of the individual employee: his muscular system and coordinating neural mechanism, the limbs and torso and their normal patterns of movement. Later critics of scientific management were often unfair in labeling Taylor's methods mechanical

[9] Significantly, they failed to evolve comparably rational methods for determining an appropriate division of labor and how finely specialized the work should be. Thus, even within the organizational system as they defined it, there was a fatal flaw.

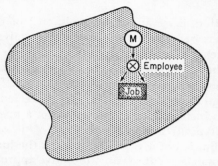

Stage 2 in the Development of Administration
The manager's job: training the individual and evaluating job performance

and nonhuman. Several in this scientific management movement endeavored to build their techniques on a solid base of
physiological knowledge, in some ways perhaps more scientifically
founded than many of the quasi-scientific pronouncements (scien-
tisms) of those who professed a knowledge of the fundamentals
of leadership and motivation. Here, however, we are getting
ahead of our story.

Management as Applied Psychology

In more recent times scientific management has spawned its
highly vocal detractors. The critics argued with vehemence and
conviction that the administrator was being misled into thinking
his job was simple or capable of being rationalized; that, actually,
the manager is not dealing with students eager to learn (the
protagonists of human relations would have substituted the
word "machine" for student). The employee is often not so
malleable nor is he so passive as scientific management assumed.
Rather, managers must cope with feeling, reacting, hating, and
loving human beings whose responses are frequently irrational.
While logically they should produce more if work is made easier

(by simplification, more automatic tools, etc.) or their incentive to work is increased (by more assurances of advancement and greater income), realistically, they frequently do the opposite. Even worse, they form informal groups or unions committed to frustrating the manager and restricting output. Thus, while a machine may go faster if the load on it is decreased or the energy going into it is increased, an employee is not a machine, and the manager should not treat him as one.

This is the burden of a vast literature on the human relations movement in management. As an alternative approach, the application of clinical and social psychology was proposed. The manager's job was to find ways of motivating individuals and groups. From the same environment dealt with by the proponents of scientific management, very different conclusions were drawn. In all fairness, however, there had been changes in the community. Not only had unions become more successful, but employees were better educated and more demanding. Persisting labor shortages of the war and postwar period may have made labor less manipulatable and less amenable to "rationalistic" approaches. These, then, were some of the new challenges to the manager:

1. Find better means of communicating with employees, since emotional elements and previous experience tend to distort what the subordinate hears his boss saying.
2. Find ways of appraising the emotional state of the employee, since tensions, predispositions, and irrational fears interfere with effective work. (Counseling and interviewing are frequently the therapeutic techniques specified.)
3. Use the social group to motivate the employee by channeling its energies into constructive rather than destructive projects.

The manager became an inspirational leader, a therapist, a confidant, a builder of a more healthy psychological environment. All this occurred as the enormous impact of Freudianism and psychology in general spilled over into industry in the 1940s and 1950s.

The applied psychologists have tried to rebut almost all the

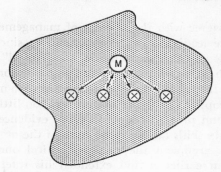

Stage 3 in the Development of Administration
The manager's job: motivating employees and the group

tenets of what they regard as the outmoded "classical" theory of management (theory X to McGregor).[10] They tended to play down the job or standards of performance. Douglas McGregor has even argued that the manager should not always receive direct information on the performance of subordinates.[11] According to him, it is more important that the subordinates learn (with the help of a responsive coach) to take responsibility for setting their own goals and assessing their own progress toward these objectives. Through a process of interlocked meetings and guidance sessions, subordinates should be encouraged to establish objectives for themselves and to ask for whatever help they need in meeting these "targets." By providing a climate conducive to "self-actualization" and by avoiding or limiting the use of authority or any emphasis on dependency, the manager would make it possible for the subordinate to achieve a high level of motivation, enthusiasm, and loyalty.

This point of view has come under increasing attack. In a sense,

[10] The most cogent statement of this position is found in Douglas McGregor, *The Human Side of Enterprise,* McGraw-Hill Book Company, Inc., New York, 1960.
[11] *Ibid.*

those who disagree with the concept of management as applied psychology are leading a counterreformation, since their target was, in its day, an effort to undo the "mechanical" or "engineering" approach to administration and organization. Those who would reverse the trend believe there has been too much emphasis on helping people to grow and mature and too little attention to productivity and profits. They ask, What evidence is there that these leadership skills facilitate the goals of the organization? To this economic argument they add an ethical one: Just as the manager in an earlier period extended his interest to aspects of the employee's life that were outside the working relationship, so too the manager as applied psychologist is unduly concerned with the "inner life" and the psyche—areas deserving even more privacy than leisure-time pursuits and questions of loyalty.

The result of this disillusionment with human relations has been a resurgence of emphasis on nonadministrative functions for the executive: those which, superficially at least, appear more compatible with the concept of the professional and a fixed body of knowledge as distinct from behavioral skills. For example, the present emphasis on operations research as *the* science of management suggests this conclusion, as does the ready response given to the association of administration (we would say "managerial activity") with "red tape," self-perpetuation, waste, and unproductiveness.

A CHOICE OF ROADS AND ROLES

What, then, is the manager's job; what is the nature of administration? These questions must be answered before we can effectively design managerial training programs or evaluate the work of the manager.

Historically, there is a diversity of answers. The manager is like a father or a political leader, and good administration is justice and the right proportion of reward and punishment. Alternatively, the manager is a teacher who uses conditioning and clear instruction and grading to get the job done. More recently, the manager has been conceived as a therapist-counselor who manipulates the group and the psychological environment for the individual. Each of these roles projects a very different picture of what the manager does with his time and energies.

Confounding the choice is the rising chorus of critics who cry "a plague on all your houses." They would have the manager return to an earlier role of overseer-pacesetter, at least at the lower levels of the administrative hierarchy.

There is also, as indicated earlier, the new scientific management school which would banish most supervisory action from the repertoire of the manager, at least at higher management levels. They envision the manager as a technical decision maker, assuming that the organization *qua* organization will take care of itself. Managers become adjuncts to computers and behave much like the economists' earlier view of the entrepreneur who appraised the risk element (today we speak of probability or degrees of uncertainty) and then optimized the quantities of labor, land, and capital he combined.

We argue that none of these "schools" provides a realistic basis for a science of administration. It will be our task in the succeeding chapters to establish some basis for such a study and some of the directions it can take. In the process, we hope to give back to administration, as the core of managerial activity, some of the status it has lost in these belittlements and controversies.

We have examined the multiple sources of confusion over the nature and value of administration (or management) as a profession, occupation, or skill. Our objective, however, is not to explain the lack of status or the misunderstanding concerning managerial action, if indeed these evaluations are correct. Rather, it is our endeavor to provide an analytical framework and more operational concepts to describe administration or management as an organization process.

The statement is often made that management is an applied subject; that just as engineering draws upon theories in physics and chemistry, management draws on theories from economics, psychology, and sociology. Unfortunately, the analogy is not a good one. Although the manager can learn something about dealing with individuals and groups from these "mother" disciplines, they do not provide a completely acceptable theory of the nature and functioning of organizations. Until there is such a theory, there can be no conceptual basis for describing administrative actions.

The New Challenges to Management

The thoughtful reader may ask appropriately if it makes any difference if management is correctly perceived. If, the argument might go, in order to appear professional, management stresses its own technical knowledge and its critics berate "red tape," "conformity," "office politics," and all the other supposed concomitants and products of administrative behavior, what does it matter? Good managers, whether the definitions and the critics are right or not, will continue to be good managers, and poor managers do not deserve a better fate.

Unfortunately, the real work of a manager is not this simple nor justice this assured. Large organizations, schools of administration, and governments are paying a high price for their inability to *measure managerial behavior*. Vast sums are expended on consultants and selection and training programs when there is no generally acceptable way to assess whether or not managerial performance has been improved. Promotion and salary progression systems (based on merit rather than seniority or nepotism) and a vast testing program all resemble a huge inverted pyramid that is constantly becoming larger. The narrow apex on which it all rests—the assessment of managerial performance—has not enlarged. These programs are all precariously balanced on an exceedingly fine point: highly subjective and universally suspect personnel assessment techniques.[12]

[12] The literature on the fads and foibles associated with "merit rating," "performance appraisal," and the related arts is a vast one. There is widespread conviction that at best these devices can stimulate individuals to try to improve themselves, and at worst they are subject to every human whim, caprice, and prejudice. They are not objective measures of performance.

Most companies hope that the very bad manager will obviously "look" bad and the very good one will not be missed either. Logically, the odds are in that direction, but, after spending time in large organizations, one wonders whether the guilty and the innocent are judged correctly in a high enough proportion of cases to warrant such optimism.

There is ample reason to seek both a theory of management and a method of implementing it that will provide generally acceptable measures of managerial performance. These are the touchstone of improvements in the distribution and use of managerial resources, just as certain engineering and statistical techniques and theories have been the source of technical advances in the large-scale organization.

There are several other reasons, if more are needed, to justify increased exploration of management science. American business and American educational institutions claim an expertise— expert knowledge and skill—worthy of export. In the world race for economic growth and for the allegiance and stability of lesser-developed sectors of the globe, United States management "know-how" is a crucial factor. Because our institutional scale and technical ingenuity have been so enormous, no one has questioned whether our managerial skills are really exportable.

The most important justification for administration research is the need of the manager himself. At present, managers are confused: Are they being "too soft" or smothering individualism by being too authoritarian? They are uneasy about the hodge-podge status of the dealing-with-people component of their job and wonder if it is really worth doing, particularly when so many technical and strategic problems pose more tangible challenges. If they are technically trained themselves, they resent the platitudinous, frequently patronizing content of much managerial training, and they seek more systematic knowledge based on disciplined, quantitative methods rather than on elusive psychological concepts. Most of all, they want the job satisfaction that professionals expect: that of dealing with interesting problems, using tools they have been trained to use that will have predictable consequences in a comprehensible environment. This has been expressed by Professor Simon:

> The pleasure that the good professional experiences in his work is not simply a pleasure in handling difficult assignments; it is a pleasure in using skillfully a well-stocked kit of well-designed tools to handle problems that are comprehensible in their deep structure but unfamiliar in their detail.[13]

Also there is need for a *language* to describe administration and organization and to discuss its problems. The manager is handicapped when he must rely on a language or concepts developed to make comprehensible the direction of foot soldiers and primitive workshops.

The problem is posed by one relatively new manager:

> I am running into all sorts of difficult administrative problems on this job, but other than saying that I have problems, I find it difficult to talk to my boss about them. I don't know what words to use to describe my situation. Sure, if we spent ten hours talking, I think I could communicate some of the difficulties, but I want something more precise to diagnose what is going on, something like the terms we have for discussing technical work.

It would be paradoxical indeed if the modern organization that thrives on accumulations of knowledge could not find some way of providing a terminology for this field.

There is still another reason for seeking a valid science of management. Although the computer's role in substituting for managerial skill has been emphasized, there is good evidence that the administrative aspects of executive jobs are becoming more difficult. This is the result of what anthropologists have observed in many cultures. As technology becomes more complicated, the problems of coordinating the various parts of any process multiply rapidly. In other words, as the division of labor progresses,

[13] Herbert Simon, *The New Science of Management Decision,* Harper & Row, Publishers, Incorporated, New York, 1960, p. 40.

more and more managerial inputs are required to provide the coordination between the increasing number of steps or stages. Many of the newest developments of industrial science make this trend even more pronounced. For example, the evolution of solid-state components in the electronic industry—the miniature building blocks that contain analogies of resistors, transistors, and the like—decreases the tolerance than can be permitted between any two parts of the electronic equipment. No tampering or modifications can take place since these components are "frozen." This reduced "leeway" or "play" is evident in most modern technology; it is, in fact, the primary characteristic of completely automated processes. Similarly, communications between interdependent groups must be that much more effective. We shall return to this problem in the next chapter, as we look more closely at the interrelationship between technology and the manager's job.

CONCLUSION

A useful theory of administration, then, must have the following characteristics:

1. It must be consistent with a realistic view of the nature of organization processes; hopefully, in fact, it will be derived from them.
2. It will enable the organization to describe explicitly the managerial behavior required at any given position in the structure, and that behavior will be a function of the position.
3. It will describe managerial behavior in a language that provides sufficient objectivity to be useful in training, counseling, and appraising the performance of administrators on the job.
4. Its concepts must enable us to distinguish between the effect of the manager's personality and the situational constraints on the supervisory processes being evaluated.
5. Our theory should not only enable us to relate managerial "motions" to specific technological requirements of the work situation but also to predict the impact of broader cultural factors on the

type of supervisory practices that will be successful in a given situation.

To develop such a framework for administrative skills, we must ask whether the organizational context within which the manager operates has been correctly assayed by those who have been prescribing principles of good management.

The Modern Organization

Much of the confusion and controversy over what is good management has its source in the failure to comprehend the relationship between what the manager should do and the nature of organizational processes. In the previous chapter, we have endeavored to show how various prescriptions for the supervisor were a product of certain assumptions about what the organization itself was like. Thus, all the philosophies, schools of thought, and methods of "good" management described share a common and fatal flaw. None of them reflects any development over the years in the concept of managerial behavior or administrative activity. Contemporary organizations are enormously different from the almost primitive workshops produced by the first industrial revolution. By "different" we mean something more than their obviously larger concentrations of increasingly complex equipment and trained personnel.

THE SECOND INDUSTRIAL REVOLUTION AND THE ROLE OF THE MANAGER

Associated with the first industrial revolution was the growth of large factories, equipped with power-operated machinery. While there were exceptions, most employees, as individuals or in small groups, tended machinery, and their productivity was a function of how hard and fast they worked and whether the equipment kept operating.

While we often associate with the second industrial revolution engineering developments such as automation, it had its beginning before the days of servomechanisms and computers. It was heralded by the recognition that work (or productivity) is a function of *systems,* of integrated equipment operation as well as integrated employee coordination. The major difference from the first industrial revolution is the emphasis on closely timed coordination of work processes in space, as distinct from discrete jobs. The critical elements that the manager must maximize are the continuity, regularity, and periodicity of the process, *not* individual employee bursts of speed and energy expenditure.

The second industrial revolution is really the awareness that the organization is not just a human replica of a factory building, containing a number of individual workmen and their overseers or therapist-leaders. The organization is networks or patterns of sequential work operations that serve to link production stages, staff and line personnel, and hourly workers. Work and systems are synonymous. The individual's contribution has no value except insofar as it is made at the right time and place in a sequence. In order to function, the organization must arrange for that contribution to occur at the right time and place.

Scientific management, as we have noted, contributed a great deal to the design of equipment and the related physical movements of workers. However, in some of its applications, particularly at the managerial level, it impeded constructive use of human resources. We refer to the emphasis on compartmentalized function. The exciting new computer technology is breaking down the barriers between these arbitrary divisions and functional specializations. In department stores, the activities of the sales person can be linked to accounting, billing, stock room, warehouse, buying, and advertising. In the factory, many formerly independent work operations are tied together by continuous-processing equipment, where individual steps, functions, or batches lose their identity.

But there is no need to cite the newest technology. In any organization in which there is a division of labor, there is a process by which material, ideas, people, or papers come in, have something done to them in one or many interlinked stages, and then pass out the door to a customer. A flow or work system is created wherever there is a sequence of operations performed in a regular or predetermined order by separate individuals.[1]

Thus far, we have concentrated on the work of the organization as a flow process. The same is true of the jobs supervised by the manager. While supervisory manuals often assume that these are purely individual tasks involving some kind of *man-machine* or *man-paper* relationship, the actual pattern of job performance turns out to be very different.

Many jobs that were once assumed to be man-machine or man-paper in structure are actually much more complicated, and the supervisor who believes that he is in charge of a group of relatively independent workmen is in for a rude awakening. This was evident even in the now dated Western Electric Studies.[2] It would have done the manager little good to concentrate on individual performance; he should have been concerned with the overall pattern of coordination among wiremen, soldermen, and inspectors.

Managerial jobs are expected to involve the ability to conduct relationships with other people. But, interestingly, little attention has been paid to how to manage managers; it would appear that the challenge and problem of administration stop at the first level up from the "bottom" of the organization. Recently, as the relative proportions of jobs in the total labor market have changed and more technical and professional positions have been created, there has been a spurt of interest in the supervisory problems posed by these employees. Usually such employees are viewed as unique because of their educational backgrounds and high skill. Actually, their work patterns are becoming the norm

---

[1] See Eliot D. Chapple and Leonard R. Sayles, *The Measure of Management*, The Macmillan Company, New York, 1961, pp. 18–45.

[2] F. J. Roethlisberger and William J. Dickson, *Management and the Worker*, Harvard University Press, Cambridge, Mass., 1939.

in contemporary organizations.[3] This norm consists of complex interaction patterns extending to many points inside and even outside the organization.

It would be paradoxical indeed if the activities of the manager did not reflect this second-industrial-revolution concept of flow and system. Weber, like Taylor and the countless experts on industrial management and administration that followed, all tended to minimize this challenge of administration. To them, management consisted of placing the right man in the right job and making sure he did what he was supposed to do. Close observation, training, and well thought-through rules would take care of any coordination problems.

But when we look at contemporary organizations, we see that the major task of the supervisor is to coordinate, to integrate, to maintain sequential patterns in the work flow. When we get inside the office or factory building and behind the organization chart, we find that this is crucial to the success or failure of the business.

This, then, is the reality of the contemporary organization, as a greater division of labor has been introduced and technology has worked its transformations. But when we look at management theory, what do we find?

The Traditional View of the Manager

The "experts" in scientific management and administration, for the most part, still consider an organization and a manager in highly abstract, static terms. In their theories and prescriptions, the manager has a nicely bounded, compartmentalized job. He is given ("delegated") authority commensurate with this responsibility and a group of subordinates presumably able to help him to do the work assigned to him. They, like him, can be evaluated simply in terms of whether or not they complete the assigned work—how effectively they combine resources to achieve the

[3] For example, in a study of professionals in organizations, it was found that the satisfactions desired by subordinates were *not* controlled by their superiors. W. G. Bennis et al, "Authority, Power and the Ability to Influence," *Human Relations*, vol. 11, pp. 143–155, 1958.

maximization of a service, a product, or some combination of human satisfaction and economic goods.

In this view of the manager's job, he directs, persuades (motivates?), or cajoles those who are responsible to him to do his bidding. The manager receives instructions from his superior and passes them on, making sure that people do *what they know they are supposed to do and are responsible for doing*. The only possible flaw in the system is illegal action on the part of the subordinate (he ignores or distorts an instruction)—grounds for disciplinary action in the old school and psychosocial motivation in the new—or a communication breakdown occurs (an instruction is lost, misunderstood, or arrives too late). If the manager or his subordinate succeeds, he receives credit in terms of approval or promotion or increased income; at least, he avoids disapprobation. The hallmarks of this view of the organization are discrete entities. Each person has a *job*, with a clear beginning and end, to do and for which he is responsible (and by which he can be measured). The individual makes discrete decisions within the confines of his delegated authority.

On the surface, the process of rationalization that endeavored to apply scientific methods to human affairs (as well as to physical phenomena) has proceeded at an increasing pace. Not only can production work be segmented "rationally" so that workers can be trained in a matter of minutes or hours to perform preset motions, but the interrelationships of machines and even of engineering drawings to machines can be programmed so that ideas or plans can be converted "automatically" into action and finished products, with little human intervention or decision making. Further, there is an increasing number of new management skills, e.g., operations research and PERT, that imply a constriction of human ingenuity in favor of tight control: programmed decision making. Finally, the organization itself, with its increasing size, levels, and mushrooming standard operating procedures, suggests not only a structural pyramid but a social mechanism like that which built the original pyramids: a small number of influential planner–decision makers and a much larger number following rigid orders.

One of the most serious problems stemming from the traditional view of organizational behavior is the use of *end-result* measures to appraise performance. There is a totting up of wins and losses as if the individual were responsible for everything that happened on his job, and there is a concomitant failure to observe and evaluate how the game was played.

> . . . it is not correct to describe a research department manager as responsible for his firm's new products, a sales manager for the sales figures, . . . , a safety officer for the prevention of accidents. . . . Each of the employees contributes by his work to the outcome mentioned. But he cannot by himself be said to be responsible for that outcome.[4]

While there are a few haphazard efforts to appraise the behavior of the subordinate as distinct from the final result, many managers still rely on other, often costly methods of control.

Current management texts and by-products such as organization charts (with their neat pyramidal structures) and terms such as "delegation" and "staff" tend to encourage the mechanistic view, which merely confuses the façade with the reality.

REALITY: THE ORGANIZATION AS A SYSTEM

Actually, successful managers in a modern organization carry on a job process very different from the one described in the preceding section. However, they often have only vague concepts of this process themselves and find it very difficult to describe it to others, especially to their subordinates.

Simultaneous equations are a more appropriate analog for the organization process than the simple stimulus-response assumptions of the previously described legal model. The latter, like the classical economists, envisions the manager selecting the quantity of each variable that he will utilize to maximize profitability or success. In reality, the actions of each manager affect all the groups around him, and they must make adjustments before

[4] Elliot Jaques, *Equitable Payment,* John Wiley & Sons, Inc., New York, 1961, p. 61.

he can shift his own efforts. As one or another group makes what are, for him, less than optimal moves, our manager must make compensating moves. These, in their turn, affect still other groups, and so our peripatetic manager must go around the circuit again, securing new agreements, commitments, and assurances from those he had committed to something else only shortly before.

The manager who does not recognize this iterative pattern can anticipate failure. He does not comprehend the modern organization but, instead, sees things in "blacks" and "whites"; he expects to have available all the resources he needs, when he needs them, to do what he has to do (i.e., the "authority"), and he expects others, upon whom he depends, to do their work so as to effectuate his activity. In reality, solving problems in a modern organization is a matter of flows, of processes. Decisions are the product of actions through time on the part of many people. People are not responsible for compartmentalized specific functions or actions but for participating in and influencing a series of relationships.

The individual manager does not have a clearly bounded job with neatly defined authorities and responsibilities. Rather, he is placed in the middle of a system of relationships, out of which he must fashion an organization that will accomplish his objectives. There is no "standard" interface; rather, the relationships differ, depending on the objectives and the position of the other groups with whom he must achieve a working pattern of give and take.

Good managers instinctively know this. We have been impressed in field work by the degree to which the managers who have been "successful"—meaning rapid promotions and a reputation for being dynamic, forceful accomplishers—were able to move from the usual shibboleths about their jobs to a dynamic concept. Unfortunately, they lacked a language to facilitate their own self-understanding, and they apparently had even greater difficulty communicating it to others, say to subordinates. There was no means to accumulate knowledge and build on the successes and failures of the past.

Thus, decision making is not a discrete event; rather it is a *continuous* and *intricate process* of brokerage, as one observer has called it. As changes take place in the group and in other groups and even outside the organization, there are generated pressures that call for responses. The responses are compromises and marginal adjustments in decisions that reflect the very different and ever-changing interests and points of view of the parties to the decision. This will be enlarged upon in Chapter 12.

We have been trying to present a systems concept of the manager's job that stresses interrelationships as distinct from discrete responsibilities and individual choices. One notably self-assured and successful manager described this process well:

> My people get directed [told what they should be doing] on the basis of pressures: pressures from people doing work for them and for whom they are working and from whom they must get certain approvals. These pressures determine the priorities in their jobs; they direct their attention—they even force their attention. You see, we live on the basis of communication, a man's ability to keep in touch with all the parts of the organization that can affect him.

In the past, management and organization theory has had to struggle with the exceptions to the rule that the manager had authority equal to his responsibility. Thus the staff expert or specialist, through various scholastic devices, has been incorporated into the job of manager. "Dotted lines" and special distinctions between functional and nonfunctional authorities had to be invented—cumbersome distinctions at best. Similarly, the union and collective bargaining relationships were brought in via the back door. These, too, were special exceptions to the rules about what a manager does and how he does it. One happy result was the creation of a special subfield of management: industrial relations.

The change in the supervisor's activities was in part anticipated by the innovations introduced when unions become more potent within the plant. With the growth of unions, supervisors learned new patterns of coordination that bore little resemblance to the orthodox boss-subordinate pattern of human relations. Advance consultation, negotiation, "trial balloons," exchanges of favors, collusion to avoid the interference of higher-ups—all were added to the repertoire of the successful manager.

Unfortunately, the basis for a false dichotomy has been reinforced, even institutionalized, by business schools themselves. They have created separate courses and departments labeled "management" and "industrial relations," or more recently "human relations" and "organizational behavior." The courses often deal with the same topics concerning managerial behavior; only the prescriptions are different.

Surely these makeshift efforts to bolster unrealistic theory will encounter increasing difficulties when they are stretched to include still newer developments. The boundaries of the firm itself have become permeable. The union, the government negotiator and auditor, the industrial consultant, and the subcontractor all come in from the outside. Increasingly, all of them work within the physical confines of the firm but have no simple authority relationship with the manager.[5] Any effective theory of managerial action must be able to incorporate such relationships as these. For example, the computer is now moving from the back room to the front office, and many operations must be tailored to its technical limitations and requirements. The computer specialist, who may work for the computer manufacturer, spends an increasing portion of his time in the firm, dealing with internal matters affecting the operation of this enormously expensive and demanding piece of equipment. Its requirements are beginning to shape the activities of many who thought they were far removed from its impact.

Dual Allegiance

The myth has been perpetuated that industrial organizations are characterized by single lines of authority—good, clean, clearcut relationships—that, while hospitals may be schizophrenic, with their dual administrative and medical hierarchies, and the

[5] See Margaret Chandler and Leonard R. Sayles, *Contracting-Out: A Study of Management Decision-Making,* Columbia University, Graduate School of Business, New York, 1959.

union member is caught between the initiations of his leaders and his boss, the manager has no such conflicts.

This is very naïve. Dualism or trebleness is hardly unique in industry, although there may be frequent efforts to disguise its existence by weasel words such as "functional relationship." The maintenance supervisor is often in the position of responding to both the production superintendent of his division and the chief engineer. The plant personnel man takes orders from the plant manager and the corporate director of industrial relations. The engineering manager reports to the head of a project and a supervisor for his field of specialization.

Thus, a theory of administration based upon a kind of Euclidean geometry (only one line can connect two points) is unrealistic. Relationships among managers must be considered as a function of space and time, not two-dimensional surfaces.

One can make the generalization that, as technology becomes more complicated, the number of specialized groups within an organization and the number of bases from which decisions can be made will increase. These developments place greater strains on the manager. The so-called staff-line exception to the "normal" chain of command comes close to being the rule. Similarly, the types of organizations that are supposed to be special cases, such as hospitals with their *parallel* chains of command (e.g., administrative and medical) and universities where the staff (e.g., teachers) initiate for the line (administrators), turn out not to be special after all.[6]

CONCLUSION

As Durkheim predicted, there are economic and social costs associated with the benefits of greater division of labor. Methods of management associated with one form are useless in another; this is just as true in the military or government as in private

[6] Amitai Etzioni and others have written about the supposed deviancy of these types of "professional"-dominated organizations. See his *A Comparative Analysis of Complex Organizations*, The Free Press of Glencoe, New York, 1961.

business.[7] Even the Chinese Communists are not immune to this relationship. While overpowering force, militarily imposed discipline, and unquestioned authority can build pyramids and temples, it cannot manage a modern interdependent agricultural or industrial complex. Might does not make right; nor does it make coordination, as the Chinese are discovering to their sorrow and starvation. The Soviet Union has long since learned this lesson and is now exploring a variety of techniques, as substitutes for commissariate directives, to integrate and administer the diverse parts of its economic life (including education in business administration).

This trend was foreseen by the liberal economists as well as such wise observers as Walter Lippmann, who some years ago observed that the trend in the division of labor makes monolithic control of the individual untenable.[8]

Further reflection of this is provided by a recent British study. The researchers compared manufacturing organizations having highly advanced technologies with those utilizing simpler technologies. By advanced technology they meant companies using continuous processing and sophisticated controls providing for great regularity and predictability. This predictability and tight control was accompanied, however, by a very high density of management compared to less sophisticated unit-, batch-, and even mass-production-type organizations. Obviously the greater need for coordination, the extent to which operational difficulties represented matters of great urgency, *increased* the administrative load.[9]

An impressive, systematic study of the organization of the modern army also shows that modern technology is associated with a whole new array of administrative problems:

[7] Morris Janowitz finds styles of military leadership shifting as a function of new military technology. See his *The Professional Soldier*, The Free Press of Glencoe, New York, 1960.

[8] See Walter Lippmann, *The Good Society*, rev. ed., Little, Brown and Company, Boston, 1943.

[9] Joan Woodward, *Management and Technology*, Department of Scientific and Industrial Research, London, England, 1958, pp. 16, 27.

> The technology of warfare is so complex that the coordination of a complex group of specialists cannot be guaranteed simply by authoritarian discipline.[10]

The reader will note a paradox here. Increased specialization, as we have already observed, decreases the margin or leeway permitted individuals or groups who must coordinate their efforts; greater synchronization of effort is required. Yet this reduced opportunity for individual deviation is not accompanied by increased monolithic authority. It is only when we look at the real job of the manager in the modern, complex organization that we can resolve this seeming contradiction between the need for conformity and the requirement for discretion.

[10] Janowitz, *op. cit.*, p. 43.

Empirical Studies
of Managerial Behavior

A few studies of managerial behavior have been made. However, the sum total of such research is a very modest one.[1] Assembly-line workers and machine tenders have been more popular subjects for inquiry than managers. Furthermore, most of the studies have concentrated on the manager's response (or that of his subordinates) to questionnaires. These tell us something about perception and values but little about behavior.

Although writers on the subject of management endeavor to express their generalizations in profound terminology, a few have noted the complete absence of real data to support their contentions:

In the literature on administration most of the writing is not even concerned with results in the form of observed and classified facts, but merely with generalizations from limited experience and with principles which in some instances are clearly stated as "axioms" or "propositions," but which in most cases are nothing else but per-

[1] Professor Robert Dubin has undertaken a useful task in endeavoring to summarize this handful of studies in his article, "Business Behavior Behaviorally Viewed," in G. B. Strother (ed.), *Social Science Approaches to Business Behavior,* Richard D. Irwin, Inc., Homewood, Ill., 1962, pp. 11–56.

sonal opinions. . . . [Further] concepts like planning, coordination and control are of very limited use when we want to describe in an observational study the daily work and actual patterns of behavior of a managing director. Most of these concepts do not fulfill the qualification of operational concepts that they should be synonymous with a clearly defined set of operations. . . .[2]

Carlson is also referring to the intricate abstractions surrounding most position guides for managers: the highly legalistic "authorities" and "responsibilities" that have no behavioral counterparts. He says that nearly all organization charts and job descriptions belie the true state of affairs regarding actual performance of work. Organization charts imply that contacts are limited primarily to the lines connecting the boxes, but the relationships necessary to get the job done are much more complex. The maintenance people and the production people are in separate columns, but something must "connect" them if the organization is to be maintained, even though there is no such line on the diagram.

Similarly, job descriptions are highly misleading. They list all the responsibilities of the manager, implying that he can do all these things by adept use of the time he spends at his desk and with his subordinates. He has responsibilities for this and that decision, this and that activity, but the dynamic elements of his job are left unspecified. Yet these elements truly determine what the position requires from the incumbent in the way of administrative abilities. Thus, the descriptions include little reality, which may explain why most lie dormant in unused files.

We shall refer here to three studies of the actual behavior of managers. One was done in the United Kingdom by Burns and the other two are United States researches by Quentin Ponder at Columbia and Walker, Guest and Turner at Yale.[3]

[2] Sune Carlson, *Executive Behavior*, Strömbergs, Stockholm, 1951, pp. 17, 23.
[3] Tom Burns, "The Direction of Activity and Communication in a Departmental Executive Group," *Human Relations*, vol. 7, pp. 73–97, 1954.

Quentin Ponder, "Supervisory Practices of Effective and Ineffective Foremen," Ph.D. dissertation, Columbia University, New York, 1958.

Charles R. Walker, Robert H. Guest, and Arthur N. Turner, *The Foreman on the Assembly Line*, Harvard University Press, Cambridge, Mass., 1956.

PATTERNED SEQUENCES
OF RELATIONSHIPS

In one sense, these few studies prove the obvious and confirm the cliché: Management *is* working with and through other people. Burns, for example, concluded that the middle managers he studied (department managers, production and design engineers) spent 80 per cent of their time in contact with other people, both inside and outside the organization.[4] Other research would suggest that this figure, while not necessarily representative, is not unduly high.

In the more precise studies of Ponder at Columbia and the Yale group, where literally every minute was accounted for (as distinct from Burns's research which did not involve such careful observation, the data show that 50 to 80 per cent of a first-line supervisor's time (in manufacturing) is spent in direct, face-to-face contact with people.

These men also spend a good deal of time moving around the shop. In many cases, they themselves manipulate materials and tools or inspect parts or materials. All this reduces the time remaining for interpersonal give and take. Even so, the Yale group's study concludes that, in highly mechanized, rationalized operations such as an automobile assembly line, verbal interaction is an important component of the job.[5]

However, when we look more closely at the data, we are able to go substantially beyond this documentation of the obvious. Some of the generalizations one can make, and the supporting data, follow.

Table 1 shows the daily distribution of time and contacts for the supervisors studied by Walker, Guest, and Turner in an automobile plant and Ponder in an electrical equipment manufacturing plant. While there are obvious differences in the distributions, the essential similarity of the overall pattern is rather remarkable, suggesting that the division of labor and

4 Burns, *op. cit.*, p. 78.
5 Walker, Guest, and Turner, *op. cit.*, p. 89.

Table 1
A Manager's Day: The Pattern of Relationships

Relationship[c]	Daily frequency of contact		Average duration of contact, minutes		Total minutes per day		Per cent of total day	
	Yale[a]	Columbia[b]	Yale	Columbia	Yale	Columbia	Yale	Columbia
Own subordinates	114	47	¾	1⅛	89	65	18	14
Own group leader		13		1½		19		4
Other supervisors	23	9	1½	2	33	17	7	4
Other supervisors' subordinates	6	6	¾	1½	4	9	1	2
General foreman	7	4	4	3⅓	28	12	6	3
Department superintendent	3		5		15		3	
Materials handling	5	11	1	1	5	11	1	2
Inspection and quality control	8	6	1¼	1⅔	10	10	2	2
Standards and methods	1	7	1	3	1	22	1	5
Maintenance, production control, and other misc. staff and service personnel	20	38	1	2	24	77	5	16

Notes:
a Walker, Guest, and Turner give data for only one supervisor (p. 86).
b Ponder's data are for 16 hours and for 12 high rated and 12 low rated. All these were merged and divided by 2 to obtain distribution for an "average" supervisor in his sample for one day (pp. 111–113).
c Some of the categories in both have been combined to increase the comparability, since there were differences in the categories for staff and service groups used by the researchers.

accompanying organization structure tend to be rather similar for these two plants.

High Activity

One interesting point in these studies is the recognition that the typical manager must be an enormously active person. While certainly some managerial jobs are the exception, the managers studied had to be able to undertake, maintain, and successfully conclude a staggering number of contacts per day. Ponder's supervisors averaged 457 contacts per 8-hour day, and the Yale study's carefully observed manager was not far behind with 387. This is a striking coincidence, because one study concerned an automobile assembly plant and the other an electrical equipment manufacturing plant in which the work activity was much closer to a job shop than to a mass-production assembly line.

Most contacts averaged only one or two minutes in duration. We should expect that higher-level executives would show significantly lower frequencies and longer durations. Even here, however, as Burns and Carlson have shown, the activity level is high because the total time in contact with other people is so great.

The supervisor must deal with a great number of people, not just immediate subordinates but staff, service, and other levels of management and adjacent supervisors. The details of the breadth of his contacts will be discussed later.

Thus, even on the basis of this limited information, we see that it is misleading to conceive of the manager as primarily (1) a human relations counselor or (2) a thoughtful planner–decision maker. The manager, when acting in a managerial capacity, is uniquely and profoundly *active,* whether sitting at a desk or restaurant table, walking through a sales or shop floor, or handling a telephone. In the contemporary organization, he expends enormous quantities of energy dealing with many different kinds of people.

Obviously the executive must think, or use his intellectual powers, but this must be an integral part of his interactional behavior. Administration inevitably means constant or almost constant contact. If the manager conceives of these contacts as interruptions or "frictions" that will eventually, or would in an ideal organization, disappear, he is certain to find perpetual frustration and dissatisfaction with his lot.[6]

Wide Variety of Types of Contacts

It was noted earlier that management activity is often compared to that of a squad leader. The manager keeps his men going. If we now look in more detail at the previously cited studies, we see that a large share of the contacts have little to do with motivating subordinates, what is narrowly conceived as leadership skill.

The Columbia and the Yale data show that there are great variations in the duration of contacts: Some are exceedingly short, lasting but fractions of a minute, and others extend for significant portions of an hour or longer. Our own limited study of executives in an engineering organization suggests even greater extremes: split-second interactions and discussions lasting several hours. Even more striking is the observation that interactions between the manager and his own subordinates are, on an average, among the *shortest*, if not the shortest, contacts. Again documenting the obvious, a large number of contacts must be something other than permissive, two-way-communication, non-directive discussions.

At the same time, it would be inappropriate to assume, as do many of the small-group problem-solving experiments, that all contacts are brief exchanges of data. Negotiations with other departments or outside vendors or a union representative may take a long period of time as compared with telephoning a requisition. There are also self-evident differences in the internal structure of these contacts.[7] In some, the manager does most of

[6] From the point of view of executive selection and placement, it is useful to distinguish between individuals whose basic personality makeup permits this high interactional behavior and those whose energy and aptitudes are not adequate for such positions.

[7] See Paul Lawrence, *The Changing of Organizational Behavior Patterns*, Harvard University, Graduate School of Business Administration, Boston, Mass., 1958.

the talking; others are more evenly divided; and in some the manager is primarily a listener. One can also observe differences in *who initiates the contact*. For some parts of his job, the manager goes into action *after* someone goes to him, e.g., a subordinate with an equipment failure or a staff specialist reporting on control statistics reflecting the department's performance for the previous day.

In other words, the manager must have at his disposal a repertoire of actions (and inactions). He must learn and be capable of undertaking (the two are distinguishable) a wide variety of types of contacts, and he must be available to receive still others. The concept that managerial activity is a unity, that there is a homogeneous leadership method used in "dealing with people," is a myth and a deception. The manager, like the good actor, has many "lines" and many types of "exits" and "entrances," and their pacing varies tremendously. At times, he must be able slowly and even tediously to explore a subject in great detail with an associate; at other times he must move with lightning speed from contact to contact if his job is to be handled successfully.

Breadth in Range of Contacts

It is worth repeating that we are discussing managers in contemporary, complex organizations, of which the large company or government agency is a good example. In these, the supervisor is *not* dealing primarily with his subordinates. Very likely one-fourth or less of his time is spent in interaction with subordinates, with the remainder devoted to working with other levels of management or associates and staff and service groups.[8] In the Yale and Columbia studies, for example, even these first-line

[8] Ponder notes that the more effective supervisors were those who worked more intensively with these widely dispersed specialists, whereas those failing on the job endeavored to work more within their own groups. Furthermore, the less effective supervisors tended to have a greater quantity of contacts with their own subordinates than did the more effective managers. *Op. cit.*, p. 116.

supervisors spent only from one and one-half to two hours of the working day with their immediate subordinates.

Recently we observed a number of managers in the engineering development services division of a large corporation. Many of them maintained contacts with as many as thirty distinct groups under as many separate managers. Here is a partial list of the types of groups with whom these managers "coordinated," to use an ambiguous term covering the multitude of managerial relationships.

◆ The subordinate group, reporting directly to the manager

◆ The manager of the manager, and often the next two levels of management as well, who, in theory, directly supervise the actions of the manager we were observing

◆ Groups for whom the manager is doing work, who have in a sense contracted out some part of their activities to him

◆ Groups to whom he, in turn, contracts out work, because they are more expert or better equipped or staffed to complete the work

◆ Groups from whom he secures parts, materials, or services, some of whom may be within the formal boundaries of the organization and some outside vendors

◆ Groups who assist him in making such acquisitions or who must prepare facilitating papers, such as purchasing, accounting, etc.

◆ Groups who control the use of or access to equipment, space, and other resources that the manager must borrow or use in the course of his work

◆ Groups who can help him when he has problems with personnel or with financial or technical aspects of his work

◆ Groups who ask him for special help in areas where he has technical expertise and for whom he can serve as a "consultant"

◆ Groups who are working at an earlier stage in the overall technology or work-flow process, from whom the manager will receive ideas, materials, semicompleted designs or objects and for which he must be prepared

◆ Groups to whom he will send what he has processed in the way of ideas, materials, designs, or semicompleted parts and who want to be prepared

◆ Groups who are doing things in other parts of the organization that directly or indirectly impinge on his activities and with whom, therefore, he wants to keep in touch

◆ Groups who can help him predict changes in personnel, organization, finances, or level of business activity

◆ Groups who can facilitate his contracts with and help him to comprehend the behavior of bosses, customers, etc.

◆ Groups from whom the manager must secure approval for the work he is doing and his method of doing it

CONCLUSION FROM EMPIRICAL RESEARCH STUDIES

From this type of data and from studies of the organizations produced by the second industrial revolution, it is clear that some of the older management myths have to be discarded in the light of the realities of the contemporary organization. Several current field studies have already questioned the primacy of vertical relationships, contending that there has been too little attention paid to the human relations that go crosswise in the organization, rather than following the "chain of command."[9] But we can be even more explicit in identifying "old wives' tales" of management theory. Among these can be included the following:

1. A manager should take orders from only one man, his boss. (Most managers, in fact, work for, i.e., they respond to the initiations of,

[9] Henry A. Landsberger, "The Horizonal Dimension in Bureaucracy," *Administrative Science Quarterly*, vol. 6, pp. 298–332, 1961. (A study of three British factories and the relationships among middle managers.)

Robert Guest and Frank Jasinski, "Technology and Organization: Two Case Studies" (mimeographed), Yale Technology Project, 1960. (A study of an American automobile assembly plant and one other unidentified factory, which emphasizes the contacts between managers at roughly the same level.)

George Strauss, "Tactics of Lateral Relationship: The Purchasing Agent," *Administrative Science Quarterly*, vol. 7, no. 2, pp. 161–186, September, 1962. (A study of the "horizontal" relationships between purchasing agents and other members of management in twenty-four companies in the Buffalo area.)

many people who are customers for the services they render or who are in a position to make demands upon them.)

2. The manager does work himself only under exceptional circumstances; the good manager gets all his work done through the activities of his subordinates. (The manager himself must carry on many of the relationships with "outsiders" in order to negotiate for the materials and services he receives and to participate in the procedures by which his activities are evaluated by specialized groups in the organization.)

3. The manager devotes most of his time and energy to supervising his subordinates. (The need to interact with many groups outside his own keeps the manager away from his subordinates a significant portion of the time.)

4. The good manager manages by looking at results. (The modern organization has so many interdependent parts that the manager could not wait for results if he wanted to; others who were being affected would be at his door. But even without these pressures, the costs of waiting to find out "how things are going" until the results are seen would be enormous. Furthermore, most "results" are joint products and cannot be assessed against a single individual. Consequently, methods of continuous feedback are required.)

5. To be effective, the manager must have authority equal to his responsibility. (A manager almost never has authority equal to his responsibility; he must depend on the actions of many people over whom he has not the slightest control.)

6. Staff people have no real authority since they are subsidiary to the line organization. (Staff groups have very real power.)

Many other myths could be cited, but perhaps these illustrate the point that management principles have been based too heavily on organizations that no longer exist or at least are diminishing in importance.

One is never sure how many managers expect the real world to be like the out-of-date textbook or idealized instruction manual that they receive when they start work. Certainly, most managers we have seen quickly learn to file away the job description for their position, because it bears no resemblance to what they do with their time and with whom they do it. Nevertheless, there must be many cases where a manager is frustrated as a

result of expecting his job to be like the one the myths portray.[10]
Such managers would do well to listen to a highly mobile
member of middle management in a large, demanding, science-
based organization describe his job:

> I have a terrible time trying to explain what I do at work when
> I get home. My wife thinks of a manager in terms of someone who
> has authority over those people who work for him and who in turn
> gets his job done for him. You know, she thinks of those nice, neat
> organization charts, too. She also expects that when I get promoted,
> I'll have more people working for me.
>
> Now, all of this is unrealistic. Actually, I only have eighteen peo-
> ple directly reporting to me. These are the only ones I can give orders
> to. But I have to rely directly on the services of seventy-five or eighty
> other people in this company, if my project is going to get done.
> They in turn are affected by perhaps several hundred others, and I
> must sometimes see some of them, too, when my work is being
> held up.
>
> So I am always seeing these people, trying to get their cooperation,
> trying to deal with delays, work out compromises on specifications,
> etc. Again, when I try to explain this to my wife, she thinks that all
> I do all day is argue and fight with people.
>
> Although I am an engineer, trained to do technical work in the
> area encompassed by this project, I really don't have to understand
> anything about the technical work going on here.
>
> What I do have to understand is how the organization works, how
> to get things through the organization—and this is always changing,
> of course—and how to spot trouble, how to know when things aren't
> going well.
>
> As for doing a lot of planning ahead, well, it's foolish. In fact, I
> usually come to my office in the morning without any plans as to what
> I am going to do that day. Any minute something can happen that
> upsets the works. Of course, I keep in mind certain persisting prob-
> lems on which I haven't been able to make much headway.

[10] See W. R. Dill, T. L. Hilton, and W. R. Reitman, "How Aspiring Managers Promote Their Own Careers," *California Management Review*, vol. 2,
no. 4, Summer, 1960. These authors find that the successful new managers
are not so naïve. "They maintain a wide range of independent contacts to
evaluate their present position . . . not likely to rely solely on their immediate
supervisor to define tasks. . . ." (p. 15.)

Note the elements our informant has emphasized:

1. A relatively small proportion of time with subordinates
2. Little importance of concepts such as authority, power, and planning
3. Need for relationships with literally dozens of people, and many of these difficult negotiating contacts
4. Use of certain unspecified cues for deciding where and how to apportion his scarcest resource: his own time
5. Relatively slight importance of technical sophistication
6. Fast "footwork"

CONCLUSION

A manager in a contemporary organization has many tasks to perform besides the one of motivation, and he deals with many people besides his subordinates. In an earlier age and in smaller organizations that lacked the proliferation of staff and service groups and coordinative responsibility for adjacent or parallel-line groups, the manager may have been able to give primary consideration to supervising subordinates in the completion of their relatively simple and homogeneous tasks. Today, our increasingly white-collar, technical, and professional organizations have managerial problems whose complexity dwarfs these more primitive forms. Activity, involving a wide range of problems and of contacts throughout the organization, is the salient feature of the modern managerial position.

Many of the criticisms of the contemporary manager's lack of virile independence, of stand-up-and-be-countedness—in contrast to his presumed wish to be submerged in team play—stem from a basic misconception of the manager's job. The operations-analysis enthusiasts, on the other hand, show little awareness of the problems of operating an organization. They conceive of the manager as a small-scale version of the entrepreneur–risk taker who gambled his (or someone else's) money on the astuteness of his decision making in the market-place (or the smokey hotel room).

But these virtues of decisiveness, willingness to assume risk, nerves of steel and a poker face shield are of little importance in operating an organization (although they may help the president when he faces the investment bankers).

Realizing that, in fact, a manager's job requires *primarily* human relationships is not the same thing as believing that a manager is primarily concerned with being nondirective.

Human relations and the behavioral sciences have often failed to produce more realistic appraisals of managerial activities than those provided by the industrial engineer, economist, or political scientist. Little or no recognition has been given to the effect on a manager's job requirements of changing technological systems, organization design, or any of the complexities introduced by diverse, large-scale, highly specialized organizations. In these, as we shall see, the manager has to maintain a multitude of diverse relationships, and these are both a function of and shaped by the specifics of system and process.

The satisfaction the executive used to derive from clear lines of authority, deciding what to do and seeing it done—and no "shilly-shallying"—the clear rules and uncluttered divisions of responsibility and labor are gone. They never existed in government, in hospitals and universities, or in laboratories and most service organizations.[11]

What is the result? It does little good to say that the manager must have patience, be a skillful persuader, and learn his way around an organization that bears little resemblance to the chart that has been drawn up to represent it. Rather, we need some objective, conceptual means of describing these types of managerial positions in terms that have substance and more operationality than "the ability to get along with people."

[11] See Morrie Helitzer, "How Do Businessmen Do in Washington," *The New York Times Magazine,* May 7, 1961, p. 67.

4

Programming the Manager's Job

We can now be specific about the function of the administrator. His primary purpose is *not* transmitting orders downward to subordinates, although he occasionally does this. His primary purpose is to maintain the regularity or the sequential pattern of one or more of the work processes underlying the division of labor.

The inability to describe adequately this *active, dynamic, interpersonal* aspect of administration in operational terms stems, in large part, from misconceptions concerning the nature of an organization. It is easy to be misguided by the legalistic theories of the corporation or the analogies drawn between companies and older military models or the Catholic Church. All these suggest a hierarchy in which basic decisions are made at the top and are converted into more specific plans, orders, and finally actual operations as they move downward through successive levels.

There is good reason to conceive of an organization from the bottom upward; this is the way an organization structure should be designed.[1] As long as a single individual can do all the work necessary to complete some task, such as the plumber or account-

[1] Eliot D. Chapple and Leonard R. Sayles, *The Measure of Management,* The Macmillan Company, New York, 1961, pp. 18–45.

ant who is in business for himself, no organization is needed. But once a division of labor is necessary, when specialization occurs, organization is required to coordinate and integrate the activities of the various people who together make up the work system. The nature of those activities and the specific form taken by the division of labor determine the job of the administrator.

A similar view is that of a well-known industrial psychologist:

> It seems to me strange that the function of holding the organizations together is not more heavily weighted in job descriptions of executives. Usually we read that they collect information, make decisions, see that the decisions are carried out, and the like. Observing executive behavior, it seems to me that most time and effort is spent in holding the thing together as a single working unit. Most organizations, properly started, will largely direct themselves except for periodic, crucial decisions. In terms of importance, decisions catch our eye. In terms of time and effort, and perhaps of equal importance, the holding-together has slipped us by.[2]

In a recent book, the author endeavored to convey a similar picture of the managerial job as one of stabilizing work systems in response to recurring disturbances of one kind or another:

> The objective of any organizational structure is to minimize the incidence of deviations from the established interaction patterns of the work process. The realistic administrator knows complete stability is a never-to-be-achieved utopia. Equipment will always break down; employees will always be absent; and changes in procedures will be introduced continuously. Work will not always come through on time, or when it does, the quality may be so poor the normal process time must be increased significantly. Rush orders or a flood of work may press upon his unit. Whatever the type of fluctuation, his interaction patterns have to change. He may have to spend more time with individual workers, supervisors in other departments, engineers, mechanics, maintenance men, or various persons in control positions, such as production planners or factory cost controllers, who occupy a place in the paper-work flow of which the line supervisor also is a

[2] Mason Haire, *Modern Organization Theory*, John Wiley & Sons, Inc., New York, 1959, pp. 302–303.

part. And, as a result, less time is available to maintain other vital contacts.[3]

In shifting from a static-legalistic or group-dynamics description of the manager's job to one that is more consistent with the actual operation of contemporary organizations, there are several objectives. The results of the Carlson, Burns, Ponder, and Yale group studies are interesting in roughly characterizing the nature of these jobs. However, it is not sufficient for us to know the gross quantitative dimensions of a given managerial position (e.g., the manager is in contact with 18 people, on an average, each day, the ratio of initiations to the total is 34 per cent, the durations range from 5 to 50 minutes, etc.). These do not provide specific guidance in making such managerial decisions as the following:

1. The criteria that ought to be established for evaluating the performance of incumbents
2. The desired translation of organizational arrangements, and changes in these, into predictable patterns of managerial behavior (i.e., such questions as, "If we merge these two departments, how will it affect the department manager's work load, where can he get along without additional help, and where will he need bolstering?")

The first step is to develop a more useful scheme for classifying the manager's activities. Aside from the simple counting already described, the managerial job has been divided into dealing with people and dealing with production. Casual observation suggests that the two are only occasionally separable. Similarly, the distinction between planning-idea activities and those related to immediate problems lacks operationality, as do many of the efforts to ascertain the amount of delegation and non-directiveness incorporated in the way orders are given and information sought.

In other words, we are seeking *a notational system* to describe the underlying rhythms of the human relations processes that make up the organization. These are movements of people in

3 Chapple and Sayles, *op. cit.*, p. 39.

time and space. As noted, we must go beyond the simple statement of who sees whom to a fuller representation of the administrator's behavior as a function of technology and structure.

On the basis of our field observations, we propose that managerial work be operationally classified into three major categories
of activity. It should be repeated that classification systems,
particularly in the field of management, are not hard to come by.
It is a favorite pastime to find new, more elegant (and often
more abstract) ways of breaking up wholes into parts. However,
the categories below provide us with certain distinctive analytical
tools and are integrally related to the behavioral processes of the
executive. By implication we are suggesting that some other
schemes do far less.

I. The Manager as a Participant in External Work Flows

As already stated, the contemporary manager spends a large
portion of his time interacting with other managers (peers or
near peers). Here he is providing the connective tissue that
helps to hold together the specialized subparts of the organization. Unlike the simple organizations in which this function
could be performed by the next higher level in the hierarchy, the
complex organization assumes that lateral relationships will be
plentiful. While there are exceptions, in general these are *pair*
relationships which the manager conducts himself; i.e., they are
two-person contacts.

In our research, we have identified a number of behaviorally
distinguishable external relationships in which managers are
likely to participate. As we shall see in succeeding chapters, each
has a unique interactional pattern associated with it and a
number of predictable human relations problems. These relationships can be related to other empirical studies of managerial
behavior.

The patterns we observed were these:

1A Contact with work-flow stages that *precede* the one or ones directly supervised by the manager

1B Contact with work-flow stages that *succeed* the one or ones directly supervised by the manager

2A Arrangements to *sell* or transfer internally held or produced goods, services, or personnel to other parts of the organization

2B Arrangements to *purchase* or receive goods, services, or personnel from other parts of the organization

3A Continuing relationships with groups (or managers) to whom the manager's own subordinates are supplying services or support

3B Continuing relationships with groups (or managers) from whom the manager is receiving service or support

4A Contacts for the purpose of giving advice, counsel, information, or skilled assistance on difficult problems

4B Contacts for the purpose of requesting advice, counsel, information, or skilled assistance on difficult problems

5A Contacts undertaken to evaluate or appraise the work or activities of other organization groups

5B Contacts undertaken in order to respond to the requests and activities of groups (or managers) who are appraising or evaluating one's own area of activity

6A Relationships designed to limit or control the decisions made by other managers in accordance with certain general policies or strategies adopted by the organization for the purpose of maximizing certain gains

6B Relationships of response to groups or managers who are seeking to limit or control the manager's decisions in accordance with larger organizational policies or strategies

7 The relationship characteristic of managers whose groups are supposed to be isolated from the main stream of interaction and work flow of the organization

In succeeding chapters, the dimensions and specific use of these categories of managerial action or response will be described in detail, and this terminology adopted:

1. Work-flow relationship
2. Trading relationship
3. Service relationship
4. Advisory relationship
5. Auditing relationship

6. Stabilization relationship
7. Innovation relationship

At the same time, hopefully, the internal logic of the terminology and the location of the "break points" between categories will become clear.

II. *The Manager as a Leader*

While it may appear that we have slighted this activity, any undue deemphasis has been only to redress the balance. Clearly the manager has the job of getting his own immediate subordinates to respond to him as a leader or initiator. This behavior is distinguishable from the preceding external flow relationships in that it involves largely (but by no means entirely) contacts in which the manager (leader) endeavors to secure from his subordinates a group response, i.e., to initiate simultaneous action for them. The distinction then is between pair or two-person relationships and what the anthropologist has called "set events."[4] The latter are one of the hallmarks of leadership and are essential to the construction and maintenance of any institution. As many have observed, it would be impossible to maintain an organization that was composed entirely of two-person or chain-type interactions. An apt statement of the reasoning is this:

In all organizations of any size at all, the flows of materials, people, and messages quickly fall into patterns, or "channels." One has only to make a circle of a hundred points and to connect each point with all the others by a straight line to realize how quickly an unpatterned flow of communications and transportation would break down; even in a small organization, this has the makings of a colossal traffic jam. The simplest way to order these flows is to establish a chain, so that each individual only communicates with two others, but this is both slow and highly vulnerable to breakdown that paralyzes the entire organization. It is safer, faster, and more economical to divide the members of the organization into groups having in-

[4] Eliot D. Chapple and Carleton S. Coon, *Principles of Anthropology*, Holt, Rinehart and Winston, Inc., New York, 1942, p. 37.

dividual spokesmen through whom all flows into and out of the group nominally pass, and to gather the spokesmen into groups with spokesmen of their own, thus establishing the familiar pyramidal hierarchical form. This arrangement permits comparatively fast contacts from top to bottom without overburdening anyone, for it reduces the number of contact points considerably, yet it permits most of the organization to continue operations even when part is cut off. The pyramidal distribution pattern of most large organzations develops, in short, because it has significant advantages over the alternatives to it.[5]

In theoretical terms, the intragroup contacts between subordinates in a given managerial unit should be self-maintaining. That is, if the organization structure is correctly designed to facilitate the reintegration of division of jobs, subordinates act largely on the basis of stimuli provided by fellow subordinates. This the reader will recognize as the burden of the vast and amorphous literature on the "informal group," a most inauspicious notation. Work patterns involving the exchange of ideas and materials among members of the group reach some self-regulating equilibrium, what Kaufman calls a "reciprocating model."[6]

But the real world never allows this to continue for very long. Either internal friction or external change cruelly interferes with this harmonious counterpoint and the manager *qua* leader must take a hand. This, then, is where these set events come into the picture.

A leader, or a leadership group, devoting time specifically to the detection of such situations and to the issuance of messages that inhibit some actions, encourage others, slow some down, speed up others, change the directions and intensities of flows, open new channels and so on, can often end blockages, prevent jams, and thus facilitate the vigorous performance of the basic processes.[7]

5 Herbert Kaufman, "Why Organizations Behave as They Do: An Outline of a Theory," paper presented at an Interdisciplinary Seminar on Administrative Theory, University of Texas, Austin, Tex., 1961, p. 47.
6 *Ibid.*, p. 46.
7 *Ibid.*, p. 59.

The existence of these centrally issued stimuli or interactions is hardly a new observation, but in Chapter 9 we hope to show that most of the nonbehavioral literature on leadership is convertible into more operational terms consistent with our overall view of managerial action.

It is also necessary to supplement this narrow view of leadership with two more types of behavior so that the total is this:

1. *Leadership as direction,* getting subordinates to respond simultaneously to the actions of the manager
2. *Leadership as response* to initiations from subordinates who are seeking aid or support
3. *Leadership as representation* or as *intervention* for subordinates in contacts with other parts of the organization

Category 2 typically involves pair contacts again, although group initiations to the supervisor or manager are not uncommon. Category 3 is also usually a pair relationship, but here, too, the manager may seek to modify simultaneously the behavior of other managers in the organization, consistent with the needs of his subordinates.

III. The Manager as a Monitor

Related to both I and II but distinctive in its own right is the manager's monitoring activity. This simply is the method or methods he selects to appraise himself of how both his internal and external relationships are proceeding and to identify stresses and strains that may require his intervention.

In the behavioral analysis of this activity in Chapters 10 and 11 we shall distinguish a number of interrelated steps or stages in the monitoring activity:

1. Methods of detecting disturbances in the work systems in which the manager participates
2. Development of criteria for evaluating the significance of disturbances that are detected

3. Patterns of corrective action to be applied and the assessment of their effect
4. Detection of continuing (resistant) sources of disturbance in the work systems and their analysis
5. Formulation of strategies of organizational or structural change to cope with these
6. Implementation and validation of these structural modifications

CONCLUSION

These, then, are the three major activities comprising the job of the manager and its various subdivisions. Note that we really are looking at the boundary, or interface, at which the manager's job meets the jobs of other members of the organization, some of whom he calls subordinates, most of whom he does not. We shall concentrate on this interface rather than on the intellectual or emotional attributes that have so often characterized the analysis of executives: their decisiveness, courage, sense of responsibility, ambition, and so on.

In the chapters to follow we shall see how the division of labor and the structure that the organization has established serve to make predictable the job pattern of each manager in the system. Not that all will be similar; quite the contrary. There is a distinctive pattern at the interface for each manager, but this pattern can be behaviorally defined in organization terms (as distinct from psychological or mathematical or economic terms). This defining or programming converts administration into a learnable series of skills or "plays" (as distinct from unlearnable "good" attitudes or insights). More important, as we have tried to emphasize, the explication of these behavioral patterns provides the necessary benchmarks against which actual performance can be evaluated.

For the sake of exposition we shall describe managers as though they had only a single administrative pattern to perform. Obviously a manager often has work-flow relationships *and* advisory relationships *and* service relationships and others combined within his own job.

Management then is not to be comprehended in terms of general shibboleths or prescriptions for "goodness." Rather, management or executive actions should be regarded as human relationships programmable in time and space.

Most importantly, administrative behavior can be viewed in human system terms. Present interests to the contrary, an organization is not a physical or statistical entity that can be conceived (and operated) largely in nonhuman terms. While the fields of human relations and "management" have had shortcomings, their recognition of the necessity of facing up to the people problem of the organization was essentially correct. The difficulty has been to find an analytic conception of organization processes that provides a valid view of administration as an activity.

Many organizations hold together in spite of themselves. Sometimes their apparent success is due to a monopolistic position; more often it is the result of enormous expenditures of energy on the part of executives who hold the system together by "baling wire," or, to change the metaphor, never stop running to put out the "fires." As long as the organization can expand and provide ample rewards and encouragement to attract and hold the able, it works. As soon as the spirits are dampened by a major cutback or reversal, one sees the whole structure collapsing like the proverbial deck of cards.

As an alternative, in succeeding chapters we shall examine the type of calculated and controlled executive action that accomplishes results in a less crisis-laden fashion.

AN OPERATIONAL CONCEPT OF MANAGEMENT

Our objective is to go beyond the recognition of interdependence and flow and system in order to provide explicit management tools: to translate job requirements into skill patterns, to induct and train new managers to use them, and to encourage them when they are successful in learning to "play the organization."

It does not seem sufficient to stop where many astute managers have:

> Some of my managers learn—other don't—that it is not what they have authority to do that counts but rather that they are responsible for almost everything, and it is up to them to find a way of getting the job done, somehow, on time and within the budget. The whole organization is set up with everything blurred so that the ones who are going to get ahead can make time, and others will fall behind.

> On many projects we have things organized so that everything overlaps; that way someone is sure to get through.

A dynamic system of mutual interdependence still has a structure, and the manager first must be able to identify this structure. In other words, he must do more than recognize that everything depends on everything else, although this awareness, as we have endeavored to emphasize in the previous section, has some value in itself.

At this state of our knowledge, we may be able to provide the manager with the following:

1. A means of comprehending (and describing) in behavioral terms the variety of relationships he must undertake and maintain if his work is to be handled successfully. We can point out how these are distinguishable, both in his behavior and in the behavior of others, and help him to make predictions as to the types of feelings, reactions, and attitudes with which he is going to have to cope (both within himself and in others) in these relationships.
2. The means by which he can monitor these relationships both to detect when they are changing and to guide him in making the appropriate compensations in his own behavior.

In addition, the manager must have guidelines for converting changes in policies and procedures into changes in behavior patterns. For example, when top management decides that certain activities will no longer be discussed with outside customers, this affects the engineering service manager's relationship with the customer and his relationship with the specialized group producing information that he formerly transmitted or negotiated with the customer. By viewing his job behaviorally, the policy changes can be factored into his actual pattern of activity.

Another reason for proposing a more operational and explicit means of describing managerial patterns for the executive is the diversity of organization relationships that must be maintained by a single manager. For example, in dealing with one "outside" group, the manager may act in an advisory capacity, providing expert knowledge, counsel, suggestions, and criticisms on technical points. For other groups the manager may act in a support capacity, providing some necessary service to fulfill a specific commitment of the other group.

Thus the pattern of relationships—their timing and the type of contacts—varies as a function of this division of labor in the administrative sector of the organization. Without some objective and durable record of the optimal or reasonably anticipated pattern, there is a tendency for managers to adopt a single or excessively narrow array of organizational relationships. Unfortunately they are given no help by the traditional functional designations such as marketing, finance, or personnel. Knowing the technical specialization does not tell the manager how to relate himself to the organization.

5

Trading, Work-flow, and Service Relationships

We have already enumerated the array of externally directed relationships in which the manager may be engaged. Here we shall discuss the differences in the behavioral requirements of these relationships and the distinctive problems or tensions associated with each. Where possible, we shall refer to the literature, to the extent that other observers have described these work patterns.

All seven types of external relationships have some elements in common. Much of what we shall say here has been implicit in some of the earlier discussion; for the sake of emphasis, it is repeated.

Because of the division of labor imposed on the modern organization, the manager rarely controls all the resources needed to do whatever has been assigned to him (i.e., he and his subordinates together do not have all the pieces required to make a whole unit of work). Further, there are people, other than his own boss, who depend upon him and who have the job of keeping watch over him. All these conditions require the development and maintenance of particular patterns of relationships. They are not optional, extra, or necessary as good human relations; they are an integral part of the administrative task.

What we have called external relationships have been identified by other researchers in organizational behavior as "lateral,"[1] "horizontal,"[2] or just "work-flow"[3] relations (a term we prefer to save for one subtype). Whatever the terminology, certain identifying characteristics distinguish these external relationships from the usually described, garden variety of relationship: superior-subordinate. There are three such hallmarks:

1. Unlike superior-subordinate, these contacts are between managers who have a roughly equivalent position in the hierarchy. Even when there are substantial differences in status between the two, one is not the boss of the other. There is no clear-cut, established deference pattern in which one of the parties is prepared to accept unequivocally the initiations for action of the other.[4] There are substantial ambiguities in what the pattern of give and take should be.
2. It is likely that the parties to the relationship operate under different standards of performance or with differing and often conflicting objectives. While this will become clearer as we describe the dynamics of these relationships, it is useful to point out here that the reward-and-punishment system of the organization rarely produces identical short-term objectives for all groups. An elaboration process occurs in which most departments, divisions, units, or groups evolve distinctive objectives for themselves, such as making a good showing on their own budgets, securing increased appropriations, or

[1] See George Strauss, "Tactics of Lateral Relationship: The Purchasing Agent," *Administrative Science Quarterly*, vol. 7, no. 2, pp. 161–186, September, 1962.

[2] Henry Lansberger, "The Horizontal Dimension in Bureaucracy," *Administrative Science Quarterly*, vol. 6, pp. 298–332, 1961.

[3] Conrad Arensberg, "Behavior and Organization," in John Rohrer and M. Sherif (eds.), *Social Psychology at the Crossroads*, Harper & Row, Publishers, Incorporated, New York, 1952, chap. 14.

[4] In Barnard's terms, the "zone of indifference" is a very narrow one, approaching zero at the limit. See Chester Barnard, *Functions of the Executive*, Harvard University Press, Cambridge, Mass., 1938, pp. 92–94.

receiving credit for a new idea.[5] As a result of this suboptimization, external relationships have more built-in conflicts than the superior-subordinate relationship. What one party desires or expects to achieve by means of the relationship may be contradictory to or incompatible with the needs or desires of the other.

3. As a direct result of 1 and 2, these external relationships typically involve more difficult, more lengthy, and more negotiating contacts. These tend to be uncomfortable, tension-producing relationships, requiring high orders of human relations skill. (These will be reviewed in Chapter 12.)

TRADING RELATIONSHIPS

By a trading relationship we mean the process by which the terms of some future relationship are established. Because organizations are not static, a manager frequently has to expand the number of internal "customers" for the work he performs or to expand the number of "sellers" of things that he must "buy" within the organization. We shall look shortly at these relationships *after* they have become part of the normal work flow, but first let us look at their inception.

Whether or not the organization requires that a particular service group balance its own budget (by adequate internal "sales"), many such groups have other reasons for wanting to be used (particularly by important "line" departments). Similarly, a manager responsible for completing an order, project, or whatever, may have to shop within the organization for other groups that can help him. In order to establish the "terms" of this future working relationship, some contacts are required, which we have called "trading." They are not really different from those that take place between vendors and customers outside the firm or between union and management.

[5] See James March and Herbert Simon, *Organizations*, John Wiley & Sons, Inc., New York, 1958, p. 42, and George Strauss and Leonard R. Sayles, *Personnel: The Human Problems of Management*, Prentice-Hall, Inc., Englewood Cliffs, N.J., 1960, chaps. 3, 16.

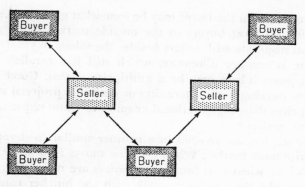

Trading Relationships
*Potential "buyers" and "sellers" seek to identify
those interested and to negotiate acceptable terms of trade*

In effect, there is a wide variety of "terms of trade" to negotiate: what, when, how, and for how much the work will be performed. Often there are efforts by "buyers" to improve the terms once they are negotiated, e.g., by asking for a few "extras" or an earlier completion date. The buyer not only supplies a budget or an approved activity (which will justify the existence of the seller), but he may also be called upon to supply waiting time, special manpower, tools, space, even good contacts with supply sources of one kind or another, or special informal favors in the area of organization politics. All are analogous to a market price.

Thus it is not inappropriate to compare these relationships to the typical salesman-customer patterns characteristic in marketing activities. The important difference is that the "customers" may not be willing to accept the going "price" or the rationing among competing users. For example, a customer may not be willing to allow the extra time required (presumably delays or slower deliveries are comparable to paying a higher price) or the budget that is requested. He may insist that he just cannot pay the price, in terms of his schedule and available budget. Thus the constraints on the buyer may be somewhat greater than those operating on most buyers in the outside market place. (There they can negotiate with others besides the salesman.)

There is another difference, which still has parallels in the market place. There may be a multiprice system. Good friends (or those offering more interesting or desirable projects) may get lower prices than organizational enemies or those requesting less pleasant services.[6]

Some services are secured in a manner similar to shopping at a favorite meat market. When one first moves into a new neighborhood (or when it is found that orders are not well handled) one takes the time to have a talk with the butcher concerning how the meat should be trimmed, the grades and size of portions preferred, how frequently bills will be tendered and paid, and what the complaint procedure will be. After that both parties anticipate that orders will flow in almost automatically and be handled routinely. On the other hand, household repairs by outside craftsmen cannot be handled so easily. Each repair requires a separate negotiation of exactly what is wanted, when, and what it will cost.

Presumably, one can differentiate services that can be handled with almost no contacts, after the initial understanding has been reached, and those that require frequent renegotiation.

Stages and Tactics in Trading Relationships

In the early stages of a trading relationship, the manager-vendor usually must undertake rather lengthy "selling" contacts. This means the ability to accept rebuffs, indifference, and a somewhat subordinate role and to meet the challenge of a "Let's see you

---

[6] In our studies of the decision process on contracting out versus in-plant maintenance, we observed great variability in the addition of overhead to various cost estimates. When it seemed desirable, the overhead added to a cost estimate could be 0 per cent of direct labor costs, and just as easily a 100 or 200 per cent could be rationalized. See Margaret Chandler and Leonard R. Sayles, *Contracting-out: A Study of Management Decision-making*, Columbia University, Graduate School of Business, New York, 1959.

prove it to me" position. Successful manager-vendors are able to describe their wares in such a way that, as one internal "buyer" put it, "They have me drooling to get my hands on what it is they have to offer." These are long contacts and require persistence.

On the other hand, in some relationships the customer does the initiating. These are instances where the service or product being sought is in very short supply. Here the manager-customer takes the initiative to convince the vendor:

1. The work will be successful, and it will enhance the vendor's prestige to be associated with it.
2. The work will be either or both (*a*) interesting and instructive for the vendor's personnel or (*b*) feasible, reasonably predictable in scope, complexity, and completion time and well within the resource capability of the vendor.

In a second stage of the trading process, the customer often increases his contacts with the vendor and lengthens his discussions in order to uncover some of the possible defects, problems, limitations, and uncertainties that were not revealed earlier. These are investigatory contacts.

I want my managers to spend enough time with these people to find out what it is they really have to offer and to "get out the water."

Now let us look at the concomitant attitudes. One constantly hears sentiments like this expressed by the vendor:

They always figure they can squeeze us on budget, saving their funds for the work they do internally.

You have to put in a substantial safety factor as to cost and specifications, or you'll never be able to deal with contingencies, and they'll keep asking for more and more for the same price.

On his side, the seller has these suspicions:

Each outside group we deal with puts a big healthy safety factor into what they are doing. You have to squeeze this out, or you'll be paying for the moon.

If you let them, they'll build everything gold-plated, make a big project of it. You have to keep after them to give you only what you really need, not something that is many times more costly and essentially useless.

They always exaggerate what they're going to do in order to get your business. Squeeze out the water first; find out what the real facts are and what they are hiding. If you negotiate long enough, you can always get it for less!

If you let them, they'll give you an old package and keep you from getting interested in something new by making the price sky-high for the development part.

To get a good deal, always show them that you're not dependent on them; that you can go elsewhere or do it yourself.

Even with these divergencies, there is an implicit understanding that the vendor will gain something extra in the way of improved know-how, some technical breakthrough, the opportunity to secure work his people are anxious to do, over and above the "price" he receives. Skilled vendors insist on this extra margin to improve the overall position of their groups in the organization, and the buyer must recognize this need.

Some managers are loathe to accept these trading relationships as a part of their job. They resent the fact that who does what with whom and for what terms is not established by some superior level in the organization or by fixed rule or formula. They are ignoring a crucial aspect of their job.

As the boundaries of organizations become less fixed, we can predict that the trading relationship will become increasingly crucial. There is no longer any clear line of demarcation between those tasks which the firm does for itself and those which it "farms out." Computer work is done in front offices, back offices, and subcontractors' offices. Even when it is done in the organization, it may be under the effective control of an outside vendor who rents or sells the equipment. Similarly, clerical tasks, scientific work, maintenance activity, and even day-to-day operations can be contracted out. Thus the manager has an ever-widening scope of trading relationships in the external world as well, not to mention collective bargaining, which is *both* inside and outside the boundaries of the firm, depending on one's arbitrary geometry. Stated in another way, many employment relationships are being converted into contractual relationships; these require "trading" ability more than traditional "leadership."

It is worth repeating that trading can be a matter of either buying or selling some function or activity, or both. Many times, but by no means always, it involves establishing a "service" relationship in which one manager provides, at specified times, activities required by the other. At times the relationship is very short-lived. The trading involves a "one-shot" purchase or sale, e.g., an arrangement to transfer a group of employees to one's own department from a preceding stage in the work flow. Agreement on terms may conclude the relationship with the other manager's group.

Many managers who are termed successful attribute this success to their constant attention to the trading elements in their job. In particular, they emphasize search activity (what marketing people might call "missionary work"). This means the maintenance within the organization of diffuse contacts that at some point could be converted into a "sale" or "purchase." (For good examples of this missionary work, see the case in Chapter 13.)

(A potential "seller"): I never miss a chance to go out to lunch with a department head who may be able to use our services. You've got to keep telling people what you can do for them if you expect to build up the reputation of your department and its activities.

(A potential "buyer"): You can't rely on written memos or reports to keep up with what's going on in the company. Many times some group is working on something which could be very useful to you,

if you knew about it. So whenever I have some free time, I wander'
around to keep current. Then when we have to farm out something
or have some difficult problem, I know where to go and, just as important, *who* to go to, who can help us.

From the point of view of organizational controls (and we
shall look more precisely at this in Chapters 10 and 11), a manager may do too much of this "empire building." The question of
balance is a general one.

In summary, there are three sequential stages in the trading
relationship. The first, "missionary work," involves widely dispersed contacts throughout the organization to seek potential
buyers or sellers. In the second stage, the actual terms of trade
are established. Finally, the parties exchange rather full information about their respective needs and capacities. Successful completion of the third stage makes it possible for both to
anticipate problems and make intelligent decisions when contingencies arise outside the scope of the original agreement.

WORK-FLOW RELATIONSHIPS

While, in a sense, all the relationships that we are describing
and for which we are providing benchmarks are "work-flow" relationships, in that they involve activities that must be performed
by different people in a relatively fixed sequence, we shall use
the term to refer only to the primary stages required to assemble
physical goods, carry out services, or complete analyses or paper
work. Later we shall deal with "service" relationships which may
at first appear to be the same thing. The difference is an interactional one. Each of the stages in the work flow feeds directly
and completely into the next stage or, in very unusual cases, into
several other stages. The stages are related in that one begins
only after the other has been completed. A service relationship,
however, is characterized by multiple feeds (or on-going commitments) to other groups in the organization and is not a next
stage.

Work-flow Relationship

Service Relationship

In the diagram above, B is in the position of receiving work (ideas, paper, or materials) from A, and when his work is added, the total goes to C. Each is concerned with the preceding stage. However, in the service relationship shown above, A′, C′, D′, and E′ all act on B′ because B′ handles an activity that neither precedes nor succeeds in the flow of work but is *internal* to one of the stages. That is, before A′, for example, can pass along its

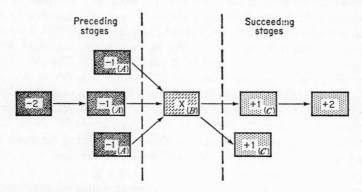

Work-flow Relationships
Manager B receives imputs from preceding work-flow stages in the jurisdiction of managers A and transmits his outputs to succeeding stages of the work flow in the jurisdiction of managers C

work to the succeeding stage in a work-flow relationship, B′ must repair a machine, ditto some reports, or run a statistical analysis. The significance of this distinction will become clear when service relationships are discussed.[7]

[7] It should be noted that there is also an internal flow of work with which most managers are concerned. Where their own subordinates have *sequential*

From the manager's point of view, these work-flow relation-ships are crucial. How much he can accomplish depends upon the condition and timing of the "work" he receives from the one or more preceding stages *and* the demands made upon him by those other managers for whose departments his department is the preceding stage. Let us look first at some of the problems in these relationships and then consider how the behavioral require-ments of this aspect of the managerial job can be specified.

Typical Problems in Work-flow Relationships

Typical work-flow problems concern timing. A great deal of in-teraction (and dissatisfaction) concerns mutual pressures to re-arrange schedules. Manager B says he cannot wait until A finishes; could A supply some of whatever he is working on or at least some information now so that B can be ready? The A's often accuse the B's of seeking advance information in order to provide excuses or rationalizations for their own failure to complete their work on time or within specifications. In other words, they accuse them of looking for "skeletons in the other's closet."

Similarly, A and B dispute whether each is doing his work in such a way as to make it easy or difficult for the next stage. Be-cause most organizational controls reward a group for meeting small-group criteria rather than larger organizational goals, each is induced to short-cut unmeasured (and unrewarded) areas that help only the outside group.

We have many examples of this:

---

relationships (as distinct from having identical work assignments), the man-ager is only an *indirect* participant in that he must monitor the degree to which the time parameters remain constant; this is not one of his external flows where he is a direct participant. At times the distinction may be blurred because the manager himself becomes one of the internal stages. For example, he has certain critical skills and asks that subordinate Jones bring him his completed work and then he, the manager, performs certain steps and gives the material to Smith who is to carry on from that point. When this occurs, the monitoring of the total flow can be handled only by the manager's manager.

The [next-stage] group over there who take the work when we are done with it are penny pinchers. Their manager doesn't care much about time or quality but only about keeping his budget down. So our own "customers" are climbing down our necks because their work is delayed or because it isn't done perfectly, and there is nothing to be done about it while that other management feels the way it does.

We are interested in developing the best . . . that is available. But those guys in the next department keep telling us just to get out something that will meet minimum specs and they can make use of it. That isn't the way we do things.

I'm awfully glad we finished our work on time. The guys [at the next stage] were just looking for an excuse to slip their schedule. Even if we hadn't been holding them up, they would have used us as an excuse.

Many managers are in a work-flow relationship with another group, i.e., the designs or equipment move from their group to the next stage, which is under another manager, while at the same time they are also committed to monitoring the next stage. When they are concerned with a number of work-flow stages, their interest extends beyond the interface.

There is another reason for emphasizing these contact patterns between adjacent stages. A few managers make the naïve assumption that people will come to them and tell them what is important for them to know. This is not true even for subordinates, who frequently lack benchmarks to distinguish the important from the unimportant, the real crisis from the minor perturbation that they should handle themselves. The "outsider" may have more reason for avoiding communication. Time and time again one hears of the need for restricting information (both organizational and technical).

If you tell people too much, they'll try to help you. Then you've got the problem and the other guy to worry about.

Never give out more information than you have to. Something that sounds innocent enough can be used against you if things should slow up.

A lot of people [from later stages in the work flow] come around on fishing expeditions, but it usually is pretty easy to brush them off. After all, something you tell people today may change tomorrow; furthermore, we have our own objectives to satisfy, and if you tell people too much about what you're doing they'll wonder why you aren't doing more to satisfy their needs.

In technical activities particularly, it may not be clear when one stage or step is completed and the next is ready to begin. Some managers may be too eager to anticipate what they will receive. This involves them in what the preceding-stage manager feels are premature contacts. In addition, they may try to discover whether what they will receive is really completed satisfactorily. As one engineering manager commented:

Frankly we can't tell those people [at the next stage] as much about our work as we would like to. They are politicians, and if they run into any troubles doing their work, they will try to use what they know about our work to prove that they got a "lemon," something that wasn't really perfected; they never are. But we also know that, if they will spend time and effort, they can resolve the problems as they crop up.

Thus managers may want to receive their new work, materials, or orders *before* or *after* the manager in the preceding position in the work flow is ready to pass it along. When they believe it is not yet perfected or complete or they are too busy with other activities to begin the next phase, they want it later. Typical are the endless controversies over whether a project is ready to move into production or to a testing stage.[8]

Designing TV Sets: A Case Example. George Strauss has provided us with a superb first-hand study of the work-flow-relation-

---

[8] See Harriet O. Ronken and Paul R. Lawrence, *Administering Changes*, Harvard University, Graduate School of Business Administration, Boston, 1952, pp. 185ff.

ship problems in the design operations in a television receiver manufacturing company. We quote some highlights of his study.

We observed the process of designing a new-model TV set, as we observed it in one company. The Engineering Department is, of course, the one most directly concerned, and it consists of five sections. *Electrical* determines in theoretical terms how the set will be made (technically: what the over-all "system" will be). *Mechanical* tries to fit the components together; it often finds that Electrical's theoretical plans are impractical or even that one Electrical engineer's theoretical suggestions are incompatible with those of another. *Chassis* designs the cabinet; close coordination is required if the components are to fit into the cabinet. This is not as easy as it sounds, since Electrical and Mechanical are constantly designing improvements which give better reception, but which conflict with the company's over-all goal of producing an ever-thinner, lighter set.

Automation designs the machinery which makes the printed circuits and attaches the tubes to it; in contrast to Electrical, which wants an ever-more "sophisticated" set, Automation wants one that is simple enough to be reduced to printed circuitry and put together mechanically. *Industrial Engineering* determines the techniques by which the set will be manufactured (other than the operations that are 100 per cent automated). Like Automation, it seeks to eliminate what it feels to be unnecessary frills.

Further complicating over-all coordination are the pressures brought by outside departments: Sales wants an attractive product that will sell easily, and Manufacturing wants a set that is easy to put together. And management as a whole is interested in keeping costs low, profits high.

Note that in this case no one section can make modifications without affecting all the others. A change in a cabinet, for instance, may require adjustments by every other section, yet each adjustment may in turn require further compensating adjustments elsewhere. Each section has its own vested interest. Electrical, with its goal of technical perfection, conflicts, for example, with Industrial Engineering's goal of manufacturing ease.

Since a new model must be designed each year, intergroup conflicts tend to reach a crescendo as the time for a final decision approaches. During the early part of the year there is little pressure to resolve agreements, and each section is free to work on its own pet projects.

As the deadline draws near, an increasing number of compromises and adjustments must be made, tempers grow raw, and human-relations problems begin to complicate the technical ones. Each engineer likes to feel that he has *completed* his end of the job and hates to reconsider his position just to please another section. No engineer likes to sacrifice his own brainchild.

Complicating all these problems are the changing status relationships between departments. When TV was new, the major problem was to design a workable set, and Electrical was the highest-status section. Today the emphasis is on sales appeal and manufacturing ease. Electrical still thinks its function is the most important one, but management seems to favor other sections when it makes critical decisions and hands out promotions.[9]

Implicit in the above case is one of the thorniest behavioral problems in work-flow relationships: uncertainties surrounding sequential positions in the flow. Managers often compete for earlier position in which they can initiate more and are thereby less confined. (This will be treated more extensively in Chapter 7.)

Although we know of no empirical studies, recent developments in the field of marketing must provide a similarly fertile ground for work-flow problems, since technicians, sales engineers, salesmen, manufacturing supervisors, manual writers, various troubleshooters, and people involved in technical development must coordinate their efforts in consummating the sale of a technical product.[10]

Behavioral Requirements

We can summarize the behavioral requirements of work-flow relationships by stating that the frequency of contact between stages should be a function of the degree of uncertainty at the

[9] George Strauss and Leonard R. Sayles, *Personnel: The Human Problems of Management*, Prentice-Hall, Inc., Englewood Cliffs, N.J., 1960, pp. 367–368.
[10] See Carl Rieser, "The Salesman Isn't Dead—He's Different," *Fortune*, November, 1962.

interface. Where timing, quality, or quantity problems are likely to occur, more frequent contact between managers is required. Where the sequence has become routine, i.e., manager B knows when, what, and how A will complete his work, the frequency can be reduced.

We can also distinguish three broad classes of relationship in terms of duration of contacts:

1. Short: B acts as a switching center, receiving or requesting information from A and transmitting it to his subordinates or even to C. All information is unambiguous, and the only crucial element (or problematic element) is timing: The promptness with which B's group or C can learn what is happening in A's stage will affect B and his group's efforts.

2. Medium: B regularly gathers data on work being done by A either through analyses of reports or through interviews of A and evaluates its potential impact on his group and on others. No immediate adjustment is required because there is a lag in the impact being felt.

3. Long: B reviews ambiguous, involved problems in sequential relationships and carries on investigations with no fixed duration.

Let us look briefly at some examples of these:

Short

A manager receives a complaint from the production floor that covers produced at the preceding stage are coming through too small to fit over the engine mount. He calls the cover department to stop the line and then informs the next stage in the flow that they will soon experience a shortage of engines.

Medium

A manager reviews a daily written report on the number of rejects of parts received from department B and notices that they exceed the established control limits. He calls the manager of B for an appointment to discuss this quality problem.

Long

A manager is asked to start manufacturing a component that has just gone through the development stage. His review of the blueprints, specifications, and test data raises a number of questions about the cost and time requirements. He assigns some of his own staff to undertake certain checks and asks for some meetings to review the status of the project.

Unfortunately, many managers do not make these distinctions and take too long to move crucial information through the system and spend insufficient time on the more difficult, ambiguous problems.

It is worth repeating that the time characteristics of the interaction are a function of the difficulty of the problem, i.e., how much interaction is required to find out what others are thinking, what is going on and why, how frequently the problem occurs, and finally how closely tied in are others whose work will be affected by what is learned.

There are many barriers to the successful conduct of these patterns of behavior. The most typical is an underestimate of the number and seriousness of problems that can occur or an overly optimistic estimate of the degree to which this has already become an established sequence with predictable limits of variation. Here are two examples drawn from an engineering environment:

We know now that we didn't spend enough time clarifying our requirements. We didn't keep checking back, and as a result the specifications, which looked good on paper, really were inadequate. So we are stuck with getting something that isn't right in terms of what we have to do with it.

The second example is a quotation from a meeting in which a high-level manager is appraising a new piece of equipment designed by his organization:

Just look at the amount of hardware where those two parts of the unit come together. The managers in charge of the respective areas didn't spend enough time together. It takes a lot of collaborative effort to come up with a good design. Otherwise you get results like these: too cumbersome circuitry, too many components, and all the rest.

There is a famous, or infamous, case in the automobile industry in which the new design of a hood was supposed to take into account the shape and size of the air filter. The hood designers did not conceive of the possibility that the air-filter design would significantly affect the new rakish line of the hood. However the two proved to be completely incompatible. A new enlarged air filter met a new lowered hood and a fit was comically impossible. By the time the lack of coordination was discovered, a number of expensive dies had been built especially for the new model, and they had to be scrapped.

The problem was attributed to location (the two groups were in different buildings). We contend that location can aggravate the situation, but the basic problem is failure to build work-flow contacts into the job of the manager. Particularly where groups are widely separated, the likelihood that chance or social contacts will spontaneously "fill in" the administrative requirements is minimal. Under these circumstances, special efforts are required to see that necessary contacts take place. (We shall return to this when we consider monitoring.) Otherwise such results as this are the rule, not the exception:

> I had a group working for me in one of our outlying locations. They were supposed to work closely with the people up here; after all, this group uses their output. Instead, there has been nothing but antagonism, no close working relationship. Everything that goes wrong technically they blame on us. They identify much more closely with the . . . which is located in the same building over there, banding together against the people in my building up here.

This middle-level manager is saying that his subordinate managers do not have the centripetal force of shared informal group membership and, although they fill adjacent steps in the flow of work, they fail to coordinate. Most work provides ample opportunities to find fault with another stage's contribution, to blame it for every ambiguous situation that creates hardships for the manager. This is unfortunately a more typical state of affairs than coordinated sequencing. Therefore, there is a major need for factoring work-flow contacts into the job of the manager.

SERVICE RELATIONSHIPS

We have already referred to service relationships in our introduction to work-flow relationships in order to clarify the distinction. In terms of the division of labor, an organization often decides to centralize an activity (called "service") rather than allow each manager to control it himself, usually on the theory that this provides for greater economy and more skillful completion of the service than would its dispersion among all the users.[11] Thus a service group manager must respond to the requests of a large number of other managers who come to him for activities needed to complete their own internal work.

In a previous study, the author and his colleague endeavored to distinguish those activities that could be centralized because they were not essential to the creation of a continuously paced, fixed time-parameter-sequence internal work flow.[12] In this study it was apparent that management often creates separate service groups, despite the fact that this prevents one or more managers from stabilizing their own work groups, since they must always rely on an outside group to balance the coordination process of the work of their own departments. However, even when a division of labor makes desirable splitting off a part of the work and giving it to a service group, one can predict a series of continuing conflicts between service group managers and managers requiring service.

[11] This is the familiar observation of Adam Smith that the economic feasibility of increased division of labor (in part, synonymous with more "service" functions outside the jurisdiction of the manager) is a function of the extent of the market; here the "market" is inside the firm.

[12] Eliot D. Chapple and Leonard R. Sayles, *The Measure of Management*, The Macmillan Company, New York, 1961, chap. 2.

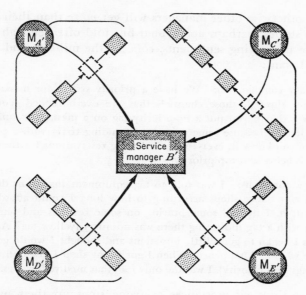

Service Relationships

Managers A', C', D', E' must each have certain activities
completed by service manager B' to fulfill
their own work-flow requirements

Typical Service Problems

It is almost an unwritten rule that service functions become scarce resources. The phenomenon can be observed in all institutions and locations: communication circuits in the military, maintenance activities in an industrial plant, a typing pool in a university, restaurant pantries, the pathology laboratory in a hospital. Often because of a chance coincidence, there is a sudden and heavy demand for the resources controlled by the service group. As a result of difficulties experienced in satisfying their needs, managers requiring service decide that they must use greater pressure or authority in order to meet their requirements; otherwise other managers will get *more* than their share. Two stories, perhaps apocryphal but told often enough to reveal the underlying sentiments, concern the military and an industrial plant:

> (A Navy commander): We have a priority system for messages going out through those channels that are overburdened. You soon discover that if you put a no-priority tag on a message it will never be delivered because somebody else is sending trivia with a priority. Before you know it, everything, including reservations for the officers club, is being sent top priority!

> (A new foreman): I was told to tag equipment that went down to the maintenance shops according to how long I could afford to be without it. I needed some bracing on some benches and sent them down with a tag indicating there was no hurry [yellow tag]. After six weeks I began to get a little impatient and thought I would go down to see what had happened. When I got to the shop I saw nothing but red tags [top priority]. I was the only fool that used yellow tags.

Under these circumstances everyone steps up their own demands to "get there before the hoarders do." This increased pressure for service makes for increased shortages, the standard problem of any rationing system. But, more important, it creates organizational problems, as the service manager is subjected to increased initiations for action and his clients experience an increased number of nonresponse situations.

In every organization the service manager has an unenviable position, fending off those who fear that their work is not getting the attention it deserves, particularly if they lack status for adequate defenses:

> Those guys wait until the last minute and then expect we'll drop everything else to take care of their work. Then when they don't get what they want, they threaten to make a federal case of it in the front office.

> Once you do something for them more quickly than usual, they expect that you'll do it every time at the same pace, and they factor into their planning the likelihood that they can pressure you into cutting the time.

I spend a good share of my time arguing with other managers who think we aren't doing enough for them. This keeps me from doing other things and often keeps my key people tied up, where we should be doing our regular work.

As we noted in our discussion of trading relationships, time is not the only variable. Cost and quality also are important considerations in many service functions. Service managers complain of being squeezed on budget and of constant pressures to add a little something extra to the work they do. Obviously the degree of ambiguity in the nature of the service determines the amount of negotiation necessary each time a client is served. Some jobs are completely routine and can be "sent out" without further contact; there is no possibility for variance. Others incorporate many unpredictable elements.

Some of these ambiguous items become weapons in the struggle and serve to make the conflict more intense. Reciprocity is a familiar phenomenon in all recorded history. Individuals establish relationships based on exchanges of good will: favors, gifts, aid, good turns, mutual protection. The typical service manager alternates between rewarding his friends and punishing his enemies (by doing their work more slowly, less carefully, or "charging" them more, where budget and cost accounting procedures allow) and favoring his most powerful adversaries in the belief that they carry most weight at higher organizational levels.[13]

This serves to outrage the less favored clients who respond by increasing their initiations directly to the service group or to a higher management which, they hope, will apply the pressure:

> The only way you can be sure of getting your work done correctly and on time is to keep needling them; you don't dare stop or your work will get sidetracked in favor of someone else's.

> Getting work done by outside groups is a pain in the neck; you have to spend so much time watching them. In the old days, when we did it ourselves, it took a lot less managerial effort.

[13] Melville Dalton has documented the most detailed account of this type of intrigue. See his *Men Who Manage*, John Wiley & Sons. Inc., New York, 1959.

There is a reasonably true adage: Shortages tend to become serious scarcities. A manager has a tight schedule into which a particular service item fits. He discovers that he is being outbid by others. He is tempted then to increase his bid, and he protests more vigorously that he cannot wait. He exaggerates the acceptable terms at the early negotiations to provide himself with a comfortable margin, in case others become too demanding, and acts on the premise that the wheel that squeaks the loudest gets the grease.

Thus, in both initial contacts and follow up, scarce resources requires constant attention. They are therefore burdensome, beyond their worth in terms of time and energy of contact.[14] Like the union leader squeezing another half cent into a package settlement, the manager-protagonist must emote with greater conviction on each successive contact.

Even then he is uncertain that the "ante" will not be raised again, in terms of what is required to get the job done. He may seek out powerful allies, perhaps the sponsor of the project or any higher-level manager who has some stake in what he is doing, in the hope that they may intervene in his behalf. Again, this takes interactional time, that is, if one is to be sure of getting there before the hoarders do.

Thus a spiral builds up: Lack of satisfactory response from the service group manager causes the client to increase his frequency of initiation of *short contacts* (needling) and efforts to dominate. In turn, this may reduce the effectiveness of the service manager in fulfilling his commitments and/or increase his nonresponsiveness. The result is a joint product of the service manager's lack of time to exercise adequate stabilizing influences internally and his increased loss of control due to emotional strain.

There is also a tendency for the outsider's point of contact to shift upward within the service function. He tries to put on

14 Often contracting out begins as a reaction to these burdens. The manager prefers to deal with an outsider with whom he has a legal relationship (enforceable by law) rather than with a colleague with whom he must maintain *human* relations.

pressure by appealing to higher levels when the lower echelons fail to provide him with adequate responsiveness. Second, the management hierarchy within service finds that higher-status— meaning higher-level—managers are better able to withstand the enormous pulling and hauling among competing users.

> Our department has the job of shifting office furniture. I found the man I had in charge of the operation couldn't take it any longer. Each department that wanted work done brought in the big brass, so on any particular day he might have three or four division heads claiming that their people had to be taken care of first. Now I make them come through me, and I make up a schedule of priorities for the immediate manager.

We have noted that service relationships incorporate a maximum of intraorganizational friction. They lack the regularity of work-flow contacts, are likely to have many mutually incompatible demands in them, and encourage temporary alliances based on reciprocity which further antagonize those who don't receive "most favored nation treatment."

Successful Service Managers

One temptation is to observe that successful managers were those who recognized the inevitable conflicts in their jobs and resigned themselves to accepting the mutually incompatible pressures and hostilities. This is an argument for insight and understanding. But, in fact, the successful managers seemed to be able to *do* something about their organizational position that contributed to the stability of their departments.

Most significantly they were able to reverse the one-way flow of originations of action. Rather than wait for the manager receiving service to come to them with demands for greater speed, lower costs, improved priorities, they go to him:

> Look here, Bill, you asked us to finish this special work in a hurry. Frankly, with our backlog, we can't touch it for days unless you can lend us some of your people or do some routine work yourself.

The successful service manager is one who can serve as a buffer for his subordinates and reduce the pressure on himself by negotiation with the managers who are demanding "better service." For example, he persuades them to change their requirements (specifications) or to provide him with additional manpower. The important thing is that he takes the initiative and takes it before crises (e.g., schedules missed) emerge and increase the pressures still more.

Not only do two-sided negotiations occur where one might expect, in terms of setting prices, dates, etc., but also in other areas. While the orthodox order of initiation is clear in service relationships, i.e., the "customer" tells the service manager what is wanted, the alert manager converts this into a two-way street:

> They came to us and said they wanted a completely new X. I told them how long they would have to wait for that kind of development job. I began discussing with them how it might be possible to modify one of our existing X's and eventually convinced them to give us one of their people and finance a small feasibility study.

> We were supposed to develop this kind of item for them. After a lot of discussions, I sold them on one that was much simpler, which was fortunate because we needed that extra time for other work.

CONCLUSION

This chapter has reviewed three distinctive administrative patterns that may be part of a manager's external relationships. These include trading, work-flow, and service relationships. We have endeavored to identify the typical managerial problems associated with each of these and to propose behavioral solutions to the most serious ones. All three constitute the major elements of the "operating work" of the organization.

In the next chapter, four "contingency" patterns will be examined. These represent structural mechanisms provided by the organization in order to *identify, solve,* and sometimes *avoid* certain predictable administrative problems.

Advisory, Auditing, Stabilization, and Innovation Relationships

In this chapter we shall complete the description of the basic administrative patterns of the manager, again using behavioral, operational terms wherever possible so that the manager knows what he must do to fulfill the requirements of his job. Here we shall look at advisory, auditing, stabilization, and innovation relationships which comprise a large portion of executive activity in the modern organization. Interestingly, these particular patterns are probably the hallmark of firms that have elaborated the division of labor at the managerial level. Traditionally they might all have been handled by the head of the organization; only relatively recently have these activities been incorporated in the jobs of lower-level executives.

ADVISORY RELATIONSHIPS

Advisory relationships are the core of what traditional textbooks refer to as "staff" activities: the provision of counsel and advice by the expert to the generalist, the manager concerned with overall coordination. Expertise may be required to solve problems in finance, personnel, production, or metallurgy. The advisory manager usually has a group of college-trained subordinates who are ready to apply their skills and knowledge to problems brought to them; at least that is the theory of their presence in the organization.

Several years ago we undertook an analysis of the advisory functions of personnel managers. Although this group represents only one specialty, there is no reason to believe that it has unique properties. Therefore we shall quote from those findings.

The Case of Personnel

The use of advisers rests on the assumption that a sharp distinction can be drawn between the three categories of information, advice, and decision making. In practice, this distinction is often blurred.

When providing information, the personnel manager simply furnishes facts that will help the manager to make sound, well-informed decisions:

1. The disciplinary clause of the union agreement means so and so.
2. The "going rate" for engineers like Jones is $650 per month in our present labor market.
3. Other companies in the metropolitan area require their carpenters to move small machinery when it is necessary in the course of their work.

Or he may play a more active role and furnish advice:

1. You are likely to provoke a wildcat strike if you give Bill Williams a disciplinary layoff.
2. On the basis of the record, Jones looks like a better bet for the promotion, since the man on the job will have to assume a good deal of initiative without close supervision.
3. If you hire Smith at that salary, you will have some dissatisfied older employees in your department.

Sometimes there is a very narrow line between providing facts and providing advice. By selecting his facts carefully, the personnel manager can actually influence the line manager's decision.

Finally, the personnel manager can make decisions:[1]

1. Don't discharge Brown; give him a warning slip.
2. Hire Green to replace the man who left.
3. Pay White $100 per week for that new job.

These neat distinctions often break down in practice. What is given as advice may be interpreted as a decision.

Historically there has been a tendency for management to turn over more and more functions to well-trained experts who have specialized knowledge in a relatively narrow field. When experts were first used to supplement the skills of line supervisors, the distinctions between information, advice, and decision making were rarely made. Management showed a readiness to accept expert advice. Often the industrial relations department, for example, actually *told* supervisors whom to hire, what to pay them, and how to answer their grievances. The result was frequently disastrous to the prestige and status of the supervisor.

In practice, it takes a strong-willed personnel manager to resist the temptation to become a decision maker. Once he has grown accustomed to providing advice and counsel, he may find himself irresistibly taking the next step and actually make the decision, e.g., "Bill Williams should be given another chance, not discharged."

It is not surprising that advisory groups seek to broaden the questions on which they are consulted. A new personnel man may be hired just to give expert advice on employment and training problems. It would be a safe prediction that he will soon seek to have his expertise used for a broader range of questions, such as wages and salaries, grievances, and reorganization problems.

Even when the personnel manager is careful not to usurp the responsibility of the line supervisor, his actions may still be misinterpreted. The following case illustrates this problem:

[1] Later we shall see that this is a shift to a *stabilization relationship*.

A grievance was filed against Gus Homes, a departmental supervisor, for failing to divide overtime equally. Homes argued that employees who failed to meet production standards on regular work should not be given overtime. The union contract said nothing about overtime, although general plant practice sanctioned equal division. The personnel director of the company, anxious to avoid any union bargaining on the overtime issue, urged Homes to change his mind. Homes refused.

Some weeks later, Homes was transferred to a less desirable job. The plant "grapevine" reported that the manager had "given him the axe" on the recommendation of the personnel director. The truth of the matter was that the manager had believed for some time that Homes should be removed from his department. The overtime situation was just one among many reasons that seemed to justify the move.

From this point on, other supervisors in the organization thought twice about refusing the advice of the personnel director. His recommendations had become cloaked with real line authority; he had become another boss.

We may have given the impression that managers who are supposed to advise aggressively seek to broaden their responsibilities and in the process thwart the line organization's efforts to maintain its unity of command. This is not always the case, however, for the managers receiving the advice may themselves encourage this.

The willingness of the personnel man to help in a difficult problem, for example, may provide the supervisor with welcome relief from burdensome responsibilities. In effect, he says to the personnel man, "Good. You handle the personnel and I'll take care of all the technical problems." Then if something goes wrong, if a decision backfires, the line supervisor can simply point out that it was not *his* decision, it was a personnel department decision.

Problems in Advisory Relationships

The line supervisor's reluctance to question the adviser's expertise is easy to understand. Top management has engaged specialists who are presumed to have the answers to difficult problems. The subordinate manager who challenges their ability feels that he is risking a bad decision for which he will have to bear all the responsibility. He may even interpret advice as a decision in order to avoid assuming responsibility and to "pass the buck" to the expert. Furthermore, he may believe that the expert is speaking for top management. Many experts are more closely in touch with the higher levels of the organization than are the managers they advise.

Paradoxically, a manager may complain that an advisory group is pressuring for increased recognition and at the same time grumble that the adviser is failing to take responsibility for decision making. As one supervisor expressed it:

> We stay away from the industrial relations department as much as possible. They're always trying to sell you on some new program or new way of doing something that makes more work for you. But then when you go to them with a problem, you can't get a straight answer from them; they won't tell you how to handle it. [Interviewer's query: But what do they tell you then?] Oh, they give you a lot of pros and cons and stuff that leave you more confused than when you went in. They are always coming around with this pet project or that great idea, which if we accept will give them a star on their chart and upset our entire operation.

Problems are created because advisory managers offer too much advice and because they do not offer enough, that is, they do not take over a problem and actually solve it for the manager in need.

They are "too free" with their assistance for reasons besides the desire to gain stature and recognition in the organization. Not only do their superiors evaluate advisory management performance in terms of number of ideas, projects, or techniques that are adopted but also in terms of their missionary skills. The advisers are encouraged to influence managers to change some of their current practices. From the point of view of the manager who has a problem, this has every appearance of being the wrong kind of medicine:

Company Y has manpower specialists who can be consulted when departments are interested in determining the personnel requirements of new operations. However, top management has encouraged these experts to recommend, as strongly as they know how, that new operations use a smaller proportion of fully trained craftsmen and a heavier proportion of semiskilled operators [through a finer division of labor]. The managers who receive this advice complain that their problems are being handled in terms of an inflexible policy rather than in terms of the needs of a particular job.

Ideally, a work-flow manager begins a new activity by requesting assistance. His own monitoring or pressure from higher levels of management or an auditing group causes him to seek outside help. The advisory manager himself or his personnel then respond to this request. However, many managements use advisory relationships as additional sources of pressures. Having failed to design adequate controls for the performance of the manager in some crucial area, they expect the advisory manager to be a kind of conscience reminding the manager to keep experimenting with management development or some other unmeasured area. Here the flow of initiations is in the opposite direction, from advisory manager to work-flow manager. These are the most troublesome advisory relationships and the most difficult to integrate into an organizational system. The work-flow manager has no incentive to adopt the ideas unless the adviser acts as the representative of a higher level of management.

The advisory manager may get himself into difficulty with other managers not only by attempting to sell "strong medicine" and new "hot" programs but also by the patterns of his contacts. He is often tempted to get around "old line" thinking by going directly to either lower or higher levels of the organization where he hopes to find a more responsive ear for his new solutions to old problems. This irritates the manager, who feels he is being bypassed by those who are too eager to earn "merit badges."

It is not unusual to find that the expert can woo away a subordinate who finds the outsider easier to consult than his own manager. There are amply documented satisfactions to be obtained by the manager who can solve all problems for his staff.

To find that his people seek an outsider can jolt the manager into a belated recognition that he is not quite indispensable. One of the frequently observed concomitants of automation is the disturbance to the equilibrium of the supervisor; he misses the frequent calls for help from subordinates who now call technical experts when equipment problems emerge.

We have simplified the advisory relationship by implying that one adviser deals with a manager and causes problems. In the modern organization, expertise is distributed among many specialized groups and a given problem can call for engineering, standards, methods, personnel, and many other types of knowledge. The boundary lines are never clear, and each group manager feels his is the real answer to the difficulty. Thus a manager may be deluged with helpers, many of whom remind him of their associations with higher company levels and programs in order to encourage his adoption of a particular solution to the problem.

To summarize the interactional difficulties in advisory relationships:

1. The adviser may take the initiative without waiting for requests from managers with problems.
2. Multiple initiations from advisory groups can place a manager in conflict over whose expertise is most valuable.
3. Advisory managers have relationships above and below the manager they are there to help; this upsets the equilibrium of the manager's position.
4. When asked to take over a problem, the advisory manager who previously was only too anxious to help may fail to respond because he would be infringing on the other manager's "responsibility" to handle the situation.
5. Advisory personnel may interfere with a manager's relationships with his own subordinates. At times, the adviser may initiate action for the other manager's subordinates. These initiations can conflict with existing orders. Even more troublesome, as we have noted, subordinates may find the advisory manager more responsive to their ideas or problems than their own manager. Such a shift can injure the leadership position of the manager and cause him to resent the interference of the outsider.

Many of these difficulties are the product of an inherent conflict between the expert and the generalist, the man of ideas and the man of action. They have different origins in terms of education outside the organization and career lines inside the organization.[2] They create communication problems at the symbolic level that accent the organizational conflicts described above.

Improving Advisory Relationships

There are methods by which this very difficult type of relationship can be handled with greater success than is usually observed. Clearly it is not enough to say that an advisory manager should provide technical counsel. The question is how to integrate his pattern of activity into an organizational process. One notably successful head of such an activity described the job interactions expected of his subordinates:

> We feel that it is our job to represent a point of view that might otherwise be lost. The typical manager just doesn't keep this . . . area in mind. We help him by getting together a lot of background material for him; we even go outside the organization and make certain contacts that will help him. Also, I expect members of this department to spend enough time with these men to learn all the "rules of the game," the way they work. My people have to be able to detect when what they are learning concerning the work of a given manager cannot be reported up the line and when he doesn't care if it gets out. I tell them all not to try to make a reputation for themselves. I can identify my best man because he has established a reputation with the engineering managers such that they jump when he makes a suggestion. But even he doesn't push hard; that's the job of the manager's manager.

Successful advisory relationships seem to be those where the adviser responds to the same distress signals as those he is supposed to help and where he is willing to see credit go to the helped department.

[2] See Melville Dalton, *Men Who Manage,* John Wiley & Sons, Inc., New York, 1959, pp. 71–108.

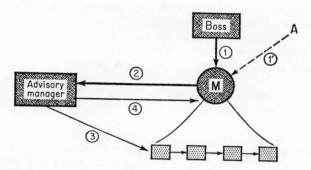

The "Ideal" Advisory Relationship
*On the basis of pressures from superiors (1) or auditing groups (1'),
a work-flow manager detects a significant problem
and seeks assistance from advisory managers (2).
The advisor investigates (3) and reports to the
work-flow manager on alternative solutions (4)*

This also means developing advisory relationships at the point
where the influence should take place. This is largely a function
of organization-design decisions. Managers have observed that
where advisers (and critics) report up separate lines of communication and are not close, in the organizational sense of the
word, to the groups they are supposed to assist, conflict surrounds
their efforts to get their views accepted:

> In the old days, *before* we were tied in lower in the organization,
> every little question concerning our area used to get blown up and
> end up in the V.P.'s office. Each manager just backed his subordinate
> managers more strongly.

The sequence of successful advisory relationships appears to
be this:

◆ The manager turns to the specialist-advisory group with his problems, largely on his own initiative, with the feeling that he can

discuss his problems freely with a sympathetic listener who will not hurt his position (have authority).

♦ The line understands what skills and knowledge are embodied in the advisory group—how far they can go—and in turn the advisory group comes to understand the needs and objectives of the line groups.

♦ The manager is aided in understanding the full dimensions of his problem and is helped to develop skills in evaluating alternative solutions.

♦ The manager increases, over time, his ability to cope with these problems in his own area; perhaps he has to call on an adviser less often. At least he regards such problems as a means of developing new abilities and insights.

♦ The advisory group develops greater acceptance for its ideas and points of view, not by putting pressure on the line but by developing confidence in its helping role and by proving in practice that it can contribute to the manager's effectiveness.

♦ The line manager gets credit for any improvements that result.

♦ The adviser is evaluated, not in terms of the number of his plans and projects, but in terms of his ability to solve problems that the line manager sees as problems.

A similar view of the managerial behavior necessary to facilitate an advisory relationship is provided by Whyte, based on his own field research:

1. The specialist builds up a certain frequency and regularity of interaction with the operating man before seeking to bring about any innovations.

2. This means, in effect, that the specialist does not simply cook up his innovation in his own mind and then move right in and try to bring it about. Instead, he deliberately withholds his innovating efforts until he has established a personal relationship which will make them more acceptable.

3. Before he seeks to innovate, the specialist concentrates on familiarizing himself with the operating man's situation and problems. Some of this is done through observation, but a good deal of it is done through interviewing. This means, in effect, that the specialist gets the operating man to explain his situation as he views it himself, and to take the initiative in their relationship.

4. The specialist tries to build his innovations into a pattern of reciprocal initiations and exchange of valued activities. That is, he is not exclusively asking the operating man to change his behavior. He is also providing opportunities for the operating man to call for help from the specialist.

5. The specialist helps the operating man with activities for which the operating man receives rewards.[3]

AUDITING RELATIONSHIPS

At almost every level in an organization managers grow dissatisfied with their ability to "keep tabs" on what is happening. The manager is concerned with whether subordinates and other groups in the organization are meeting schedules, budgets, standards, rules, and all the organization requirements for which he himself can be called to task. Initially, he may appoint a staff assistant to act as his eyes and ears in overseeing the work of others. Over a period of time, particularly at higher levels, this one man evolves into a department made up of trained watchers who know personnel practices, financial reporting, product quality, or good customer relations and who can tell whether or not these are being achieved. Thus the checking-up or watchdog activities of the modern organization are not limited to traditional "auditing." The growth of specialization has resulted in numerous groups whose existence depends upon their ability to make appraisals, evaluations, and checks that the manager himself has neither the time nor the skill to make for himself.

There are two other justifications for the use of such specialists. The first is technical: The individual manager may not see trends by merely looking at single points in time. Accumulations of samples of performance may exhibit significant properties that self-checks, each isolated from the other, do not reveal. The second is more Machiavellian. The regular superior-subordinate contacts may serve to disguise rather than reveal significant departures from desired trends. Through well-known processes of

[3] William F. Whyte, *Men at Work*, Richard D. Irwin, Inc., Homewood, Ill., 1961, p. 562.

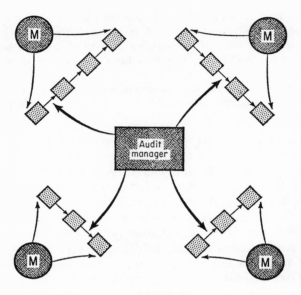

Auditing Relationships
*The auditing manager taps the work flows of other managers
to ascertain whether their activities are consistent
with specific organizational rules or standards*

covering up, filtering, accenting the "good" and deemphasizing
the "bad," successive layers of the organization serve to deceive
the higher-level managers. Therefore, functionnaires who are not
in the line are added to report directly.

Perhaps the most important reason for the proliferation of
auditing management in the modern organization is the failure
of the reward-and-punishment systems to direct adequately the
energies of managers:

> In our department store, each manager handles his own customer
> relations. It's up to him to decide on merchandise returns, for ex-
> ample. We know that most of them only give lip service to careful
> handling of customer complaints. They have learned that, over the

years, the only thing that counts as far as bonuses or promotion is concerned is their P and L showing. As a result, we are looking for some way of checking up on how they handle customers.

It is easy to see how this builds into conflict because at times the auditing manager is fighting the real payoff system of the organization as well as the emphases of other auditors.

It would be misleading to suggest that auditing relationships are designed just to provide information to higher organization levels. They are obviously meant to serve a pressure function as well. In the process of observing what is being done and "grading" how it is being accomplished, the persons doing the evaluating provide a kind of moral suasion at one extreme and an absolute veto at the other.

Let us look at these for a moment. First, there is moral suasion.

Top management wants to reduce the quantity of . . . we are using in our products, but they can't specify a fixed percentage reduction. If orders don't show any cuts, we go over the specifications very carefully. A lot more discussion is involved if this policy isn't being lived up to to the fullest.

In some instances the auditing manager has the power to hold up the activities of the groups being appraised until such time as they can satisfy the auditors. Quality control, for example, samples operations and can stop the line when certain standards are not being met.

In "classical" theory there should be no problems. The watchers use the same standards of evaluation that the manager himself would use. In practice, these standards are often ambiguous and mutually incompatible. There are few go–no go situations. There is almost endless room for maneuvering over whether or not a given manager has met a performance standard. Even in highly technical areas, e.g., the physical or engineering specifications of a component, one finds that men of competence and good will can disagree:

The test people used an improper statistical averaging method in computing their test results, which just managed to throw our work into the "unacceptable" category.

The 318 test is not designed to measure that dimension, and that's the only reason we didn't pass.

The specifications read that the product must be able to "take" certain temperatures and certain humidities. They don't say anything about the combination; only the evaluation group has interpreted them to mean that the components have to be exposed simultaneously to extreme temperature and humidity—and that's unfair!

When we leave the so-called technical areas and consider how effectively certain policies concerning employee relations, public relations, or customer relations are being met, we can anticipate a hundredfold increase in the possible disputes between auditors and the audited.

The result is animosity between them. Each side sees the other as the "enemy." This in itself may not be incompatible with the objectives of management in establishing these groups but, as we shall see, the behavioral concomitants of these attitudes serve to frustrate the objectives of auditing.

Managers are always trying to fool us, to hide data. They don't realize that we are all working for the same objectives.

We are under terrific pressure to alter our reports, to forget what we've seen. If we aren't somewhat cooperative, the group we are appraising can make life rough for us, and we'll have a terrific time getting the information we need.

On the other side of the relationship, the audited manager tries to adjust to what are often incompatible pressures from many auditing groups. In other words, he has to make trades; he cannot score equally high in the appraisals of everyone. If he provides absolutely safe working conditions, his costs will soar over his budget if he modifies his product to suit one group of engineers interested in reliability, he increases the servicing costs being measured by another group. Thus the manager keeps negotiating a delicate balance among competing objectives and ends up with a number of frustrations and fixed views on auditors.

Those guys are just paid to find trouble; they can't understand our problems. Even when you're doing everything well, they'll dig up some dirt.

They are just another barrier you have to get around. Now that we have experience with them, we can spend x dollars before they find out what we're doing.

Many of those standards are set so loose that the auditing group can apply whatever interpretation they want to them.

We keep getting more and more watchers, and watchers to watch the watchers, and none of them understand what it takes to run a department; they're all too narrow.

A student related what is almost the classic case involving suspicions of motives:

I worked in a government office that was periodically evaluated on its procedures. Whenever the team appeared, we knew we were in for trouble. The last time all our books and everything were perfect, but they had to find something wrong to report. Finally, they pulled out of the hat a violation of some provision concerning the gauge of the wire mesh that had been used in a "cage" we had constructed to keep certain documents. Apparently it wasn't heavy-duty enough, although none of the papers included involved security or could be negotiated. They just wanted to get the goods on us.

Behavior-pattern Problems

Problems are created by the manner in which auditing is conducted, the pattern of interaction between auditors and those being audited:

1. The auditor may go directly to subordinates of a manager and seek to find out things from them that the manager has not learned himself or would not reveal if he had been approached. Insofar as there is some tradition (accepted pattern) involving "going through" the manager, such a procedure violates expectations.
2. The auditor can build no regular relationship; he comes infrequently and often unannounced, and this "free floating" is inconsistent with easy working relationships.
3. On occasion, there is too much contact between auditor and audited. Collusion evolves out of such a close relationship. In exchange for not reporting certain defects that he observes, the auditor receives good cooperation, and other defects are left out in the open. The agreement is maintained by the power of both sides to embarrass the other in the eyes of higher management.
4. Many times auditors report their findings "up the line" without giving the offenders a chance to rectify the defect.
5. Those being audited are so unresponsive to questions and probes as to convince the auditors that they must be hiding serious problems. Further, in this ostracism they express such antagonism to the auditing group as to make discussion of ambiguous points nearly impossible.
6. After finding a problem, those involved often ask the auditing manager to propose a solution that will rectify the difficulty and will even help defend the solution to upper management. Many auditors take the position that this is not their function.[4]
7. Conflicting signals are a hallmark of the modern organization. The manager who attempts to respond too wholeheartedly to the defects uncovered by one auditing group finds that he is in trouble with another.

[4] They argue that one cannot be a participant in a decision or an activity and also give an impartial evaluation. An analogous situation is the union that refuses to cosponsor a job-evaluation program in the belief that this will compromise its ability to file grievances when inequities show up. Recent criticism of the public accounting field for engaging in "management consulting" is also relevant here. It is argued that, although a C.P.A. firm contends that its advisory and auditing functions are compartmentalized, it cannot help being influenced when passing judgment on those organizational decisions to which it was a party and those to which it comes as a complete "outsider."

Behavior-pattern "Solutions"

Our observations do not disclose answers for all these problems. The last, 7, is inherent in the multiplication of evaluators and in the inevitable overlapping of one area with another. One cannot affect production without affecting personnel; quality without affecting cost—or at least not usually.[5] But there are directions of improved relationship that can be proposed.

First, one needs to distinguish three quite different types of auditing relationship, for each requires distinctive behavior patterns:

1. The auditor can stop the flow of work when he decides standards are not being met, and the standards are *relatively* unambiguous and applied with little interaction.
2. At stated times auditors run checks on specific aspects of work being performed, but these are subject to negotiation and interpretation.
3. At very infrequent and irregular intervals, operations are audited on many dimensions and reports prepared. The auditor is usually a complete stranger to that part of the organization.

Short-term Auditing Relationships. Here auditing is part of the actual flow of work. Good examples are the requirement that every sales order over *x* amount go to a credit evaluator or that every *x* piece produced go to a quality evaluator. The most important determinant of appropriate behavior patterns is to whom the evaluator reports. When the pace at which the inspection proceeds directly determines the rate at which other operations progress, these should be under a common supervisor. Otherwise, there will be constant haggling over the impact of the auditing on the ability of the operations supervisor to maintain an even flow of regular, continuous work.[6] When the evaluation is via sam-

[5] We shall deal with this problem of conflicting objectives of auditing groups when we consider decision making as an organizational process in Chapter 12.
[6] In a recent book, the author and a colleague develop more explicit criteria for distinguishing between work stages that are part of a *unit work flow,* and therefore should be under a common supervisor, and those which are separable. Where a checking operation is placed under the supervisor whose

pling that does not interrupt the flow, it is appropriate to place it under the control of a separate functional manager.

Periodic Evaluations. Most cost, personnel, and technical evaluations involve frequent assessments of how operating managers are doing. We can distinguish several stages by which these are handled: the establishment of the standard, observations to determine how the standard is being met, and interpretation of the findings and use of the results.

The first and last often involve problems, because the manager being appraised does not see the relationship between the assessment and the rewards and punishments that affect him. Here is a simple recommendation:

> In the two factories where the greatest acceptance of standards was observed, standard-setting was always described as a process of negotiation between superiors and subordinates in the *operating* departments, with the accounting department serving as the recorder of the bargain. . . . The notion that standards could be established by a neutral "umpire" was rejected.[7]

Not only must the manager's manager be the one who shows by deeds that the standards being audited are important to him (and determine his evaluation of the subordinate manager), but at the end of the process he must demonstrate that he makes use of the findings.

During the auditing and interpretation of the findings, frequent and regular contacts are highly important. The auditor has to spend the time—and it is often painful time because those audited are not receptive—in explaining the standards being

---

work is being evaluated, provision is made for periodic auditing (2, in our categorization) by an auditing group manager, who sees that the other manager is actually maintaining standards. See Eliot D. Chapple and Leonard R. Sayles, *The Measure of Management*, The Macmillan Company, New York, 1961, pp. 21–32.

[7] Herbert Simon et al., *Centralization vs. Decentralization in Organizing the Controller's Department*, Controllership Foundation, New York, 1954, p. 33.

used, their internal logic, and the possible uses that the manager himself can make of the findings. In the process he must be able to respond to initiations (suggestions, criticisms) from the operating manager. In doing so, he drains off much of the hostility that normally exists in these relationships. The early stages are the hardest, when the auditors are tempted to "keep busy at their own desks to avoid unpleasant or frustrating experiences with operating people."[8]

In his study of controller departments, Simon bolsters the argument for changing the traditional interaction pattern associated with auditing relationships, where all the initiation comes from the auditor—and on a highly irregular basis—to a bilateral pattern with greater frequency:

> On the other hand, if a definite program is set up, involving regular assignments for accounting personnel requiring them to contact operating supervisors for information, the accountant may begin to arouse the interest of the operating executives in possible uses of accounting data. They may also obtain a better understanding of these executives' needs for data. When this occurs, the operating heads will generally encourage or seek out more frequent contacts with the accountants. Each begins to gain a more thorough understanding of the vocabulary, problems and methods of the other. This cycle continues until a fairly high degree of communication and use of accounting data is attained.
>
> This provides the controller's department with an opportunity to show that it really intends to provide data in useful and usable form, in terms of operating departments' needs, so that when it is asked for help, it meets such requests promptly.[9]

Whyte makes the same recommendation after observing industrial engineers.[10] Needless to say, such interactions are highly consistent with our finding that the standards being enforced

[8] *Ibid,* p. 49.
[9] *Ibid.,* pp. 49–50.
[10] William F. Whyte et al., *Money and Motivation,* Harper & Row, Publishers, Incorporated, New York, 1955, pp. 227–233.

are both ambiguous and not without conflict. Therefore, some negotiation-discussion process is inevitable, if relationships are to be satisfactory.

On the other hand, the manager successful in dealing with auditors appears to be one who is willing to continue discussions with those who potentially can hurt him and who he may feel do not understand him or his problems and who are not rewarded for doing so. The manager who retires from the field believing that there is no way of dealing with auditors is failing an important element in his job.

A crucial part of the relationship is also the willingness of those doing the judging to go over their evaluations with the affected manager before the reports go higher in the organization. With the exception of a few highly sensitive areas where any infraction may be grounds for serious discipline, it is useful to give the "offending manager" a chance to review and contribute to the interpretation and, in many cases, to initiate changes that will eliminate the need for a negative finding.

Related to this is the willingness of the operating manager to initiate contacts with the auditing manager at an early enough stage in the work process to permit changes and adjustments to be made. The ability to modify decisions then becomes a function of the quality of other aspects of their relationship and perhaps the physical location as well. Simon and his fellow researchers found that where significant geographic distance separated the two a close working relationship was next to impossible.[11]

Infrequent Appraisals. The organization may wish to minimize the relationship between auditor and work-flow manager. On the assumption that almost no cooperation is necessary and any systematic relationship can breed collusion or corruption, the auditing manager adopts the role of the stranger or outsider. This works best in the very infrequent appraisals or evaluations made by task forces or special appraisers. These relationships are not part of the day-to-day work systems but occur annually or even less frequently when unusual problems occur.

11 Simon et al., *op cit.*, pp. 51–52.

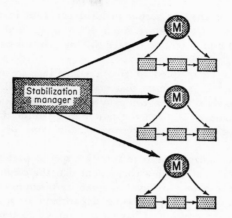

Stabilization Relationships
*Prior to initiating certain work flows or responding
to internal problems, managers must gain approval
or clearance from the stabilization manager*

STABILIZATION RELATIONSHIPS

Unlike auditing, stabilization involves advance approval. While
the auditors probe, sample, and assess (or evaluate)—what we
have called giving "grades"—those who have a stabilization function hold all the initiative. Before certain operations can be
started, their approval must be secured. Thus they also resemble
a preceding work-flow stage, in that, before certain activities can
get under way, they must be appropriately responsive. Unlike
adjacent work-flow stages, however, the interaction pattern here
is very one-sided. The stabilizing group does little adjusting to
coordinate with the next stage.

Why is advance approval necessary? The creation of these
groups is another admission that the organization has not succeeded in adjusting its incentives and controls so that managers
are induced to serve the over-all goals of the institution.

♦ A supervisor may schedule output in his department in a manner that serves his needs but thwarts other departments, and so a production control unit is created to take the initiative in establishing these schedules.

♦ A manager may be tempted to give a salary increase or resolve a union grievance in a manner that maintains the equilibrium in his own group but creates company-wide problems, and so a personnel department is given the power to establish tight limits on salary adjustments and to approve certain types of grievance settlements.

♦ An engineering manager wants to specify a special part for a new piece of equipment although a component that the company regularly stocks and can be purchased at quantity discounts would do almost as well, and so a purchasing department or a standards group is put in the position of having to approve all nonstandard parts.

The growth of stabilization groups is also related to changes in the environment in which the organization operates. The salience of labor, community, and government relations for the firm, for example, is such that top management is reluctant to allow individual managers to carry out all the steps of certain work flows. Therefore grievance settlements have to be cleared, speeches approved, pricing decisions centralized, and contacts with political figures justified and shaped by the specialist who has been most thoroughly indoctrinated with the policy position of the total organization. There is ever present the fear that the manager, left to his own devices, might injure a delicate relationship. While the individual manager handles much of the labor relations or pricing determinations, the stabilization group enters the process at a key point.

Also, these groups have been created by top management to limit the disadvantages associated with suboptimization. Because the overall balance of incentives in the organization tends to reward the manager for actions that might improve his position but hurt others or the total system, decisions are confined within limits by the stabilization group.

The groups interacting with stabilization managers often have this point of view:

> Those guys will always ask for more from you or be more rigid in what they expect you to do than they really expect to get. So it is up to the manager to convince them that he can't do any more than he feels is reasonable under the circumstances. Otherwise, he is going to be burdened with a terrific job. Keep a big safety factor in. Haggle with them; review all their figures.

And their counterparts in the other office arrive at complementary sentiments: The manager is always crying before he is hurt.

Another way of viewing the stabilization function is to recognize that the organization spawns a number of distinctive interest groups. Perhaps purposefully, management creates competing and conflicting suborganizations.

With an implicit or explicit awareness of this difference in short-term objectives and the potential victory or defeat of one group over the other, management then creates *additional* groups to ensure a balance of power, so that one does not overpower the other. Thus we have the business equivalent of the political scientists' system of checks and balances.

These new groups have the function of balancing the pros and cons and making decisions; they *do not* just advise or audit. For example, a delicate balance is necessary between the high cost of inventories (and the danger of obsolescence) and the need to maintain customer good will by quick and complete service. Unfortunately, existing control systems tend to push the groups involved toward one extreme (low inventories) or the other (high inventories). Therefore a production scheduling and planning group is created. It has the job of balancing gains and costs, of mediating between conflicting points of view of rival-interest groups.

Stabilization groups are much heavier initiators to the line than other lateral groups. In many ways they are "bosses," and the line manager seeks techniques for evading their decisions and minimizing their impact on his own situation. The usual conflicts take place over the ability of the stabilizing group to factor successfully into its decision-making apparatus the special needs of all the groups that it must control. In addition, there is the danger that the number of stabilizing groups will seriously hamper the manager in getting his job done, as each requires time-consuming procedures, reports, negotiations, and permissions.

It would be a mistake to assume that most of these, any more than most auditing relationships, involve simple go–no go decisions. Personnel managers who administer the presumably technically precise job-evaluation plans spend thousands of man-hours in discussions with managers who seek to stretch the point value for a job so that it will have an appealing salary attached to it. Since the plans are only superficially precise, there is ample justification for many of the arguments.

At times it appears that the organization, recognizing that there can be no absolute rules or measurements of who is right, seeks consciously to develop a cumbersome system that will be difficult to penetrate. The obstacle course reduces the number of successful actions in two ways. First, the process is set up so that there are many opportunities for vetoes within the system. Second, many managers will not even initiate requests because of the extensive time and energy commitments required.

Whyte [12] gives a not untypical example in a case where a large company has instituted a special procedure for ordering machine parts and repair tools that are *not* on a carefully maintained list of approved, standard parts. In other words, management hopes that requests for nonstandard items will be exceptional, thus minimizing inventories: (Note the five months required to "decide"!)

Nov. 8 General foreman requisitioned four nonstandard tool kits (cost $50).

Jan. 6 This was approved by local management group.

12 Whyte, *Men at Work,* pp. 467–468.

Feb. 8 Divisional level "standardization committee" recommended delay until an engineer could appraise the effect of using such kits on manufacturing warranties.

At unspecified later dates, the following sequence:

1. The engineer recommended that the purchase not be allowed.
2. Divisional management reviewed and upheld the engineer's decision.

Apr. 4 Requisition was returned to local management.

In another company we found that a dozen contacts were necessary to procure the company airplane to bring in needed parts. Again this was part of a rationing plan. It resembled the operations of the Wage Stabilization Board during the Korean crisis. Both unable and unwilling to reduce wage controls to a simple rule or formula, the Board discouraged increases by providing for a lengthy, cumbersome, and frustrating procedure.

Improving Stabilization Relationships

The more successful stabilization relationships are characterized by a more constructive role for the manager who must deal with the stabilization group. For example, before issuing an edict with respect to standard parts or work schedules, the stabilization manager calls in departments that will be affected. He may develop a tentative proposal and go over it with some other supervisors, who then have the opportunity to initiate changes where they can be justified.

It is worth noting that, while these behavioral adjustments serve to moderate the frictions inherent in some of these lateral relationships, they by no means eliminate them. Chapter 8 will summarize some of the continuing human relationship problems with which the manager must cope in organizations having many such groups.

In conclusion, we should note that the creation of stabilization groups is usually a sign of centralization, i.e., higher management lodges initiative for certain decisions with these groups rather than allowing it to be dispersed through many work areas in the organization. Presumably the stabilization manager can be held to tighter standards of performance than could the many managers who would be making the same decisions. This purpose has been identified by the political scientist Kaufman:

> The usual way of reducing self-containment (i.e., centralizing) is the removal of some activity of the subgroup vital to the continuation of the subgroup's basic processes, and the lodging of that phase of its operation in, or directly under the control of, the central leadership. . . . This becomes an especially effective way for the leadership to ensure that its cues and signals will take precedence in the subgroup over those from competitive sources. . . . As one might expect, leaders tend to seek out those activities equally vital to all their subgroups. . . .[13]

INNOVATION RELATIONSHIPS

The organization creates certain groups that, unlike the others just described, are not intended to have regular interaction with the major work flows (what have sometimes been called "line"). These groups embody so-called "scarce values" that are easily lost or dissipated. For example, an advanced development group often can be lured or cajoled into "fire-fighting" operations (and, in the process, lose its long-term point of view). These specialists can be helpful in crises, but this orientation keeps the group from devoting itself to the less easily evaluated (and less easily rewarded) research functions. Because of the temptations and pressures of the organization to handle today's business today, groups that are supposed to take a very long-term point of view frequently find themselves developing close working relationships

[13] Herbert Kaufman, "Why Organizations Behave as They Do: An Outline of a Theory," paper presented at an Interdisciplinary Seminar on Administrative Theory, University of Texas, Austin, Tex., 1961, pp. 59–60.

with work-flow managers. The result is that "scarce values" are lost or at least become still more scarce.

For maximum effectiveness, a *minimum* of contact with other parts of the organization and maximum autonomy are probably desirable. The leaders of such innovation groups must *not* find their rewards (prestige, promotions) in increased visibility and recognition from the operating parts of the organization. Rather, the organization must provide alternative sources of reward (and objectives). Further, these managers cannot be expected to *sell* their contributions to other parts of the organization and be evaluated on the basis of acceptance and use.

Social science provides the underlying logic for establishing these groups. All work groups tend to adopt a somewhat stereotyped view of their work, based on their own experiences, backgrounds, and place in the structure. Common norms, symbols, and a perceptual bias decrease the likelihood that true innovations that in any way conflict with established practices or views will develop. This is the reason for "trend thinking." For example, once a design group concentrates on an automobile tail fin, the fin is likely to receive more attention and become more elaborate with each passing year. Most radical departures from present practices come from marginal members of the organization; in our example, this would be a so-called "advanced design group."

Difficulties emerge when the innovation manager must obtain data or equipment or borrow personnel from other parts of the organization, since there is no collaboration that he can trade in return.

In one sense, these innovation groups represent the extreme of professionalization in the organization, insofar as their standards of performance can be set by outside reference groups. While advisory, stabilization, and auditing groups frequently rationalize their failure to achieve satisfactory working relationships on the basis of others failing to comprehend their own professional objectives, innovation groups can be allowed these outside identifications. In fact, the organization establishes them in order to gain the value of disciplined, systematic expertise, unaffected by the pressures or standards of the internal system.

Except for the managers of innovation groups, the organization is concerned over excessive separation. As noted, advisory groups, for example, do not work closely enough with the day-to-day problems of other managers but sometimes seek to "innovate." However, innovational relationships can deteriorate because the manager is coopted by other more powerful groups seeking his skills and services to help meet standards being imposed by stabilization or auditing groups. This increased interaction serves to frustrate the organizational purpose of the innovation relationship.

Unique administrative devices may be necessary to reinforce and emphasize (or symbolize) the special position of the innovation group and to facilitate its own work patterns. These include provisions for flexible work hours on the premises, pay and promotion systems adjusted to professional norms rather than internal job-evaluation plans, and provision for contacts with outside colleagues.

CONCLUSION

Unfortunately, much too much ink is wasted on the "needs" of professionals in large organizations. As we can now see, except for the work areas that we have termed "innovational," experts, specialists, and professionals are engaged in advisory, auditing, and stabilization jobs. The requirements for and satisfactions from these jobs should be derived from successful interrelationships with other work systems. In fact the successes (and failures) of these groups should be measured (monitored) in terms of their ability to fit into the organization as an operating system. Too often they are measured by purely internal technical standards of performance and competency. However, their specialized knowledge and skill are useless unless they are integrated into work systems.

Thus in designing these jobs, in training incumbents, and in evaluating their performance, dynamic behavioral patterns must be stressed. Another reason for our emphasis on behavior is the subtle differences among these administrative patterns. For example, an advisory manager can become an auditor with a slight shift in his relationship to work-flow managers. At times, such shifts are accidental in that the manager is not aware of his role requirements. More frequently, the move away from the anticipated division of labor is deliberate. The source and direction of these motivated "adjustments" in job patterns are explored in the next chapter.

chapter

7

Dynamic Shifts in
Administrative Patterns

For the sake of exposition, we have made two simplifying assumptions. We have referred to a manager's administrative behavior in a manner that would suggest that each has one such
pattern for dealing with the rest of the organization. In addition,
these relationships have been treated in static terms, as though,
once established, they remain relatively fixed. Neither is realistic,
and we shall now remove these artificial constraints on our theory
of administration.

COMPOSITE JOBS

Most managers have to fulfill a myriad of administrative patterns.
For example, manager Y is a succeeding stage in a work flow,
receiving data from manager X, and in the same work flow he
precedes Z who takes his completed reports and uses them in a
quarterly report for division heads. In other work flows, manager
Y may have a different position. In addition, he has a small group
of subordinates providing clerical services for X, Z, and other
managers. Because a great deal of data flows into his department,
manager Y also has been given certain stabilization functions;

that is, he must initial all requests of a certain type after checking that they are in accordance with both existing policies and inventory levels.

To be effective in this position, manager Y must be able to shift his interaction pattern in accordance with the requirements of each activity. This is often more easily said than done. One can observe certain incompatible combinations of administrative roles. For example, and this is a classic case, it is not difficult to predict that the manager who audits certain aspects of the work of colleagues will have difficulty in an advisory relationship, in which they must voluntarily come to him with all problems exposed for the world to see. Similarly, a manager servicing other groups may have problems in securing their response to and acceptance of his stabilization activities.

In other words, there are conflicts between the parts of administrative activity. Where compliance from others is expected, it is not easy to maintain an informal give-and-take relationship in which information flows freely. The organization may elect to sacrifice adequate intelligence in exchange for greater conformity, or just the reverse.

CHANGES IN ADMINISTRATIVE PATTERNS

The manager does not typically hold fast to a given distribution of administrative relationships. As we shall see, he tends to shift their internal balance in a predictable fashion. Some of these shifts may be due to the ambiguity associated with most managerial jobs. This is not the place to belabor the obvious: the abysmal inadequacy of typical managerial job descriptions. These are phrased in such vague, nonoperational terms as to leave the manager who is told he must take "responsibility" for this function and "coordinate" that one and "contribute" to a third in the position of having to make his job "out of whole cloth." Furthermore, as countless observers have noted, most managers' managers do little to clarify what is expected of their subordinates in the way of performance and behavior, although they may give many cues as to what is expected in the way of appropriate attitudes, dress, and styles of life.[1]

More importantly, the manager discovers that his job can be made more or less appealing (satisfying, rewarding, even possible to accomplish) by adroit adjustments in his pattern of relationship with outside groups.

The various managerial relationships differ in their relative attractiveness and in the ease with which they can be performed. We observed a noticeable shift from more difficult to less difficult patterns. Below are examples of these shifts.

Typical Dynamic Shifts in Administrative Patterns

SERVICE
→ADVISORY
→AUDITING
→STABILIZATION

ADVISORY
→INNOVATION

1. Service relationships tend to shift toward an advisory pattern. For the manager in charge of a support group, being on the receiving end of constant demands means lower status. The service manager soon "discovers" the need to help other groups prepare their work for the support function in ways that expedite the function, and, in the process, he gains prestige and an easier, more satisfying organizational position.

2. Advisory groups seek to become auditors. Lacking the appropriate response from the other party who may reject his proposals and initiations, the advisory manager seeks eventually to be able to appaise the work of others and report this to upper management. If he is assigned this function, he knows that he will receive a better hearing and be shown more deference by those with whom he is supposed to work. Corporate responsibility for certain activities often implies this type of auditing relationship where technical activities are appraised.

[1] See W. R. Dill, T. L. Hilton, and W. R. Reitman, *The New Managers,* Prentice-Hall, Inc., Englewood Cliffs, N.J., 1962.

3. Where he cannot become an auditor, a manager with an unsatisfying advisory relationship to other projects may seek to move into the primary work flow, where he becomes a *preceding* or *succeeding* stage. The other managers can no longer ignore his technical specialty, they must deal with his group before they do their own work, or some part of their completed work moves directly to the former advisory manager. In this new type of position, he does not have to wait to be asked nor experience the stress of having his opinions ignored.

4. A stabilization relationship improves the auditor-manager's position. Now other managers *must* go to him before they act in order to obtain his permission. He discovers that there is much less stress in these interactions just because he can reject plans put forth by other managers. We have also observed managers of support groups who sought this type of relationship with those who they felt were misusing them. They sought permission from top management to set forth a number of explicit criteria for the work they were doing, among which would be the requirement that managers intending to use their services get their approval for what was to be done and the way in which it was to be done.

5. Advisory group managers who are not able to improve the responsiveness of other managers to their interactions often endeavor to shift to an innovation role. In terms of our operational definition, this means that they want the organization to recognize that it is *not* their job to get others to listen to them or adopt their knowledge. Rather, they work independently of other parts of the organization. This eliminates the need to engage in strained contacts in order to induce others to approve projects or to support their work or accept their findings. (Unfortunately, the organization may find that this isolation does not facilitate the overall objectives of the business. In general, there is less call for this autonomy than the manager of such a group would have us believe; to be of real value, most work has to be coordinated and undertaken interdependently.)

The Struggle for Status

Another way of looking at these shifts is to make the general observation that a manager wants to move to a position in the structure in which the balance of initiations favors him. Most service managers find their work onerous insofar as many other managers can put pressures on them while they have little ability for rebuttal. Their policies of rewarding friends and punishing enemies is an effort to right the balance, to some extent.

In a large insurance company the Underwriting Department was clearly the most prestigeful unit. Its position was a function of the ability to refuse to respond to requests for aid from other parts of the organization, no matter what the emergency. At the same time, the manager always felt free to go to other parts of the organization for assistance whenever he was in trouble, and they usually gave it.

The circuit designers had been a very important part of the television development activity. With the reduction in the number of new designs associated with the policy of standardization, other groups no longer responded to suggestions and proposals of this group; in fact, increasingly they were the ones told what to do.

The design engineers in an electrical equipment company were the most discontented group. While formerly they had been able to initiate directly to top levels of the organization, the creation of many new staff groups progressively narrowed the sphere of their activity, and their initiations.[2]

Thus, prestige or status can be given operational meaning; it is a function of the pattern of administration, the lateral relationships among managers that we have been describing. It depends on the number of people who can make demands on the manager compared with those to whom the manager can initiate demands (with a reasonable chance of appropriate responsiveness).

Professionalization

Sociologists have observed the efforts of many occupations to become "professional." This is really the phenomenon we have been describing. In organizational terms, a professional is an expert whose decisions are not challenged, who has limited initiations made to him, and who is assured of a desirable response when he initiates. The safety director wants to be recognized as a professional because this means that others cannot

2 Conrad Arensberg and Douglas McGregor, "Determination of Morale in an Industrial Company," *Applied Anthropology*, vol. 1, pp. 12–34, 1942.

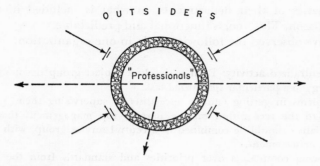

"Professionalization" means the effort on the part of a group to decrease the number of initiations to which it must respond and to increase the responsiveness of outsiders to its demands

go to him and tell him what to do and, when he sees a hazard that needs correction, the manager to whom he sends a notification will respond with alacrity.

The means of attaining this increased status are multiple. Dropping activities that do not enhance prestige is one such technique, and, analogously, claiming tasks that the organization already accepts as indicative of status is another. Similarly, restricting the job to those with recognized "professional" training facilitates the claim to such prestige. In addition, moving one's position in the work flow (at which certain decisions have already been reached) to an earlier stage (where one must be consulted before, not after) is an appropriate tactic.

THE SERVICE CYCLE AND BOUNDARY SHIFTS

We have been describing shifts in the managerial pattern used by supervisors in relating themselves to other parts of the organization. We can also observe changes in the actual physical boundaries of their departments, in what is included in their jurisdiction. This, too, is functional and predictable.

I have observed the following cycle in one organization:

1. Decentralized activity: Each major line project group devotes some energy to a particular specialized task.
2. Problems in getting enough specialists or supervising them, giving rise to the recognition on the part of top management that the specialists should be combined in a central service group, with their own management.
3. Growing complaints over priorities and standards from the users of the service.
4. Bootlegging of the service by project groups who quietly establish their own specialized service under their jurisdiction.
5. Sudden recognition that the service has become too decentralized, as everyone has his own, and a new decision to put it all "under one roof." And the cycle is repeated.

Similarly, managers seek to get under their own control "needed" activities in the preceding or succeeding stage in the primary flow of work, where their absence can be identified with instabilities. Contrariwise, there is an effort to shift to someone else's jurisdiction jobs, people, and activities that demand more managerial time and effort than they are worth (in terms of providing equilibrium for the managers).

Dynamic Changes in Boundaries

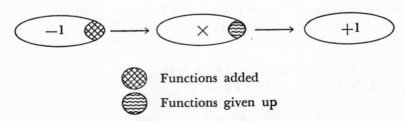

▦ Functions added

▧ Functions given up

At times, succeeding stages are just eliminated; the manager finds that he can go directly to a group one or more stages removed from his position and thus expedite his work flow. Sometimes these "jumps" are improvements; at other times they serve to cut out important way stations from the information stream.

The organization has a permeable, not a rigid, boundary. Thus managers dissatisfied with the work of a service group and unable to gain direct control may try to shift the activities to an outside contractor. Giving an outsider a part of the work is a technique for converting a human relations management problem into a more legalistic problem. Whereas negotiation is necessary with an insider, an outsider can be threatened with legal penalties if he does not do what he is "supposed to do" on time, in the right way, for the right price, etc.[3] The responsiveness of the outsider to initiations seems more assured than that of the insider who often has multiple defenses against threats and pressures.

It should be noted that many of the problems over jurisdiction are the result of ambiguities in technology. We usually think of jurisdictional conflicts as arguments by selfish trade unionists over the installation of metal doors and that sort of thing. But consider the complexities of determining "correct" lines of demarcation between the construction stage, equipment installation stage, and operation stage at a missile base or tracking center. In the process of getting electronic equipment to function adequately, it is almost impossible to specify where the *next* stage in the flow of work begins. As work frictions multiply, managers, like workers, jockey to control certain steps and be relieved of responsibility for other steps, in order to increase the stability of their own operations.

SEQUENTIAL POSITION

There is ample room for arguments over sequential position in the work flow. Some of the most interesting cases in the business literature revolve around problems of reversals in position.

[3] See Margaret Chandler and Leonard R. Sayles, *Contracting-out: A Study of Management Decision-making*, Columbia University, Graduate School of Business, New York, 1959.

Group A is accustomed to doing the early work on a project and passing along its semifinished results to group B. Now, because of some change in the situation, the B's initiate to the A's. Considerable conflict ensues as the A's find it difficult to adjust to the new situation.

A careful study of the human relations conflicts that beset the development of a new electronic component illustrated many such incidents.[4] For example, development engineers thought they should be giving assignments to the industrial engineers, whereas the latter thought the direction of initiation was the reverse.

Auditing groups, for example, say that they could be much more influential if they were called in to look at the work *before* it is completed. While in abstract theory they have as much right to reject or accept something after the fact as before, only the naïve would assume that the two provide equal opportunities for the staff views to be considered. One particular auditing group found that its work load was substantially increased as a result of having its office moved:

> When we were right next door, the engineers would come in and check their plans with us at a very early stage. Now that we've moved to another part of town, they don't bother to see us until there is a *fait accompli*. Undoing their work is enormously more expensive and, of course, charges are more difficult to impose on them than when we could discuss things early in the game.

One finds confirmation for this in the literature. Personnel departments that participate in the decision flows on contracting out before a serious issue arises are more influential in the process than those called in afterward.[5]

Purchasing agents want a chance to discuss specifications and delivery dates with engineers *before* procurement orders are writ-

[4] Harriet O. Ronken and Paul R. Lawrence, *Administering Changes*, Harvard University, Graduate School of Business Administration, Boston, 1952, pp. 205–206.
[5] See Chandler and Sayles, *op. cit.*

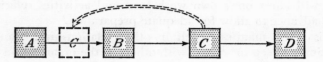

Managers often endeavor to shift their position in the work-flow sequence to an earlier stage position.

ten.[6] In other words, they want to participate in the first step in the sequence as well as the second. When they do not, they must just respond to the initiations of the engineers who are clients. Thus, in one sense, a shift in position can change a one-way interaction pattern, i.e., all initiations or all responses, into a two-way pattern involving mutual give and take, negotiation, and persuasion. There is the same concern with position in the action sequence in the work flows themselves. Here the interest is not in influencing the other party but in helping oneself. At the juncture point where work moves from one jurisdiction to another, the manager receiving the project or material or design from the previous stage often tries to insert himself into the flow before completion of the project in order to get a chance to prepare for what is coming. In many cases this is formally recognized and made part of the flow.

For example, the project engineer in development work expects the manufacturing plant people to be in contact with him rather early in the development stage in order "to get on board" and start preparation of the facilities and skills they will need when the work shifts from development to manufacturing. It can be made even more explicit when the next stage is invited to send men to be trained by the earlier stage. But in many cases there is still ambiguity in this anticipatory response. There is a jockeying for position, a struggle to be taken into the confidence of those whose

[6] See George Strauss, "The Tactics of Lateral Relationship: The Purchasing Agent," *Administrative Science Quarterly*, vol. 7, no. 2, pp. 161–186, September, 1962.

work will affect one's own work load and activities sufficiently far in advance to allow for adequate preparation.

This desire manifests itself in other relationships. Managers take time to keep in contact with others in the organization who, while not directly tied to them in the flow-of-work process, are sources of information on new technical and organizational developments. In moderation, this effort to be *au courant* is a healthy sign. However, if managers spend an inordinate amount of time in tapping the grapevine and gossiping, it signifies either a very insecure personality or a disrupted, threatening organization that imposes unwieldy self-defense mechanisms on its members. Many organization changes result in long periods during which individual managers seek to learn the dimensions of the new system in which they are now operating.

Although rare, there are also instances of managers wanting to push themselves further toward the end of the sequence. One manager complained bitterly about such a colleague:

> The . . . group ought to be sending people to us now so they can learn how this equipment operates but they are not. This means we are going to have continual trouble with them after they get it, because they won't know one end from the other, and they'll be up here for help every day. And it is twice as hard to provide help when the equipment is out there.

How and when delicate negotiations are conducted are affected by the organizational position of the participants. Here is an example of a manager who had certain auditing responsibilities:

> We are in the middle, really a bridge. The X department depends upon the Y department to carry their work through to the next stage of completion. Many times Y complains that they can't do it the way the X people have designed it; it just won't work. If they really can't, of course, it will look bad for the manager in X and will involve a whole lot of changes. I always used to investigate for X to see if there wasn't some way for Y to do it, and frequently I could knock Y's arguments and goad them into doing it. I am still in the middle, but now I work for a man who also is over Y, and he expects me to

tell X now that it just can't be done. I find it hard to do because I can see that Y is just making the thing unnecessarily difficult, but I am "boxed in" by the organization.

The manager engaged in auditing is often caught in the middle. As a project or an item or design moves from one stage to another in the flow of work, changes are introduced. The item at some point fails to meet certain cost, performance, or other standards, and the manager in whose jurisdiction it is when the "failure" occurs endeavors to show that a mistake at an earlier stage is the cause. He argues that, if they would change their specifications, methods, equipment, or whatever, he could do his job so that it would meet the standard. Here again there is usually ambiguity, and the position taken by the staff group depends upon its position in the total flow of the organization: whether it is tied in with the early- or later-stage group.

INTERNAL READJUSTMENTS

We have been describing external-relationship shifts. Managers may find it easier to revamp their internal work flows. A typical example is this. Each of a group of engineers has been negotiating for work done by a vendor group and then monitoring this work after it becomes a service relationship. Given difficulties in these interactions, perhaps because the service group is endeavoring to evolve a stabilization relationship, the overall manager of these engineers changes his internal division of labor. He appoints one man to maintain all liaison with the service group. This changes the jobs of his own engineers; they must now factor this man into their flows and cease their contact with the service group. It is important that the service group be appraised of the shift because their people must make complementary adjustments in their interaction patterns.

We have belabored this small change in some detail because many of the problems of organizations reflect an inability to introduce change efficiently. This does not mean that changes are not taking place along the growth axes specified above but rather that they are never fully incorporated into the managerial interaction patterns. The result is that many managers perform *both* the old and the new and then complain:

> You never know who you should see on this thing around here; it takes half a day just to find out what the organization is when you have a problem. I waste time being shifted from one person to another.

AN EXAMPLE OF DYNAMIC SHIFTS

To be more concrete, let us look at some of the administrative changes that might be initiated by the manager of the packaging function in a large corporation. (The following is based on an actual case.)

Initially his job consisted of recommending (advising) the type of package design and materials for the company's products. Over a period of time, the manager discovers that he is often not consulted, is consulted too late to be effective, or is not given "enough leeway" to make effective recommendations, and so he endeavors to make these changes:

1. To secure acceptance for his participation in early discussions concerning new designs for company products so that packaging needs can be considered with other requirements. (Change in flow sequence.)
2. To add designers who will draw up preliminary specifications for packaging rather than have this function carried on in the industrial design department. (Change in boundaries.)
3. To require all engineering managers to get approval from his department before changing the physical shape of the product. (Addition of stabilization pattern.)
4. To establish a small group to do research on better packaging materials and maintaining durability at lower cost. (Addition of innovation pattern.)
5. To evaluate existing product designs, shipment sizes, and routing

policies and changes in them for their impact on packaging costs. (Addition of auditing pattern.)

6. To serve as a transmission link to connect the engineering design department to purchasing for the ordering of packaging materials. (Addition of new work-flow sequence.)

7. To request that the shipping department be shifted from the jurisdiction of packaging to production on the grounds that packaging does not handle routine business. (Change in boundaries.)

8. To be available to assist cost reduction committees. (Addition of advisory pattern.)

9. To eliminate the practice of the production department requesting packaging studies by having such studies originate in the cost reduction committees. (Decrease in importance of service pattern.)

10. To require that all contacts with outside testing laboratories which evaluate packaging materials be handled by packaging personnel. (Change in boundaries and shift of position in work flow.)

As can be noted, the changes that this manager is endeavoring to establish would shift him into more prestigious and less deferential positions among the various administrative patterns and work-flow sequences.

SIGNIFICANCE OF DYNAMIC CHANGES

It may be worthwhile to evaluate the significance of these dynamic shifts of administrative patterns. They highlight the oversimplifying assumptions of organizational devices such as static job descriptions and production-scheduling techniques. More importantly, they help the manager to become aware of his own drives and the strategies of others with whom he must interact. They also help the organization to predict changes and to prepare to evaluate them in order to distinguish those it wishes to encourage and those it would extinguish.

For example, upper management can become aware at an earlier date of the trend toward the decentralization of certain service or support activities. A trend toward an increasing number of stabilization relationships may inhibit or retard quick adaptability on the part of managers who must get clearance from such groups. Therefore early detection of shifts that serve to increase the number of these types of contacts can avert costly reorganizations at some later date. Also these dynamic, self-generated changes in the structure of work are just as important elements in the real organization at any moment in time as the formally announced reorganizations. In fact, they should be taken into account in formal reassignments.

Finally, a manager may detect increasing difficulties in his relationship with the X department. An ability to distinguish between those problems created by changes in external circumstances (technology, market requirements, personality of key figures) and changes in the organizational position of the groups involved is crucial.

Most of the changes in managerial patterns and boundaries are not announced on the bulletin boards; they just occur by the dynamic processes described here. Only the most naïve manager thinks he can know what his relationships with others must be by reading the formal pronouncements.

We can summarize all these shifts in jurisdiction and function by saying that groups seek to evolve equilibrium relationships with their environment and eliminate sources of instability (such as unbalanced interaction patterns or complicated techniques for getting their share of some scarce resource).

Many morale and motivation problems stem directly from these evolutionary structural changes. Each group is like the total organization in that it seeks to flourish in its environment. Unfortunately, these group efforts often conflict with comparable exertions on the part of other groups.

CONCLUSION

The administrative patterns of a manager are constantly changing, and these changes take place whether or not there are formal changes in his job duties. Most of the shifts are initiated by the manager himself to facilitate his own managerial job, by emphasizing relationships that are more satisfying and easier to maintain and deemphasizing (neglecting or eliminating) relationships with other managers that are difficult and tension-producing to perform.

The manager accomplishes this by subtle transformations of the functions of his department and by shifts in the actual boundaries of his own jurisdiction, in his position in the sequence of various work flows, and in the internal differentiations (in the division of labor) within his own group or area.

The efforts that each manager makes to accommodate to the pressures of the organization come into conflict with those of other managers. The result is a dynamic and often ambiguous organization structure. Any realistic instruction to a manager must take into account this movement and conflict if it is to give him appropriate techniques for comprehending and dealing with the organization as a process or system of human relations. His must be the skills of improvisation, virtuosity, and flexibility, but all within the context of a systematic analysis of his position in the organization milieu.

8

Total Impact of External
Relationships on the Manager's Job

We have described the behavioral components of the various lateral or external relationships with which the manager in the complex organization must cope. This is a good time to take stock of the total impact of these relationships on managerial requirements for skill and time. In summary, these parts of his job provide challenges and impose constraints not usually viewed as an integral part of administrative behavior. Yet we have implied, perhaps should insist, that they comprise a crucial and, in many cases, the major share of his work load. They also represent the basic parameters of the human relations *system* within which the manager must operate and with which he must contend. Most are set by technology and the division of labor.

THE QUEST FOR STABILITY

The internal pattern of most of these external relationships (where successful) is evidence of the high premium placed by managers on the *stability* of their own internal work systems.

In order to avoid disturbances to their work areas, they endeavor to gain advance information on technical and organizational innovations with which they will have to cope. Most of the negotiations with auditing, stabilization, and service groups are designed to avoid internal disruptions in work pace. Many managers engage in missionary work, as noted in our discussion of trading relationships. These external contacts are maintained in an effort to secure for their departments a work load that will iron out the "ups and downs" of their production cycles.

Unfortunately, some managers do not accept these interaction patterns as an integral part of their job. They deeply resent the need to spend time negotiating for services, prices, standards, personnel, purchase delivery dates, etc. (Some spend a disproportionate amount of their time on one or more patterns that are personally satisfying.)

Most of the participants in these relationships are under cross pressures, either because the organization has consciously willed it, in the case of auditing groups, or because of easily predictable dynamics: the ever-present scarcity of certain resources, such as space, maintenance time, etc. Furthermore, nearly all involve outsiders, not only outside the immediate jurisdiction of the manager, but frequently outside the manager's manager's jurisdiction. This means that the various participants are themselves being evaluated by controls that are different and often incompatible. In addition, the manager is likely to be dealing with an individual he knows less well, sees less frequently, and with whom he is less comfortable. There may also be substantial ambiguities in the role relationships in these contacts. Individuals coming together from different hierarchies have the problem of establishing their relative rank and status. Under these circumstances, what is the impact on the manager's behavior in these flows?

Time Required

These are time-consuming contacts; they last longer individually and must be repeated more frequently if the desired results are to be accomplished. As one manager described one of his subordinate managers:

> To me one of the clearest indications of the ability of the man is the way he handled the . . . problem. The staff group that had to approve the work wanted him to take off six weeks and have his group build a full-scale working model. X spent four weeks discussing this with them, as much as two hours a day. Unlike many managers in this situation, he was not belligerent, but he was believable and coherent, letting them know that he understood they had a job to do too. After many counteroffers, he convinced them that they could get the information they wanted in a few days, using simulation. Now, all those talks took a lot of time, but the settlement saved several thousand dollars. He was able to save that because he laid the groundwork carefully.

It goes without saying that the manager cannot use his "authority" in most of these contacts. He deals with people in quite separate organizational units or with those who outrank him. Furthermore, there is little likelihood that he will be rewarded for passing upward through formal organization channels a request that was not honored. His boss expects this kind of action to be the exception, not the rule. It would create enormous delays to wait until the question reached a common crosspoint, and the effort to go over the head of the man with whom he was negotiating would make further relationships that much more difficult.

Negotiations Involved

A second characteristic is evident in the case cited above. Not only are these long, repeating contacts, but they are also negotiations. Trading, compromise, give and take are the order of the day. Many, if not most, of the subjects dealt with have no fixed, objective answer even in a technical environment. Interpolation and judgment mean differences of opinion, and the manager must expect to engage in extended bargaining. Failure to do so would probably place him at a substantial disadvantage, as the man on the other side of the desk may overstate his original position for the sake of bargaining.

Many so-called technical data really consist more of conventions, assumptions, and rules of thumb than one is first likely to realize. Methods of calculation of costs, accuracy of test equipment, size of sample necessary to obtain valid results, appropriate margins of error—all are subjects for debate and trading. The manager who believes that the facts speak for themselves and that he can be passive after presenting them is self-deluded.

A carefully executed case study of the development of a new electronic device contains examples of situations in which the appraisals of test results by an auditing group were not accepted. The inherent ambiguity in many technical questions is magnified by the assumption that the evaluator has any number of political axes to grind.[1]

Negotiation becomes an element in so many of these managerial patterns that we shall go into the techniques in some detail here.

Sophisticated managers place great stress on negotiations as a way of life. They negotiate with groups who are setting standards for their work, who are performing support activity for them, and to whom they wish to "sell" their services. However, negotiations primarily concern costs, specifications, and time. It is also worth noting that the realistic manager recognizes that the terms of any agreement are not fixed *but always are subject to reopening.* Effective negotiation is something more than being willing to sit down and talk. It requires, among other skills, the following:

1. An ability to generalize about the pacing of the discussion as it relates to the personality of the man across the table, to determine from his behavior if the situation is getting better or worse, and to change the balance of activity to increase or decrease the pressure on the other party

[1] Harriet O. Ronken and Paul R. Lawrence, *Administering Changes,* Harvard University, Graduate School of Business Administration, Boston, 1952, pp. 205–206, 208–209.

2. An ability to identify and distinguish important objectives that the other party must meet because of his symbolic goals or the real controls operating on him—and to separate these from secondary requests or demands
3. An awareness of the uses and misuses of inflated bargaining position (from which one gradually recedes), fixed lower limits, and whipsawing, obtaining concessions from one group to enlarge one's gains with another
4. Knowledge of the usual sequence of negotiations:
   a. Movement from exploration of the situation to identification of problems to solutions and the concomitant changes in emotional levels
   b. Value of spaced versus extended contacts
5. Uses of ceremony, outside scapegoats, and other bargaining techniques
6. Awareness of the difficulty of getting people to reopen what to them is completed work: the completion barrier

All these are examples of the behavioral guides to negotiation skills.

Many observers naïvely assume that labor-management negotiations are unique in that the contract promotes so many areas of ambiguous interpretation. Such conclusions underestimate the ability of intelligent human beings to find exceptions, loopholes, unfounded assumptions, uncontrolled variance, and all the rest.

Sometimes the degree of ambiguity in the situation almost destroys the motivation to negotiate:

> I feel so helpless when it comes to negotiating for . . . . I feel very strongly that we need more and that we are entitled to more, but there is no way to prove it. On technical problems I can "snow" them when I have to, but not here. There is nothing to get your hands on.

Ability to Deal with Hostility

Many people hold up well during negotiations until it becomes apparent that the other side is becoming hurt and angry. A manager has to be willing to incur the displeasure of many with whom he must maintain working relationships in such activities. There are times when he must flatly reject pleas for assistance; must turn down requested approvals, modifications, or specifications (that he controls); and otherwise anger or disappoint other managers. Some jobs have more than their share of this type of requirement. The manager may find himself resisting not only the insistent demands of a fellow manager but his boss and boss's boss as well. They implicitly threaten not only the loss of an easy, comfortable working relationship but, if the manager should be proved wrong in his unwillingness to acquiesce, potential reprimands and penalties from higher management. Many managers resist enormous pressures in order to fulfill the objectives of their position.[2]

There are two reasons why a manager must be willing to incur displeasure and withstand pressure:

1. The very objectives of his position may be to hold the line if possible.
2. But just as important, if he concedes too easily, it will make matters worse for himself. As it is, because of tremendous pressures for results, everyone is probing for weakness. And everyone puts it, "I know I shouldn't try to pressure them, but the extra needling can make a big difference."

By the ability to deal with hostility, we mean that, operationally speaking, the manager retains his normal pattern of behavior, of relating himself to other people—those with whom he is negotiating as well as subordinates—even when he detects that his stand is creating animosity and substantial tension. This does not mean, however, that under some circumstances he may not consciously modify his behavior to reduce the tension.

Another source of hostility in many external flow contacts is their sporadic pattern. This lack of continuity and regularity in the interaction pattern is upsetting to most people. While the

[2] For a confirmatory view on the need to accept hostility, see W. R. Dill, T. L. Hilton, and W. R. Reitman, *The New Managers,* Prentice-Hall, Inc., Englewood Cliffs, N.J., 1962, p. 14.

quantities do not have to be fixed absolutely, in general it has been found that good human relations are a function of relatively stable interaction patterns, both in the frequency of contact and the balance in initiations.[3]

Many of the contacts in the relationships described are with people who are seen only occasionally, when a certain need or problem arises. Because these contacts are sporadic, there is less likelihood that commonly agreed-upon norms of behavior will result. One of the most frequent "norms" in most organizations concerns reasonable secrecy and mutual protection from higher levels in the organization. Since some of these contacts require inspection and auditing, and many staff people have easy access to top-management levels, as part of their "intelligence" function, these norms are violated.

Selling

Over and over again one hears of a manager's salesmanship: interesting outsiders in a new project so that they will support it, convincing support groups to lend a hand and give special priorities, dealing with staff groups who must be convinced that there are reasons for special exceptions to be made. The manager cannot expect that his single statement of "fact" or belief will be taken at face value. As already indicated, there are too many ambiguities even in technical subjects, and there are too many jaded skeptics conditioned to special pleading. To be convincing and win the concessions, privileges, or support needed, the manager must be willing to sell—to engage in extended, persuasive contacts.

Assumption of Risks

Refusal to change a decision even when pressured by very-high-level managers "on the other side" means assuming risks as well

---

[3] See Eliot D. Chapple and Leonard R. Sayles, *The Measure of Management,* The Macmillan Company, New York, 1961, pp. 155–160; William F. Whyte, *Men at Work,* Richard D. Irwin, Inc., Homewood, Ill., 1961, p. 561.

as being able to cope with hostility. Clearly, the manager who is asked to change his decision by managers several levels above himself and who "holds his ground" is taking substantial risk. If he is proved wrong, he has committed a grievous fault and attracted the attention of powerful people who will not be sorry to see him penalized. Many times managers are required to authorize an outside group to go ahead before they are *officially* or *legally* in a position to do so. To wait until they have the authority (meaning adequate budget, organizational approval, etc.) would create a great delay:

> Production had stopped and it was necessary to get official approval for the change before things could start up again. I told them to go ahead on my say so. At first they were reluctant—the rules are clear on this—but I told them I would take all the blame if the change didn't go through.[4]

> I am always in the position of getting people to waive the formal requirements. Recently a manager said he couldn't without the authorization of my boss. I told him I could sign for my boss. I just had to get that approved that day. Of course, as soon as I could, I went to my boss to make sure he was in agreement with my action.

Gamesmanship

Much administration appears to stimulate gamesmanship. For example, less than complete communication is often the objective. Too much information transmitted can result in such situations as these:

> It gives the other group just the reason they are looking for to slip their schedule and blame us.

> It gives that . . . group ideas about where our equipment is likely to run into difficulties. There are things we naturally want to keep from them, and you have to be careful how you talk to them.

[4] For a similar case, see W. F. Whyte, *op. cit.*, p. 441.

Brief Contacts

The manager must learn to exercise restraint not only in his emotional reactions and his communicativeness in these external flows but also in the duration of his contacts. While there are times when long negotiating contacts are required, there are other rather routine matters that should be handled with dispatch (what we have called "switching" contacts). A key manager's telephone is always ringing, largely with requests for information from people who must use or evaluate the work he is doing. Frequently, the information they want can be transmitted in less than a minute or the caller can be referred to a more fully informed subordinate. To extend the conversation keeps the manager from engaging in other, more critical activities.

Personal Participation

Many contacts are a matter of foreign relations, and it may be inadvisable to use subordinates and their time as steps in the process. These are more difficult contacts, and risks must be assumed; for this reason the manager may place himself in the flow. However, good managers train subordinates to handle a heavier proportion of such contacts.

Long Chains

Because these flows take the manager into foreign jurisdictions, outside his own part of the organization, frequently many more contacts are required to accomplish a given objective, i.e., to terminate a given activity. In part, this is because he may be dealing with a less familiar section of the organization, in part because of the requirements of protocol, making some pretense, at least, of going through channels. For the new manager, these chains are even longer until he learns his way around. A typical manager must maintain relationships with dozens of work areas outside his own, with rapid organizational changes that make it difficult to keep up to date on whom to see for what and how to establish contact with him. This is another reason, then, for the heavy drain on time and energy imposed by external flows.

Resistance to Pressure

In these relationships, the manager is subjected to pressures of various kinds. He must learn to resist or discount many of them.

> In everything around here there is some "fat," something added for safety's sake. When someone tells you he needs something by September 1, it usually means October. This holds for cost estimates; there is something added to protect the "seller." On specifications, too, they promise less than they expect can be delivered in order to be sure.

Thus there is danger that a spiral can be created by crying wolf so often that eventually, in order to convince another group in the flow of work that something extra is needed, a manager must be able to mount a major performance. One still hears:

> They called up and said it was urgent, but then they sent one of the lower echelons in the department to see us about it, so we knew it couldn't be very serious. When it is, the boss himself appears.

Disturbances from Without

These external-contact channels subject a manager to disturbances originating in other parts of the organization. For example, pressures on service, stabilization, and auditing groups resulting from their own "crossroads" organizational position are transmitted to still other managers through these external flows. The "contagion" is spread as the manager to whom the strains are transmitted passes them along to his subordinates and other groups with whom he is in contact. This also occurs when outsiders change the rate at which they interact with and handle the work of a given manager's area.

For this reason it is difficult for a manager to predict the time and energy demands that will be made on him, when he will be called upon to set aside days, even weeks, for critical negotiations.

Many, if not most, of these relationships have built-in conflicts. They are not based on an assumption of cooperation or teamwork but involve checking, auditing, approving-disapproving. This means that they are subject to greater variety. What may be a short, easy interaction this week may involve long, stressful conferences next week. Insofar as the manager participates directly (and does not just monitor them), he must be prepared with surplus time to handle the difficult periods. Where his subordinates are expected to participate, they also need this available time.

NEGOTIATIONS WITH OTHER HIERARCHIES

While Americans pride themselves on informality and absence of status consciousness, there are very real limits on the degree to which either exists. Organizations also differ in their maintenance of rigid status lines requiring that, with few exceptions, status equals should interact.

This poses problems when the manager must leave his own area of the organization and negotiate with a manager in another hierarchy or chain of command. How does he go about handling a problem involving another part of the organization and perhaps more than one level of management in that unit?

While it may not be necessary to go "up and over," following the lines of the formal organization chart until a common supervisor is reached, it may be advantageous to make the initial contacts at a relatively high level. This avoids the following problem:

> I was negotiating with Crompton for a better break on what they were going to charge us for that special order. We eventually reached an impasse. But then I was stuck; if I went over his head to his boss,

the chances were good that they would stick together and the boss would support his man. Furthermore, Crompton would be sore; he figures I don't trust him. So what could I do?

On important problems involving groups that are not accustomed to working together, the initial contacts might well take place between relatively high levels of both groups. These two could then refer details to a subordinate manager and his counterpart in the other unit. They would negotiate most of the outstanding questions, unless they met difficulties. In that case, the manager who was taking the initiative could then propose that they both refer the matter back to their superiors.

When there are serious difficulties, a still higher level in the organization may be brought in, as a last resort.[5]

CONCLUSION

This summary of the behavioral implications of lateral relationships for the manager suggests an important conclusion. Given the inherent difficulties of these parts of his job, the manager cannot afford to be unsure of the dynamics of his position. He must be able to distinguish what actions will be required of him and what he can anticipate in the way of behavior from the other managers who surround his group in the organization.

For this the usual static terminology of traditional organization theory is inadequate. Look at the possible meanings of the frequently used "staff" job prescriptions: The staff man's job is to assist, advise, and counsel with managers who have decisions or problems that relate to his area of experience. What does this really mean? Here are just some of the possibilities:

1. Before making decisions of type Y, managers seek the advice of specialist X. The managers initiate the contact. If we observe the

[5] William F. Whyte and Allan R. Holmberg, "Human Problems of U.S. Enterprise in Latin America," *Human Organization*, vol. 15, no. 3, p. 19, Fall, 1956.

impact of these discussions, we find that the managers do not consistently follow through in the direction proposed by X.

2. Same as possibility 1 except that the behavior of the managers after discussion with X is fully predictable in terms of X's recommendation.
3. Specialist X initiates contacts with managers, offering his services, and on occasion managers discuss their pending problems.
4. Managers are required to obtain X's approval before going beyond a certain point in the work flow. During these contacts, a great deal of negotiation takes place over whether the proposed action of the manager is within the rules or policies being "enforced" by X. Many contacts are frequently necessary to resolve these questions.
5. Periodically X asks to review the recent actions of managers. He meets with them and their subordinates. At some later time he discusses his evaluations with the manager, and the two of them agree on modifications of his assessment. X then meets with the next higher level in the hierarchy to report on his findings.

Such a list could be extended with many permutations and combinations. Perhaps we have omitted many important hybrids that are more typical of contemporary organizations than those selected. However, these few categories should make the point that discussions of who has authority over whom are not really sensible. These are not legal-contractual relationships but work-flow-process relationships. They differ in the point in the flow at which X enters and the events that precede and follow his action. They also differ in the source of origination of the relationship and the pacing and pattern of the X-manager contacts. Some are simple give-and-take discussions in which personality differences will probably determine who is the dominant figure. Others, because of structural differences in the relationship, involve extended negotiating sessions that may stretch over many contacts and many weeks.

The time and energy that the manager must allot for these contacts and when and how he uses them in the course of maintaining his other relationships are crucial to the role and significance of the specialist and his impact on the manager's job.

Perhaps the most important lesson the manager can learn concerns the nature of modern organizations. Most Americans and

Western Europeans are brought up to believe that consensus and unity are an essential ingredient for any successful political, social, or economic institution. But this firm belief in oneness does not square with the facts. Companies, like all large organizations, have built-in divisions, and even in the proverbial "long run" they tend not to be eliminated. The manager must anticipate that more than one team will be playing in his organization and not find this immoral or upsetting.

chapter

9

Administration as Leadership

A manager has subordinates whom he can direct and over whom he has superior status. They are, in general, measured by the same reward-punishment systems as he is; therefore, negotiation and mutual compromise with them may not be necessary, although this distinction can be debated. In some ways, subordinates are similar to lateral groups or peers:

1. There are instances where there is no clear status difference and, in some professional groups, the subordinate may outrank his less well-trained boss.
2. The subordinate may have sources of satisfaction very different from those of his boss. He may not have the same interest in higher productivity, for example, and where the subordinate has subordinates, he may be under cross pressures—the familiar "man in the middle" problem.
3. The superior who expects that, to get compliance, he only needs to tell his subordinates what to do is in for many disappointments. He must use a variety of human relations techniques if he is to be successful in mobilizing the energies of his subordinates.

Even granted that there may not be the hard and fast distinction between lateral and hierarchical relations that we have

142

implied heretofore, relationships with subordinates pose some new problems and administrative patterns. However, we shall be more brief in our analysis of this area because it is already well explored in our earlier text.[1]

Most frequently, leadership is discussed in motivational or psychological terms. The leader-administrator endeavors to impart certain attitudes to subordinates (e.g., respect or admiration) and to become sensitive to their feelings (e.g., insecurity or distrust). Very little of the literature gives explicit behavioral instructions to the administrator, and most instruction is not related to other organization processes.

Perhaps the most crucial element in leadership is usually given the least amount of attention, in part because it is formally seen as part of "management theory," not leadership theory. This element is the matter of *controls,* or the assessment of subordinates and their work in order to decide where the leader's intervention is required to minimize problems. We shall devote most of our attention to this area in Chapters 10 and 11, observing that it also relates to the manager's participation in the lateral administrative patterns previously discussed. What the leader does will be seen primarily as a function of how things are going, not of abstract and static conceptions of "democratic" or "autocratic" ways of dealing with people.

Take for example the matter of the leader, the successful "permissive manager" of a human organization. Is he a doormat? Or a martinet? If neither, as this work proves again, when, how, on what issues, does he dictate, initiate, stand firm, help or refuse help to a subordinate, redress or refuse redress to a complainant, encourage ideas not his own, or judge them down? What is the balance in time of compromise and strength, of alert receptivity and personal sway? To label leadership, after the fact, "democratic" which avoids one extreme or another is only a little better than to say with the Mayoites that a successful leader "diagnoses right" and has the needful

[1] For a summary of the leadership literature, see George Strauss and Leonard R. Sayles, *Personnel: The Human Problems of Management,* Prentice-Hall, Inc., Englewood Cliffs, N.J., 1960, pp. 105–185. The leadership material is the work of Dr. Strauss.

"social skills." Nor is it any help to take note with Weber and students of fascism that some leaders sometimes have a charm, a *charisma,* that carries them through the most oafish blunders and the most blind arrogance *for a time.* These excellent perceptions must next be turned into common comparative measures and must be checked, watched, and generalized by all the scientific observers.[2]

REQUIREMENT FOR DIRECTION OR SET EVENTS

An organization cannot function on the basis of two-person or pair relationships, as we noted in Chapter 4. There must be people who can secure from many others a simultaneous response; this is what Chapple and Coon have called a "set" event.[3] An organization would be formless and unable to act effectively if it had to depend on chains of two-person interactions to achieve its objectives. This *direction* is the essence of leadership and distinguishes it from the administrative patterns described in Chapters 5 and 6. One can easily see the advantages of the set event in mobilizing the resources of a thousand or ten thousand people. With managers initiating to subordinates as a group, a major change in direction may be effected by a number of contacts that would be but a small fraction of those required to communicate via sequential chains of the A-B, B-C, C-D type.

A distinguished anthropologist has summarized the significance of direction (what he calls authority) in social organization:

> Authority means the privilege and the duty of making decisions, of pronouncing in cases of dispute or disagreement, and also the power of enforcing such decisions. Authority is the very essence of

2 Conrad M. Arensberg and Geoffrey Tootell, "Plant Sociology: Real Discoveries and New Problems," in Mirra Komarovsky (ed.), *Common Frontiers of the Social Sciences,* The Free Press of Glencoe, New York, 1957, pp. 326–327.

3 Eliot D. Chapple and Carleton S. Coon, *Principles of Anthropology,* Holt, Rinehart and Winston, Inc., New York, 1942, pp. 37, 281–282.

social organization. Hence, it can not be absent from any single institutional organization.[4]

An additional and significant value of the set is its creation of a group among those who respond to a common superior. Not only do people learn to secure a response from groups but also to respond in groups.[5] Having a common position with reference to the source of originations or direction, subordinates develop cooperative patterns toward one another that facilitate the work process. These would be much more difficult to develop were there not a common source of authority acting on them; witness the difficulties inherent in cooperative endeavors among individuals who have not had this common experience.

Other Leadership Functions

We shall identify two complementary leadership patterns associated with these sets (or "direction," as we shall term this behavior): responsiveness and representation. The first is the requirement on the part of the leader to respond to initiations from subordinates, the reverse of the set event or direction flow; the second is typified by the leader's initiations to other parts of the organization to handle the problems brought to him by his group. These, with direction, provide the three behavioral components of the leadership aspect of administrative behavior. Some may prefer to term this the *hierarchical* element, in contrast to the lateral or *horizontal* elements described in earlier chapters. An organization cannot function solely on the basis of pair relationships that are components of the work flow, nor can it maintain itself if it must depend on leadership initiatives for every action and decision. Each plays its own role. Unfortunately, global and essentially nonoperational terms like "democratic" or "authoritarian" leadership tend to disguise the full range of

[4] Bronislaw Malinowski, *A Scientific Theory of Culture*, Oxford University Press (Galaxy Books), Fair Lawn, N.J., 1960, p. 61.
[5] Chapple and Coon, *op. cit.*, p. 281.

behavioral elements that comprise the manager's job. They also fail to provide concepts that enable us to prescribe job content in terms of organizational requirements.

DIRECTION

The giving of direction is usually associated with change. By means of the monitoring processes that we shall describe in Chapter 10, the manager detects:

1. Planned relationships and processes are not being maintained— unanticipated departures from coordinated work efforts—and he must intervene to return his part of the work system to some kind of equilibrium.
2. External circumstances have changed (perhaps just a new instruction from his superior), and his subordinates need to be redirected in what they ought to be doing with whom, when, and where.

The overall quantity of direction to subordinates is a function of the variability of the system and, of course, of the manager's ability to appraise this accurately. The effectiveness of his direction—initiations in set events—is a product of that very specific behavioral skill of obtaining simultaneous action by a group of subordinates.

Without endeavoring to summarize formally the leadership literature, it is possible to propose a number of behavioral techniques that facilitate the giving of direction by the administrator. Some typical examples follow.

Drill. Although it may seem surprising, a sometimes neglected but crucial element in successful direction is practice. The military and the church have known this for many centuries. Recruits and members of congregations are placed in situations where they are conditioned to accept initiations from a leader. At the outset, situations are chosen in which there is little likelihood that the direction will be challenged or that performance will be difficult. Over a period of time, this conditioning is extended to more marginal areas. (In Barnard's terms, the "zone of indifference" can be broadened.) Subordinates, like an audience that grows used to responding to players where the situation is obvious, grow more responsive to subtle and less easily accepted initiations as they build up experience in responding.

In the beginning, the leader may endeavor to use subject-matter areas where symbolic reactions already exist and that facilitate an appropriate response to his leadership. For example, knowing that one's subordinates are already responsive to "showing up" a particular competitor should encourage the new leader to include reference to this target in his orders. In time, subordinates tend to react to the initiations in semiautomatic, stimulus-response fashion, just as an audience becomes accustomed to the speaker, the players, or the preacher.

Legitimatization. Sociologists, in particular, have noted the process by which leaders tend to associate themselves with people, causes, or expertise to which followers are already responsive. Like the politician who wants to stand next to the President of the United States on the platform, so that the existing response can be transferred to him, the new engineering manager seeks to show his technical prowess on the assumption that his subordinates have learned to defer to such experts. Appropriate social distance—from the "boys"—and symbols of office and rank can all be used to legitimatize one's right to give direction.

Insulation from Other Initiations. Actual physical separation as well as symbolic techniques can be used to prevent initiations from other sources from interfering with direction from the leader. Such conflicting initiations, which are the source of failures in direction, can come from conditioned reflexes as well as new directions. The leader uses methods to eliminate such "noisy" alternative sources (e.g., shadow leadership), to convince subordinates that the present situation is *different* and past associations irrelevant, and to isolate his group from threatening exposures. This is handled in a more extreme fashion by religious and military orders which can use styles of dress, physical isolation, and even fatigue to increase attentiveness to directions emanating from the approved source.

Detection of Incipient Nonresponse. While this is properly included in the next chapter, we must make some reference to it here. Clearly, the effectiveness of direction is a function of the ability of the manager to detect when appropriate responsiveness is not forthcoming.[6] Again, countless observers—and folk tales as well—speak of the demoralization created by the non-responder, the gradual withering away of the authority (meaning ability to initiate) of the leader.

Adequate Training. Preparing the subordinate to respond adequately by briefing, training, and the like is an obvious support for directive leadership. This requires long contacts at the outset—a kind of capital investment which many leaders are reluctant to make.

Use of Lieutenants. Supporting the position of respected, effectual lieutenants and avoiding undercutting their position by failing to "go through" them on many matters is another technique which is often cited:

> Whenever the leader originates interaction by giving an order, and he does not transmit that order to the lieutenant, he is, by that very fact, doing injury to the latter's rank. . . . If the leader will need in the future to transmit orders through the lieutenant, he has, by undermining the latter's authority, undermined his own.[7]

Penetration. There is another requirement that may seem to conflict with the use of lieutenants and the usual conception of "going through channels." While the leader must rely on loyal

6 For an excellent empirical study of how American presidents are faced with nonresponse situations from key subordinates and the dangers that they face in dealing with them, see Richard Neustadt, *Presidential Power*, John Wiley & Sons, Inc., New York, 1960.

7 George Homans, *The Human Group*, Harcourt, Brace & World, Inc., New York, 1950, p. 430.

lieutenants, he must also make himself known to subordinates who are more than one level below him in the hierarchy. If he does not, on occasion, initiate directly to such levels, the organization may split into two or more parts.[8] A former Secretary of State, Dean Acheson, notes that members of the executive branch of the government require some personal contact with the President.[9] One industrial study described the turmoil created when contact with the top executive was terminated for some lower levels in the organization.[10]

Action. Perhaps the most important principle of giving direction is that it must result in action. To be accepted as a leader, a leader must lead actively and must not wait for others to take the initiative. This is simple but extremely important. However, the leader who leads best does not give the most orders. The skill is to adjust the quantity of initiations to the situation. As we have said, the variability of the situation (the work processes, the personalities) determines how frequently the leader must intervene. Greater intervention than is required puts pressure on and unnerves subordinates, inhibits their own initiative, and dissipates leadership energies. Individuals differ in their susceptibility to this. Both cultural experience and idiosyncratic personality factors have an effect here. Employees in some countries expect and want their superiors to keep telling them what to do, as does a "dependent" employee in our own country.

AID AND RESPONSIVENESS

To maintain receptivity to direction, the leader must be willing and able to accept initiations from his subordinates. Excessively unbalanced interaction patterns tend to be less stable, and

[8] Chapple and Coon, *op. cit.*, p. 283.
[9] Dean Acheson, "Thoughts About Thoughts in High Places," *The New York Times Magazine*, Oct. 11, 1959, p. 19.
[10] Conrad Arensberg and Douglas McGregor, "Determination of Morale in an Industrial Company," *Applied Anthropology*, vol. 1, pp. 12–34, 1942.

there are many indications that *reciprocity* is an almost universal phenomenon, historically and cross-culturally.

Subordinates need an appeals procedure, help from the leader, assurances as to their position and security, and mutual exchanges of favors and concessions or bargains, which give them some control over their work environment. These initiations to the leader (participation?) can be summarized as follows:

Organization Aid. A subordinate goes to his manager when he has a problem with which he believes the manager can assist. "I can't get any of those parts from X; he says they are all spoken for. If you go to him or his boss, your word may carry more weight." Sometimes it is just a matter of information. "Who do you see over in Y, if you really want to find out their schedule?" "Will you authorize overtime to make up for the time we lost because of the delays in getting delivery?"

Technical Aid. Then there are the straight technical questions that tap the manager's greater experience, knowledge, or skill in certain subject-matter areas. Here the subordinate is asking for information or advice. Subordinates may have many questions concerning the application of personnel policies on transfers or holiday and vacation privileges, for example.

Personal Aid. In any hierarchical organization, one of the most important questions of a subordinate is, "How am I doing?" The subordinate needs reassurance that both he and his work are approved by his boss. He also wants to add to his understanding of how the system works, so that his environment will be a rational, predictable, consistent structure.

Personal Support. The subordinate needs the manager for something more than psychological reassurance. The manager is often the means by which a subordinate can get a raise or a recommendation. Just as important, the manager is often asked to reduce the pressure on a subordinate by serving as a buffer.

Sometimes the subordinate just wants a good rationalization to give those who demand that he do their work before he completes another job. At other times, the subordinate asks that the manager himself pacify those who are placing undue stress on him and take on his own shoulders the burden of their continued requests.

Monitoring Response. Finally, a subordinate initiates a contact with his manager to provide information for which the manager has asked: progress reports, difficult problems, information as to technical feasibility, results of discussions with outsiders, etc.

One obvious problem the manager faces is distinguishing among these five types of initiation from subordinates. Many times, for example, a subordinate comes in to ask a technical question or to report on the progress of some work he is doing, in order to assay his relationship with the manager and gain renewed assurance that he is appreciated. He may be inquiring about company policies when he is really seeking support from the manager. He asks what he should do with an obstreperous, overbearing "customer," when he is really endeavoring to persuade the manager to serve as a buffer between him and the source of disturbance.

To make these distinctions and to provide the appropriate type of response, the manager needs to make available adequate time. Too short a discussion can lead to a distorted conception of what is being requested. Making time available means making it easy for the subordinate to make the contact: being in his office, not appearing rushed, allowing for sufficiently long-duration contacts so that the less evident motivations may be recognized.

While such interviewing is often described in purely psychological terms, it is possible to present objective, behavioral descriptions of the process of dealing with a disturbed subordinate. These would include assessments of the subordinate's behavior pattern at the time compared with his normal rates (i.e., how "upset" is he?), experiments in adjusting the superior's interaction pattern until it conforms to the subordinate's, and some knowledge of the typical course of compensatory reactions that the subordinate may be demonstrating.

This may still not solve the problem. Subordinates differ in the "natural" frequency with which they initiate contacts. For example, seven subordinates were observed over a twelve-day period on an engineering project. Each worked in close proximity to the manager. While there were some differences in the objective problems they faced, these are unlikely to account for the following dispersion in contacts initiated: 37, 26, 13, 12, 8, 6, 0. (It should be noted that the four highest represent subordinates to whom the supervisor initiated the most contacts.)

The manager who is unwilling to take the chance that he may be ignoring some unexpressed or deviously expressed needs for aid and reassurance from subordinates can do two things. He can initiate certain contacts himself so that the subordinate will have an opportunity to raise questions. Also, he can become more adept at drawing out the subordinate and appraising what he is really trying to tell him.

Particularly at higher organization levels, the leader may believe that contacts purely for the sake of personnel morale are wasted: "I am too busy and my subordinates are too self-reliant for such shenanigans." A particular problem in a technical environment is that the technical competency and independent work habits of subordinates result in too few superior-subordinate contacts.

This result was illustrated dramatically in the case study to which we have already referred. One of the managers believed that by leaving alone a subordinate who was having production difficulties he would express his confidence in him. The subordinate interpreted this lack of contact as lack of interest and responsiveness, and this deeply troubled him.[11] It may well be that too much emphasis on the dangers of close supervision may cause the supervisor to neglect needed contacts with subordi-

[11] Harriet O. Ronken and Paul R. Lawrence, *Administering Changes*, Harvard University, Graduate School of Business Administration, Boston, 1952, pp. 136–137.

nates. Therefore, the manager who says that he may see his subordinates only for a moment or two during an average week and feels convinced that they can handle everything themselves may be in for difficulty during a period when quick readjustments and responses are required.

Even those managers who are aware of the need to maintain this part of their job program often neglect it under emotional stress. In the study noted above, the subordinate manager, Lou, allowed and encouraged his employees to initiate contacts and was responsive and in turn initiated contacts when his own relationships with higher management were satisfactory. When he felt threatened or hurt, he showed this by withdrawing, thus engendering in his people a sense of failure and lack of respect.[12]

The subordinate who is unsure of his relationship to the leader often searches for additional means of ascertaining his position. Thus, if responses to such initiations are postponed, perhaps because of other demands on the time of the manager, they accumulate and serve to place greater drains on his time. While sitting through a sufficiently long meeting to resolve the other person's doubts may require an hour or two, successive unsatisfactory contacts can mount up to three or four times this time expenditure over a period of a month.

Not only do unsatisfied needs for reassurance lead to repeated and wasteful efforts to be in contact with the manager, they also are the source of cynical or irrational emphases on styles of dress, kowtowing to the boss, and other "magical" efforts to gain security.[13]

Whyte summarizes for us the functions served by leadership responsiveness to subordinate initiations:

> Listening behavior serves several human values for the subordinate. Often workers need to get something off their chests. . . . There is also a frequent need to feel that you control the situation you are

[12] *Ibid.*, pp. 148–149.
[13] For the anthropologists' view on the use of magic to provide greater security, see Ralph Linton, *The Tree of Culture*, Alfred A. Knopf, Inc., New York, 1957.

in to some degree . . . while the worker is talking to his superior about a topic initiated by the worker, he can feel in control of the situation. The listening behavior of the superior also . . . says, in effect, "I respect you as a person. I think you have something worthwhile to say."[14]

One of the most universal reactions of subordinates is their consciousness of the difficulties involved in getting a hearing from their own boss. Rarely are they sure that they or their problems are understood. For most leaders, then, this requires attention. However, the balance of interaction must be such as to:

1. Avoid excessive imbalance in contacts among subordinates—the temptation to see a great deal of subordinates who are "easy" to be with or readily available.
2. Avoid "undercutting" lieutenants.
3. Avoid reducing subordinates' willingness to take the risks of decision making.

Thus, as in other administrative activities that we have discussed, successful action is a product of carefully adjusted interaction patterns. When monitoring is discussed, attention will be devoted to methods of achieving this balance.

REPRESENTATION

When a hierarchy has more than two levels, subordinates are concerned with their ability to influence leaders with whom they do not have regular contact. They quickly become aware of reality: Their own superior does not control all rewards and punishments nor the channels by which these are imparted.

Subordinates are quick to distinguish managers who "aren't afraid to stand up to those guys in the front office when our interests are at stake" from those who cower before superior status. Thus, for many day-to-day problems, it is not sufficient

[14] William F. Whyte, *Men at Work*, Richard D. Irwin, Inc., Homewood, Ill., 1961, p. 393.

to encourage initiations from subordinates. Many times the leader cannot satisfy the request or solve the problem because it lies outside the resources or decisions he controls. As has been demonstrated in employee counseling programs, the employee wants more than a chance to be heard; he also wants action to follow. Thus the leader must initiate action by others (who may not be readily responsive to him, since they are superior in status).

Where the leader does not carry on such negotiations as a representative of his group of subordinates or of a particular individual, he will find it increasingly difficult to gain adequate responses to his own directions. Representation is not an easy administrative action because the leader is often aware that those who outrank him are unfavorably disposed to the matter in question. Obviously, only deserving requests for representation are honored. However, because of the many ambiguities surrounding the question of who is deserving and of how much, the leader who does not represent his group will find that an increasing share of the benefits being distributed by top management are going to other parts of the organization.

CONCLUSION

We have dealt with leadership only briefly because there is a vast literature covering this particular aspect of administration. However, *direction, responsiveness,* and *representation,* the specific elements discussed, have some useful properties that are not always present in discussions of leadership. They originally evolved out of the observation study referred to in the preface; they appeared to be the most characteristic elements in the behavior we were able to identify and distinguish from participation in external work flows and monitoring.

Some other values of these qualities are the following:

1. Many existing studies of leadership can be "factored" into these three categories.

2. These three behavioral categories provide more explicit guidance for administrators than do descriptions that emphasize value or attitudinal requisites of the good leader.
3. They are theoretically consistent with the dynamic concepts of organization process and system used in dealing with work and the division of labor; that is, they are based on human interaction.

Another important matter, in terms of successful administrative action, is that of timing: *when to act,* when to initiate. This brings us to monitoring: the manager's methods of appraising the organization to determine when his intervention is called for and when it is *not.*

Monitoring Techniques and Control Theory

In preceding chapters we have discussed the manager as a participant in a variety of external relationships characteristic of the modern, complex organization and as a leader who must fulfill certain obligations to his subordinates. A crucial component of both these administrative activities is the technique by which the manager decides when and where some *change* in his behavior is required.

As he interacts with other managers, reads reports, observes activities within and outside his own department, and talks with subordinates, he is (or should be) constantly evaluating the situation. On the basis of these *inputs,* he must decide how to adjust his behavioral *output* in such a way that the system characteristics of his part of the organization are maintained.

As we have indicated, organization success or effectiveness depends on increasing the routine nature or regularity of the work processes. Where the system fails to function smoothly and regularly, it is the duty of the manager to intervene. Intervention takes many forms: a new order, a disciplinary action, a shift in the number of men assigned to a given activity, arrangement for a meeting with a disturbed next-stage manager, or perhaps a warning to the next level to prepare for a storm.

Before we concern ourselves with what the manager can do to restabilize the system, to maintain work relationships within his own area and between himself and other managers, we shall consider the methods by which he detects the need for action. Unfortunately, many managers (and management pronouncements) assume that the difficulty is always in execution; it could better be argued that the more basic challenge is one of timing: When is administrative action required?

As we shall see, monitoring, or control, is a distinctive administrative activity (although usually badly conceived and even less well executed). However, *what* is monitored is (or *ought* to be) a function of the other behavioral requirements of the jobs being monitored. In other words, in assessing or evaluating the work of subordinates, the manager must endeavor to relate their actual behavior to the behavioral requirements of their positions.

There are several secondary functions to be accomplished by monitoring:

Reinforcement. In every organization one is impressed by the degree to which subordinates do not know what is expected of them. One of the most pervasive myths is that most managers are successful in communicating to subordinates what they want done and how well the subordinate is doing what is expected of him. Quite the contrary. In the real world of the organization, the subordinate is barraged by stimuli, both positive and negative, and is left with the problem of interpreting their possible meaning:

> When I saw our manager this morning, he seemed distant; I wonder whether he didn't like the way I handled that meeting yesterday.

> I've been told that I must finish this job by the end of the week and also to drop everything and write that report. I wonder which he really wants?

> Last time when I handled the Compton order according to the new procedure, I got a complimentary note from the division head;

this time, when I did it the same way, the sales office called me up and bawled me out.

The naïve newcomer to an organization, who expects the academic grading system and regular feedback of the school to be continued, is rudely shocked. He soon comes to wonder, "What did the boss mean—does he want me to let up on that work and shift over, or was he just telling me that I couldn't expect help from him on it?" "Was he praising me for taking the initiative or criticizing me for not contacting him first?"

On the other side, the difficulty is compounded. Many managers seek to overanticipate their boss. "Something that was said the other day causes me to think that there is going to be a big push on cutting back on . . . expenses." Particularly in a dynamic firm, where organizational change is an everyday fact of life, too high a premium may be placed on guessing the next move. The result can be erratic shifts this way and that, particularly on the part of the nervous manager who can always read a number of hidden cues into any statement by someone in higher authority. Many observers have noted the proliferation of "Just in Case" files —a worked-out "pony" to answer any conceivable "examination" question that the boss may ask. Enormous amounts of time are wasted procuring this miscellaneous (and often useless) information so that the manager can look as though he is on top of his job.

Learning takes place only insofar as the individual receives rewards for correct responses and some form of negative reaction for incorrect ones. A most crucial requirement for improved organizational behavior is that the manager be able to evaluate subordinate performance and provide regular, unambiguous assessments that help to redirect the subordinate's behavior into more desirable channels. This means that the manager must be able to detect what is being done, evaluate it, and report on it. Otherwise, no learning takes place, and there is no reason to believe that performance will improve. The machinist knows when he has produced enough for the day, kept his work area sufficiently clean, and maintained adequate quality standards, or at least most do. However, the subordinate manager is usually left at sea insofar as knowing what parts of his job should be emphasized, how they should be performed, and which of multiple and conflicting auditing relationships are most crucial.

Reconstruction. A good manager does not continue to solve the same problems. Monitoring should identify the recurring, time-consuming problems that are not solved by administrative action. These obviously require special attention, and this, as we shall see, involves the manager's responsibility for introducing change. A satisfactory theory of *planning,* in fact, should emphasize the ability of the manager to measure past performance, particularly the capacity and incapacities of his organization. Most planning is unrealistic insofar as it is not based on a knowledge of the relative strengths and weaknesses of the organization.

In designing his monitoring operations, the manager must review the organizational (structural) decisions he has made with respect to the division of labor. Here he rethinks not only the "plays" required for each of the jobs of his subordinates (to be monitored) but also the division of labor between himself and each of his subordinates. This involves three types of decisions:

1. What jobs will the manager do himself? For example, many managers maintain most of the trading relationships because they believe that subordinates do not have the status or experience to commit their departments or get commitments from other department heads.
2. What criteria are there to determine at what point the subordinate should go to the manager when he is in trouble?
3. What checks must the manager initiate himself to keep under control the work processes that pass through his jurisdiction and in which subordinates participate?

STABILITY AND CHANGE

Paradoxically, the manager's job is to accomplish both stability and change. In order to maximize the productivity of the processes (work flows) under his jurisdiction *and* maintain high

motivation among subordinates (which in turn facilitates pro-
ductive efforts), he must endeavor to minimize the frequency
with which the patterns of work flow and coordination are disturbed. In fact, the frequency of such actual or potential interruptions to the work patterns, as we have described in a previous
book, is the prime determinant of the work load of the manager.
His major objective is the development and maintenance of
work-flow routines, and these "predictable and repeated patterns of interaction" are the source of morale: the absence of
debilitating stress and its concomitant, destructive emotional reaction (what we have called compensatory behavior).[1]

In a situation requiring cooperative endeavors, whether it is a
work group, employees and managers, or staff and line officials, each
tries to develop a stable pattern of work, of interaction. When these
stable patterns are disturbed (some or many) individuals experience
stress or an uncomfortable feeling of pressure and dissatisfaction.
A breakdown in the flow creates opposition as the individuals
struggle to restore it. The expected responses from the individuals
in the sequence prove inadequate, and new coordination problems
arise.

The regularities of actions and interactions disappear when the
stress occurs, and erratic variation takes over. The difference is
obvious between a smoothly running operation and one with a
problem. Under stress, people react emotionally, and, because more
than one individual is involved, the reactions usually conflict with
each other.

Thus, a vicious circle is established. Something happens in the
work situation that causes the relationship of individuals to change
or to depart from the normal pattern. This creates a stress, either
of opposition or nonresponse, that is further complicated by higher
levels of supervision and staff specialists whose unexpected interactions, i.e., outside the usual organization pattern, irritate the disturbed work-flow relations. People get upset; they become angry

---

[1] Eliot D. Chapple and Leonard R. Sayles, *The Measure of Management,*
The Macmillan Company, New York, 1961, pp. 114–141.

with each other, and, depending on their individual characteristics, react temperamentally. These personality conflicts have direct ramifications in the work process because the emotional reactions change the pattern of contact and interaction. Joe is angry with Bill, so he does not check with him before starting a new experimental run. Consequently, a special test that should have been included in the run is left out, and the whole thing has to be done over. To complete the circle, these emotional disturbances damage the work-flow sequence, which causes additional personality stresses.[2]

The achievement of this stability, which is the manager's objective, is a never-to-be-attained ideal. He is like a symphony orchestra conductor, endeavoring to maintain a melodious performance in which the contributions of the various instruments are coordinated and sequenced, patterned and paced, while the orchestra members are having various personal difficulties, stage hands are moving music stands, alternating excessive heat and cold are creating audience and instrument problems, and the sponsor of the concert is insisting on irrational changes in the program.

For example, the engineering manager knows that he is living perilously. Any minute calamity can strike: A vital component can disappear or have its specifications changed, or a plant production line can stop when a design defect appears. Unless the manager moves rapidly and appropriately to mend the damage, the losses will multiply extravagantly.

As one manager with heavy financial commitments in a new project described it:

> The group supplying a vital component changed the characteristics of the component, which overnight threw my costs and designs into the wastebasket.

In other words, the manager faces constant internal and external interruptions. As we shall see, some of these require mere palliatives—short-term readjustments—in order to bring the sys-

2 *Ibid.*, pp. 37–38.

tem of relationships back to stability, for example, a disciplinary action (which is one type of change). Other disturbances require more drastic action if the system is to be stabilized, for example, the introduction of new methods or personnel (long-term change).

The manager's objective, then, is not a static system of human relations. Rather, he is seeking a dynamic type of stability, making adjustments and readjustments to both internally generated and externally imposed pressures. By these responses to variations in the environment, he hopes to maintain a *moving equilibrium.* The new or modified work-flow pattern may be quite different from its predecessor, but the significant element is that there should be a pattern, an observably repeating tempo in the pace with which the work moves from one employee or group to another.

COMPONENTS OF A CONTROL SYSTEM

How does the manager check or control? He looks at statistical reports of quality, quantity, turnover, etc. He inquires how people are doing, and he endeavors to "sense" when people are acting differently. Unfortunately, some of this is usually done intuitively, and there is little systematic attention to an integrated control system. In a well-developed theory of organizational change, we would expect to set forth the actual pattern of control: how frequently and with whom or what the manager checks. There should also be an integrated series of controls involving technical measures of performance (quality, quantity, etc.) combined with measures of organizational relationships.

The usual managerial reporting systems—information flows or paper flows—fail to come to grips with the real purpose of controls. Rather, they naïvely try to tell the manager what is happening or, more precisely (and less valuably), what *has* happened. Only recently have there been concerted efforts to distinguish significant events for the manager. (As the historian long ago learned, no one can, in fact, describe everything that has occurred.)

But even this improvement fails to assist the manager because the critical element is lacking: the identification of those situations that require his managerial action. The important element is not to distinguish unimportant from important but to distinguish events or trends that require managerial action from those situations in his jurisdiction that do not, at that particular time at least.

It is not adequate to know that the XYZ department is in trouble. Good controls tell the manager *what action on his part* is needed to remedy the problem. This means that there must be built into the system a general theory of cause and effect. Thus the total monitoring and change system has several interrelated components. They include:

1. The manager's intellectual conception of the work processes that he should keep "in control," i.e., what he is going to monitor
2. The operational methods by which he checks, monitors, and appraises these processes
3. Criteria for evaluating the significance of what he observes (when and where an emergent problem requires some type of managerial action)
4. A description of remedial actions (short-term corrections) that the manager takes, the channels through which he moves and the techniques he uses, to bring his work processes back to equilibrium
5. Criteria for identifying recurring or "high-amplitude" disturbances that are too heavy a drain on his managerial resources and process effectiveness
6. Methods of coping with these disturbances: the introduction of organizational (long-term corrective) change

WHAT TO MONITOR

In our limited field investigation it was clear that the managers observed had very divergent conceptions of their monitoring activity, and few had thought through the dynamics or the logic of the process. Thus a major share of the monitoring problems were due to an inability to define *what* was to be monitored or controlled. This intellectual exercise is the first step in the sequence of evolving a monitoring system.

Managers intuitively recognize the need for moving toward stability. This can be observed in many of their actions, e.g., the desire to anticipate changes and prevent them so as to minimize the impact of outside disturbances. Nevertheless, there is need to improve the techniques for translating the parameters of the work flow into managerial controls. One of the reasons for this shortcoming may be the currency given to the concept of "management by results."

The Fallacy of Management by Results

A widely held belief is that the good manager manages by results. This is presumed to foster maximum delegation, prevent excessive supervision, motivate subordinates to accept responsibility, and save the supervisor's time for really important matters. While much of the material in this and the next chapter explains why results are not an adequate basis for management control, the list below summarizes these reasons:

1. Looking only at results encourages subordinates to engage in behavior that may be destructive to organizational relationships. A subordinate may benefit but the coordination necessary to meet overall organization goals suffers.
2. Such an emphasis encourages excessive competition for scarce resources, such as space, personnel, parts, maintenance facilities, and leads to neglect of the unmeasured aspects of a job.
3. It is difficult to pinpoint the cause or source of problems. Looking at results simply does not give one enough information. A man missed the schedule, the budget, or the specifications. But who is at fault, where did the problem occur, and what can be done to prevent its happening again? In most cases, the manager is at a loss to answer such questions because his feedback information tells him only that there is a problem. Typically, everyone and everything conspire to hide the blame or shift it to others. Measuring results encourages

"buck passing," "balloon squeezing," and "account poaching"—terms used by managers themselves to describe the illicit behavior in which they engage.

4. There is an increased number of instances where "crisis" measures must be taken because the manager has waited too long; a potential loss has become an actual failure. By the time the results are in, it is too late to do much about it.

5. Many times good performance is not identified—only failures.

6. For many groups such as staff, service, and administration, results are not easily assessed in dollars and cents. These groups find it difficult to justify their existence under this method of management without wasteful demonstrations of "programs" that they have initiated.

Two Examples of Defining Work in Organizational Terms

The alternative to monitoring *results* is organizational measurement: regarding work as a coordinated series of human relations. The manager then endeavors to appraise how work is proceeding through the system. Work is defined in terms of how the organizational system is sustaining itself in the face of various externally based buffetings and internally based shortcomings. Controls can be made consistent with the nature of the work and other systems concepts, rather than being something "tacked on," as are most traditional managerial controls.[3]

Type A. The manager is in charge of a group of subordinates each of whom must maintain an interrelated series of relationships outside the department. Thus the subordinates work independently, and the coordination is in terms of external groups.

The work flow of this group can best be viewed as the dynamics of the individual subordinate's job ($\ldots S_1 \ldots$) described operationally. Here is a hypothetical example (a, b, c, $\ldots$, n are outside groups):

[3] For a more complete theoretical analysis of the development of organizational controls and their relationship to traditional controls, such as cost accounting, see Chapple and Sayles, *op. cit.*, pp. 69–78.

1. $a \rightarrow S_1$ (Receives request from a)
2. $S_1 \rightarrow b$ (Solicits information from b)
3. $S_1 \rightarrow c$ (Contracts part of work to c)
4. $S_1 \rightarrow a$ (Keeps a informed as to status of work)
5. $S_1 \rightarrow n$ (Coordinates work with other interested parties who share responsibility)
6. $S_1 \rightarrow t$ (Writes final report)

Similar patterns would be disclosed for subordinates S_2, S_3, . . . , S_n.

Once this pattern is known, the manager is in a position to establish measures of the rate at which work progresses through these various steps or, contrariwise, the points at which delays occur. These may be disclosed in a number of ways: complaints from b, c, . . . , n; repeated need for managerial intervention at point 4; etc.

Many times certain "subresults" suggest themselves as appropriate controls. For example, one of the steps in the flow process may be that a subordinate is supposed to check schedules with b and report to c if there are to be delays. The number of missed schedules, related to the total number of schedules, accumulated at c is thus a check on the ability of S_1 to maintain this part of his job.

The failure to consider the dynamics of the positions being monitored can have effects such as those described by a recently transferred recruitment manager:

> When I moved into this job I discovered that my subordinates were meeting all the objectives management had established for the job in terms of the number of people being processed. Furthermore, the whole thing was running pretty smoothly. But there was a big backlog of ill will toward this department in the rest of the organization because the departments that we were supposed to service were being kept in the dark as to our activities. Our men had no interferences, just some background grumbling, and they were the whole boss. I made it my business to start checking on the extent to which these department managers were consulted and kept informed on what we were doing.

We have oversimplified for the purposes of illustration. Each of these stages is not simply a contact; it may involve prolonged negotiation or the solution of technical problems. However, the point is that the manager does not wait to see what happens at the point $S_1 \rightarrow t$. He seeks to develop measures of the flow process to disclose where the normal tempo of S_1's job is being disturbed. This knowledge of the dynamics of the system also makes it possible to know what disturbances to expect when it becomes necessary for him to introduce changes, e.g., that will make it more difficult to contact c at the required time.

Type B. An analogous flow can be derived for managerial jurisdictions in which the manager is concerned with maintaining the rate of progress of a project or series of projects through successive stages over which he himself has jurisdiction. Typically one or more subordinates work at each of these stages. For the manager to be successful, work must progress continuously with minimum hindrances through these stages or positions:

$$P_1 \ldots P_2 \ldots P_3 \ldots P_4 \ldots P_n$$

The manager should develop measures that will tell him how this flow process is proceeding and where there are emergent difficulties.

As one rises in the hierarchy, the likelihood of monitoring individual subordinates as such diminishes, as the subordinate's job (each subordinate being a manager himself) is always to manage one or more work-flow systems. The upper-level manager is particularly anxious to monitor the intersections of these flows, i.e., the point where the jurisdictions of two or more of his subordinates meet. Monitoring the boundary regions, or interface, makes it possible to detect coordination difficulties.

Where the division of labor requires that the activity, product, or idea move among several groups, the monitoring of the process or operation can be done without scrutinizing the internal group activities. Rather, the monitoring is focused on the individual who moves among the groups. Many observers have noted the existence of such liaison or contact people; it is often said that they serve to hold the organization together. (Where two groups maintain a relationship to one another through the activities of an individual who interacts in both, they are said to have a *tangent* relationship.)[4]

Many of the special task forces and committees in organizations reflect at least the implicit recognition of the critical importance of these interface or boundary positions. These contrived solutions to organizational sore spots are, in fact, what anthropologists have described as associations.[5] Associations are made up of individuals who belong to the several subsystems of an institution (or several institutions) and who have an indirect relationship to one another through the one or more individuals who interact in both institutions.[6]

Further justification for monitoring the interface, as a means of controlling organizational relationships, can be expressed more quantitatively:

> An organization system may be regarded as made up of sub-systems or unit systems within which interaction occurs with a relatively high frequency and where only a limited number of persons interact with any frequency outside. . . . In developing a mathematical model, one isolates, and then establishes the characteristics of the equilibrium of the sub-systems. Provided these systems are stable, one can then concentrate on describing the relations of the individuals who are tangent to other sub-systems as constituting the minimum total organizational system.[7]

[4] See Eliot D. Chapple and Carleton S. Coon, *Principles of Anthropology*, Holt, Rinehart and Winston, Inc., New York, 1942, pp. 337–338, 419–420.
[5] *Ibid.*, p. 418.
[6] Another good example of an association is a trade union. Departmental groups of employees who normally do not interact with one another have a tangent relationship in that a common management initiates orders to all of them. When they are disturbed by various grievances, they first endeavor to regain equilibrium by acting on the liaison or tangent person, viz., the manager. When this fails, they seek an improved compensatory mechanism, an association or union to which they take their complaints.
[7] Eliot D. Chapple, "Quantitative Analysis of Complex Organizational Systems," *Human Organization,* vol. 21, no. 2, p. 69, Summer, 1962.

Without this simplifying technique, the problem of controlling the behavior of a large organization becomes so gigantic as to be impossible.

Thus the manager watches the intermediaries, the liaison people, outside contact men, and staff groups at the focal point of networks of demand, to assess how these junctions are operating as switching points in the circuitry of the organization. By watching their motions and detecting significant departures from normal, he can identify shifts in the parameters that define the operating characteristics of the organization.

BEHAVIORAL TECHNIQUES FOR MONITORING

Let us look briefly at the traditional methods used by managers to answer the question, "How are things going?" As we shall see, most are time-consuming and inefficient and do not provide good control, i.e., show the manager how and where to act. However, it is useful to consider systematically the actual behavior of the administrator who is engaged in monitoring. It is usually assumed that these methods are obvious or intuitive; they are not. We observed four different methods of obtaining information for control purposes:

1. Contacts initiated by the manager
2. Contacts initiated to the manager
3. Observation
4. Review of numerical records

Contacts Initiated by Manager

Every so often I call the other group and ask how my people are doing. At least twice a day I contact every one of my people and ask them how things are doing.

Once a week I have a meeting which includes everyone in the group and we review the status of all the projects.

Once a week I meet with my group leaders to check where we stand on all the work.

The best way to make sure your orders get attention is to call them every few days and just needle a little.

I have in my tickler file a list of all the orders that are most crucial and most likely to be delayed so that, well in advance of when we need it, I start calling to see how things are coming.

Note the great variation in frequency (from once a week to twice a day) and the differences in the degree of preplanning versus random checks. These differ too in the time consumed, for the manager doing the checking and those checked, i.e., subordinates, outsiders, etc. Meetings are time-consuming for both manager and subordinate, but they also permit the manager to be responsive to upward initiations.

Contacts Initiated to Manager

I get feedback on how my people are doing from some of the other managers they contact.

We know we're in trouble when we get a call from one of our support groups.

I have my subordinate check with me when he feels he has a serious problem that may cause us delays.

When the boss comes down, I know we've got trouble.

Managers seem to make less use of these contacts for monitoring purposes than they do of contacts that they initiate. It should be fruitful for the manager to maintain records on the frequency with which he is called for assistance, not only by his own subordinates but by outsiders (in external flows). Such calls identify trouble spots and/or individuals who are seeking reassurances. (These are the contacts described under Responsiveness in Chapter

9.) The latter often indicate potential points of breakdown in human relationships.

Ideally, where the manager uses contacts initiated by others as part of his monitoring system, he should program them in advance, specifying the precise conditions under which he wants to be notified. Some managers endeavor to establish standards to determine when it is appropriate for a subordinate to go to them for assistance.

> I don't want subordinates bringing me general problems. I want them to be able to show me that they have tried to solve them. This usually means that they have gone out and seen all the people involved—and I don't care how high they have had to go. Then when they come to me, it is with a very specific question, such as how can we get Jensen to change his mind.

Other managers confirm this desire to have subordinates roam widely in the total organization before calling for help.

> I want this man to refuse to accept the first excuse he gets when they claim they can't meet a standard. He should get in there [to their department] and find out what they are doing, how they make their calculations, and just what is really going wrong.

Other managers want to be notified "as soon as there is any sign the man is in trouble or meeting difficulties."

As an alternative to this direct method, many managers give incomplete assignments with some built-in ambiguity so that the subordinate will be forced to check back more frequently.[8]

We should also include in this category the interventions of upper levels of management who are operating their own monitoring systems. On the basis of their interpretation of the manager's performance and of external events, in the wider organizational environment, they may intercede. The information that they bring to the manager and the requests that they make of

---

[8] Franklin D. Roosevelt was reputed to have used this method of assignment giving in order to hold in check the many dominant personalities in his "brain trust."

him are an important part of his monitoring system. He pays a great deal of attention to this kind of signal. Similarly, changes by customers in the specifications for his work and reports given him by staff groups auditing his activities provide important information that should shape his behavior.

Observation

At least once a day I walk through the department and just look at how things seem to be going.

In my area you can tell a lot just by observation; the project we are working on involves building a model. You can actually measure how fast it is growing.

By looking, you can tell whether a man is finding the right circuit by trial and error or working it out first on paper.

I have my people turn in their manuals, and I can judge a good deal from these.

I ask for written progress reports monthly. Every so often I go with one of my men when he is contacting a manager in another area. I like to watch how he handles himself, how persuasive he is.

One of our most pressing problems is customer service. We have a far-flung organization, and I have been very disturbed about the growing number of complaints from the field. Yet I am frustrated in learning more about what is going on. If I start asking questions of our top management in that area, they get the idea I have no confidence in their abilities and am investigating them. I find I get the best information by ignoring the paper reports they prepare and going out into the field and just looking and talking to people.

Most observational methods of appraising how well things are going appear to be highly intuitive. Few managers have worked out clear-cut systems, although it should be possible to arrange more careful samples of time and the items to be observed.

Review of Numerical Records

> Every week I get from one of the record offices a listing of the items we are supposed to have received, and I check these against my records.

> I check the amount expended under our budget against the number of weeks elapsed.

> I look at the amount of overtime that has been authorized.

> We establish certain mileposts for the budget and for stages of the project, and periodically I check where we are against those.

> I compare the amount of work we handled last year with the amount we are handling this year—and we graph this.

> I look to see how many days he missed last month.

These are traditional checks for a manager: how much has been done, how much has it cost, how many days has it taken to do it, how many times did things go wrong versus right. Computations of personnel absenteeism, tardiness, etc., could also be included here.

Critique

The most serious weakness in monitoring information is the omission of statistical checks. By these we mean more sophisticated measures of system and personnel performance than simple arithmetic quantification. The methods of monitoring that have been described range from the very time-consuming techniques of personal interactional explorations to the more automatic observation or quantification of certain outputs.

The purpose of seeking this information is not for its own sake but rather to determine the manager's time distributions. He programs for himself a series of certain routine checks that should involve a minimum of time. The major use of the manager's time is taking action to remedy emerging problems, as defined by his monitoring. For this reason, he needs a method of distinguishing data that indicate all is proceeding as well as can be expected and evidence that his intervention is required.

The data do not speak for themselves. At one level of the continuum, we have already indicated some of the difficulties of interpreting one's own manager's cryptic comments. "Does he really want me to change that plan?" Similarly, the manager must decide what is normal with respect to subordinate performance levels; the rate of progress of his projects, both internally and externally; and his relationships with other critical (for him) members of the organization.

Frequency of Checks

Most managers do not even consider the importance of *frequency* of checking.

The inherent variation in the technological and human system being monitored should determine the frequency with which these checks have to be made. For example, here are two extremes in the monitoring of work-flow relationships:

> Once the project is set up and we know what they want us to do for them, I hardly ever check with those people [the "sponsoring" group] and we rarely get any calls from them. I guess the reason is that there is a good deal of technical leeway in the part of the system we are designing, both in the timing of the completion of our work and in the specifications [i.e., how it will perform and its physical characteristics]. Even if we make lots of changes or get into a good deal of trouble, it isn't going to affect them very much.

Thus the properties of the system have to be explored statistically before the frequency of monitoring can be determined. Instead, we find that extraneous factors seem to determine the kind of monitoring. When the manager has a large number of subordinates (a wide "span of control") and cannot find time to see any of his people for very long, he is likely to make less frequent checks (i.e., to delegate more) than when, in the same type of organization, he is freer to undertake closer scrutiny.[9]

Similarly, when geographic or spatial factors make checking difficult, the superior is more inclined to exercise less of it:

> In Creole [Petroleum Corp., Venezuela], we observed that the Venezuelans making the most rapid progress in supervision seemed to be concentrated particularly in lake construction and drilling. These two activities had one important factor in common: a geographical situation which made it impossible for North Americans to exercise close supervision. The U.S. superior could not just drop in on his subordinate to see how things were going. . . . He could commandeer a launch for an inspection trip—which would mean perhaps a half a day spent in travel. . . . Or he could consult with his subordinates before and after they went out onto the lake and otherwise turn over the full responsibility to them.[10]

EVALUATION OF CONTROL INFORMATION

The reference to statistical controls points up the critical problem of distinguishing between variations (actual from planned) and significant deviations (or change). The latter are an indication that the system is changing its operating characteristics, which is vitally important information for the manager and normally requires him to act. Random or chance variations, on the other hand, are expected. There are a hundred and one reasons why

[9] These were the findings in a study of patterns of supervision among store managers within the Sears, Roebuck company. In stores of identical size and merchandise, managers who had more subordinates reporting directly to them, because they had fewer levels in the organization, provided less close supervision than managers with fewer direct subordinates. See William F. Whyte, *Men at Work*, Richard D. Irwin, Inc., Homewood, Ill., 1961, pp. 88–89.

[10] William F. Whyte and Allan R. Holmberg, "Human Problems of U.S. Enterprise in Latin America," *Human Organization*, vol. 15, no. 3, p. 31, Fall, 1956.

work systems vary from their expected performance characteristics. The manager cannot, nor should not, expect to deal with every one. In fact, there is good evidence from mathematical statistics that efforts to "overcontrol" such flow processes as we have described tend to accentuate the instabilities rather than damp them.[11]

There is, for example, the manager who is always "sensing" that something is wrong in his relationships with one or more of his subordinates. He calls frequent conferences or has interviews. Quite aside from the time consumed, the excessive number of probings unsettles the subordinates. Under such close surveillance, they think that they are suspected of something and not trusted. This type of supervision can be more harmful and surely more wasteful than indifferent, "insensitive" management. Unfortunately, the damage is not detected by the manager because he has converted the smoke into fire by creating a problem that justified his attention.

Here is a typical situation. A manager receives an anonymous letter claiming that personnel relationships have badly deteriorated in one of his subordinates' jurisdictions. The manager begins probing into the department much more closely; he requires long reports from the supervisor and interviews him extensively. This sudden change in the relationship with his boss unsettles the supervisor. In addition, the extra work of the investigation leaves him less time for intradepartment personnel work. Both this situation and the pressure of time hurt the supervisor's relationships with his subordinates. The manager finds that his prophecy was confirmed.[12]

The concept of statistical measures in monitoring is essential because of the need for relating the magnitude of the disturbance to the characteristics of the total distribution. If a manager is monitoring the number of mistakes a subordinate makes, he

---

[11] The magnitude and frequency of "random" variations in work-system performance are a function of the built-in imperfections of technology and structure.

[12] The self-fulfilling prophecy is a classical problem in social science.

should look not just at the raw score of quantity of errors but rather at the ratio of errors to total exposure. Similarly, some conception of the boss's normal behavior, e.g., the frequency with which he initiates contacts to ask questions about how things are going and raises problems can tell the manager when the boss is really worried and when he is just doing his "rounds." A subordinate's performance becomes significant when it deviates greatly from the norms established by the manager and from the subordinate's normal behavior. When the number of requests for aid increase, training procedure may be at fault.

Some inputs require little analysis. The knowledge that one's costs will go up by a significant amount because a major component is increasing in price is rather easy to evaluate (as to its importance, not as to what to do about it). Similarly, gross changes in budgets, performance standards, and the like have a clear meaning for the manager. Even here there is an implicit theory of limits. Small changes (or oscillations) in any of these can and should be ignored, and "small" is measured again in terms of a statistical concept, not arithmetic.

CONCLUSION

By monitoring, the manager tries to keep the system functioning as a system. He constantly adjusts his movements and efforts to avoid breakdowns, accomplish quick returns to normal, compensate for unexpected occurrences, keep operations running smoothly, ferret out potential sources of trouble, and make changes that will reduce the frequency of work interruptions. Whether he is engaging in disciplinary actions, selecting a new employee, assessing the adequacy of a new method or piece of equipment, his objective is a smoothly functioning operation.

The manager requires as part of his control apparatus a theory of significant differences that will enable him to place certain limits on the occurrence or amplitude of the phenomenon he is observing. This requires a knowledge of the limits on normal or expected variation, given the inherent nature of the system (i.e., the work methods, personalities, etc., involved). He then hoards his managerial actions for the significant deviations in the system and avoids becoming, himself, a source of upset where none existed before.

From the point of view of organization design and the specification of managerial actions, it thus becomes possible to set forth explicitly (and thus control and check the performance of) managerial surveillance actions. These include operationally definable patterns for how, when, and whom to check, as well as techniques of data analysis to ascertain significant differences. This becomes another step in the process of making managerial actions less art and intuition and more science, but within the realm of human relationships. For example, we can distinguish those checks that require the manager to take action, those that are initiated to him, and those that come from reports. All, however, require organizational analyses, i.e., a knowledge of the time dimensions of the work-flow system to be controlled, prior to the elaboration of the checking and evaluation procedures.

Unfortunately, looking at the whole array of existing monitoring techniques in any organization, one is convinced that most are the product of impulse and expediency. Almost no effort is expended in relating the information sought to a conception of the organization as an integrated system. Instead, a strange assortment of unrelated and unrelatable "data" are accumulated from which the typical manager tries to deduce what is taking place. In part, the elaboration of accumulated information also reflects the efforts toward professionalization on the part of many staff groups who are successful in shifting themselves into some type of auditing relationship. Nearly every manager is openly dissatisfied with what he knows, and he feels frustrated that he cannot really find out "how things are going" unless he spends a great deal of time personally surveying the scene.

Most managers have their favorite index by which they spot trouble, but most of these smoke signals create as much trouble as they reveal, like the "Just in Case" files which are the product of managers who believe:

You can tell whether a man is really doing a good job and on top of his department by throwing an unexpected question at him about his unit. If he has the answer at his finger tips, you can rest easy because you've got a good man there.

Such procedures are a far cry from the assessment of significant deviations that we have proposed as a crucial element in any monitoring system.

However, the most serious barrier to the development of adequate monitoring procedures is the failure to comprehend the primary purpose of controls. In our systems view of work, the function of controls is to assess the degree to which the organization is operating as an organized, reciprocating process. The manager seeks to identify the points where disorganization, breakdown, or disintegration is occurring in order to devote his interventions to returning the system to normal equilibrium. Assessment of organizational-process variables as distinct from "results" is a crucial requirement for the modern manager.

Introduction of Short- and Long-term Changes

One of the manager's major responsibilities is to determine, by means of monitoring, when and where changes are required to maintain the continuity of the work-flow process. Such changes are of two types: short-term adjustments (to alleviate a single situation) and long-term changes (changes in structure to correct recurring problems). (Interestingly, most job descriptions make the gratuitous assumption that the organization will function as planned and do little to guide the manager in selecting remedial actions when disturbances occur.)

SHORT-TERM CHANGES

The manager's monitoring is frequently rewarded by the detection of events—deviations, in our terminology—that require his attention. These can be many things: an employee performing at an unsatisfactory level, a sudden shortage of a vital part or an increase in price, a notice that he is over his budget or behind on his schedule, or an upset boss or irate "customer."

181

A political scientist has described these problems in dynamic terms:

> Difficulties develop because their [employees of an organization] activities get out of phase with each other, interfere with each other, nullify each other, or perhaps even all three. . . . It requires selective inhibition of elicited individual effort, so as to regulate the timing, intensity, and direction of the flow of materials and communications and thus prevent jams and breakdowns.[1]

Corrective or Stabilizing Action

One task of the manager in the control-change sequence is taking corrective action where significant deviations have been revealed. Here, too, we can be explicit about the interaction pattern required. This is the "short-term" intervention.

The phrase "short term" does not mean that corrective action can be applied or is completed quickly. It refers to changes that result from, and last only as long as, administrative intervention continues.[2] Long-term changes are more durable since they result from modifications of the organization's structure.

We can, in fact, write sequences of remedial action that the supervisor takes (or should take) in endeavoring to return the work-flow system to a stable state. Some of these patterns also involve outside contacts, which may serve to bring the system back to normal. For example, the unsatisfactory pacing of the activities of a service department may be creating internal problems. The manager may move through his superior or other channels to bring the tempo of these activities more in alignment with his needs. Or additional personnel may have to be secured through recruitment channels or permission to work overtime secured from higher management in order to adjust to pressures for increased output.

[1] Herbert Kaufman, "Why Organizations Behave as They Do: An Outline of a Theory," paper presented at an Interdisciplinary Seminar on Administrative Theory, University of Texas, Austin, Tex., 1961, p. 45.
[2] See Eliot D. Chapple and Leonard R. Sayles, *The Measure of Management*, The Macmillan Company, New York, 1961, pp. 48–64.

From the point of view of the organization as a whole, the manager operating these controls also must be required to alert his manager and others who may be affected by the departures from equilibrium of his system. This enables them to take complementary actions to prevent the disturbance spreading from the jurisdiction of one manager through the entire organization. All these actions can be prescribed and quantified interactionally.

Initially, the manager may notify his manager, "customers" for whom he is working, next-stage managers in the flow of work, etc. He may also be required to consult auditing or stabilization groups, or they may have first identified the significant departure from desired norms.

The next step is usually the endeavor to return the system to equilibrium. Sometimes the manager can do this by his own direct intervention, e.g., assigning an employee to work overtime, calling out of town for a critical part, delaying the start of the next batch. But frequently the manager cannot simply give an order. He must either start a well-established sequence of contacts to provide the adjustment or engage in a less routine effort to change the behavior of one or more other members of the organization.

> [After the detection of such situations the manager's job is] the issuance of messages that inhibit some actions, encourage others, slow some down, speed up others, change the directions and intensities of flows, open new channels and . . . end blockages, prevent jams, and thus facilitate the vigorous performance of the basic processes of the organization.[3]

Channels of Remedial Action

Most efforts to compensate for work-flow interferences require numerous and difficult interactions. A careful study of an IBM manufacturing plant in the 1940s revealed five distinct routines for dealing with parts shortages that were impeding production.[4]

[3] Kaufman, *op. cit.,* p. 59.
[4] F. L. W. Richardson, Jr., and Charles R. Walker, *Human Relations in an Expanding Company,* Yale University, Labor and Management Center, New Haven, Conn., 1948, pp. 74–79.

Interactionally, these were very similar to grievance procedures: a series of contacts with those who could expedite the flow of parts. Alternative channels (involving still higher levels of management) were invoked when previous procedures failed. Three of the channels involved the use of special expediters and the regular organization channels; two others involved short-circuiting, contacts between managers who usually did not deal directly with one another. The complexity of the process is revealed by the details of the five distinctive procedures:

1. Expediting foremen representing assembly operations in production control inform other foremen and expediters representing machining in the same department that there is a shortage of parts.
2. Expediting foremen for assembly notify the head of production control.
3. Foreman calls the assembly head who then goes to the head of production control or to the plant manager.
4. Assembly expediters talk directly with machining foremen.
5. Head of production control goes to machining foremen.

Every time such a procedure is invoked, valuable managerial time is absorbed. Further, because these are emergency measures, initiated under great pressure and by people not frequently in contact, emotional reactions may result. These create additional losses in managerial energy and time.

Obviously, management needs to develop monitoring methods to determine when such remedial measures are becoming excessively costly. A vicious spiral appears when the absence of continuous work flows creates the necessity for the use of remedial channels such as these. Their use, in turn, creates additional upset and more breakdowns. These, in turn, act as pressure on line management to increase further their use of short-term remedial measures until the organization literally falls apart from the internal stresses that have been set up. We shall deal with this problem in the next section.

Thus far, we have made the implicit assumption that the administrative challenge is largely one of finding the time to go through the appropriate channels to accomplish the necessary adjustments. The manager does not find life that simple.

Many of the managers with whom he will have to deal, because of the crisis, operate under very different incentive and control systems. Similarly, the manager's own subordinates, whose behavior may have to change, respond to internally generated informal group pressures that may deter them from responding immediately to the manager's call for redirected or greater effort. The manager's problem then becomes one of achieving a behavior change.

Behavior Changes in Individuals

This is the area encompassed by most treatises on supervision and human relations: how to get people to change their behavior. Here are the well-documented (but not so well-understood) techniques of negotiating, interviewing, counseling, disciplining, training, and utilizing group meetings and improved communication techniques. Most of these techniques can be described behaviorally in terms of the kind and frequency of contacts necessary.

Some of these methods primarily involve relationships with subordinates. But, as we have noted, managers in complex organizations have many relationships outside their command group. How are outsiders influenced to change their behavior so as to remedy a work-flow problem? Many of the techniques of "conversion" were already reviewed in Chapter 9, and we shall not list them all here. Often just the frequency of the monitoring activity itself serves as a pressure. For this reason, such checking activities need to be rationed. But stronger measures are also available.

Some managers are very skillful at developing *exchange-of-favor relationships* whereby they build up a credit to be called upon in an emergency. Others rely more on forceful salesmanship or skillful devices whereby the other person "thinks of the idea first." A persuasion used by many managers is the offer of certain complementary assistance: "If you'll ask your people to work overtime, we'll handle the clerical part of the job in our shop so that you'll have that much less to do." "If you can get us this design in three months, we'll take care of all the paper-work formalities and put that promise in writing."

At times, a triangular rather than a direct route may be used to muster additional support, by persuading others that they have a stake in this decision, too. They may be in a better position to influence the individual or group who has to change than the first manager:

> We showed them that they would be hurt more than we would if that change went through.

> We spent a great deal of time talking to everyone who used any significant quantity, trying to get them on our side.

Another emergency measure is an investigation into the background of the problem. Many times the manager believes that if he can get enough "inside information" he can prove that some undesirable change in the work flow is not really necessary. Such legalistic explorations take a large amount of the manager's time and/or that of his subordinates.

Then there are simple, direct actions, such as placing office furniture in the corridor to convince those who allocate office space that adequate facilities are lacking. Most frequently, however, the method of influence and persuasion is straight negotiation:

> Even though this isn't up to standard, we have got to get it approved; there are a thousand men on the line being held up. Now what'll it take to convince you that this is really an exceptional case?

Successful negotiation requires the energy and interactional endurance to keep talking and cajoling and trading in the face of early rebuffs, even rejections. But the good negotiator needs more than this. He must use these same behavioral skills and expend the time to build a case. Department Y says that they are going to have to change the specifications for the work they do even if it is going to hamper manager X's work. X frequently cannot accept this bald statement. He begins his own inquiries, checking with people with supplementary technical knowledge, interviewing, getting subordinates to gather information. All this takes time from his normal activities and requires great patience. But the ability to go through such motions before meetings makes the difference between gaining concessions and changing the actions of others and failure to do so.

Resolution of Differences between Managers

Administrative theory assumes that, when there is a disagreement between two managers, there are readily available and "legally" correct means of resolving the differences. The two most often cited are the existence of rules that automatically settle the dispute and an appeal to a common, higher authority. We have observed rather little use of either. (In passing, it is worth noting that traditional management-bureaucracy theory assumes that there will be few such disagreements since each manager operates within his own sphere of influence and decision making.)

Rules lag behind a dynamic technology. It is difficult to conceive of, let alone impose, a rigid decision-making system. As a result, managers expect that even in those decision contacts where there is less ambiguity than in some technical areas, the "no rules" rule will apply. They anticipate negotiations over when and what, and for how much, they are going to get from others and expect to do the same for whatever they provide. A few "rules of thumb" grow up, such as priority for a man close to his shipping date over someone without this pressure, etc. Similarly, a stoppage on the assembly line or a potential delay to an outside customer may be given top priority.

Even when new, high-level rule-imposing bodies are created to settle routinely the difficult problems that would normally be negotiated, many managers confidently expect, "It will only be a matter of time until we find our way around that blockage; there's always a way."

Managers similarly avoid "running to the boss" for help or fiat to settle an issue, except under certain prescribed circumstances discussed below. The manager expects to negotiate his differences, convincing the other manager that he is right or exerting pressure on him through one device or another but not appealing to the formal organization to rule for him. In part, this may be just accurate perception, namely, the difficulty of getting a "ruling" from a higher level, when in many circumstances complex crossover channels are involved to reach a common supervisor.

More importantly, intervention from upper management usually means reduced discretion. There is always the possibility that the revelation of a problem will cause upper management to impose new restrictions that make one's own job less palatable and more difficult. Furthermore, the investigation that may be instituted to resolve the appealed question could disclose rather embarrassing violations of company rules and standards. Most managers have stretched or shrunk their jobs to suit their own personalities and the expediences of the situation. They know that they can always be found guilty of violating some requirement and rule, and they fear that the quickest way to lose what they have gained by uninterrupted, unchallenged "past practice" is to instigate an investigation.

Finally, it is not considered *comme il faut* to run to the boss. Managers believe that they are, in part, evaluated on how *few* problems they cause. A recent study of purchasing agents confirms this norm; it is the less successful, less adept staff manager who runs to the boss to fight his battles, who invokes bureaucratic rules, who insists that requests of which he does not approve be put in writing, etc.[5]

The absence of these two usual "quit claim" devices, rules and an appeal to higher authorities, increases the time necessary for remedial actions. Nearly all these tactics require the personal intervention of the manager. While the telephone is used often

[5] George Strauss, "The Tactics of Lateral Relationship: The Purchasing Agent," *Administrative Science Quarterly*, vol. 7, no. 2, pp. 35–36, September, 1962.

and memos on rare occasions, neither seems to be a good substitute for face-to-face discussion. And in this, as we have noted, the pressures cannot be too direct:

> We don't call in the boss or write memos that put the finger on anybody except as a last resort. After all, you have to continue to live with these people and get things from them.

Realistically, there are times when the remedial action involves notifying or calling in the boss. The manager knows that he must maintain the support of his superior (or superiors) as well as keep him informed of such things as these:

1. Matters in which the superior has expressed an interest, to keep himself informed and technically up to date.
2. Developing problems, delays, etc., that may become more serious and attract the attention and questions of still higher levels of authority. The superior usually wants to be prepared with answers to these potential inquiries.
3. Situations that may require him to ask the assistance or indulgence of his superior (because of the difficulty of the problem and the greater influence of the superior).
4. Deviations in the superior's monitoring system. For example, he may be watching the amount of overtime, missed completion dates, the rate at which expenditures are being made, particularly signals that coordination among parts of his jurisdiction is not being maintained.
5. Significant signs of progress that indicate the correctness or validity of an approach, method, or activity initiated by the subordinate and thus help to build a favorable impression of the subordinate's competence.

Tempo or Pace of Changes in Organization

Many times the problem is not simply a matter of convincing someone to do more or charge less or to permit some departure from specifications. A return to equilibrium involves the integrated cooperation of a number of people.

The most typical require changes in the tempo or the sequential pattern of the work flow. The phrase "walk through" is often used to mean that, rather than putting a request or an endorsement or an approval through the normal organization channels, the manager accelerates the process. Usually a subordinate literally carries the paper to the people who must sign or initial it. Working overtime is a similar type of adjustment to emergencies. Less frequent are the invoking of special procedures, such as use of a company plane to obtain a part that would normally be delivered by the vendor. On occasion, a whole series of meetings are scheduled or a task force assigned to handle an unusual problem. These also serve to change the parameters of the work flow connecting the various stages. The manager may insert himself into a temporary position in the work flow, for example, to reduce the pressures on a subordinate who is near the breaking point. Here he is serving as a temporary buffer.

Probably inadequate attention is given to the high costs—in managerial time particularly—associated with changes in the manner in which work is completed. Meetings drain away a great deal of time; many last as much as half a day and require the attendance of a host of managerial talent. Rarely used special procedures such as obtaining the use of the company plane may require a dozen telephone calls (perhaps purposely, to discourage its use).

Many of these short-term remedial procedures require the manager to switch quickly from one outside group to another and in the right sequence. Changes in one specification obviously have ramifications for other groups who are working on the same project or using the same part. A delicate sense of timing is necessary.

> As soon as we discovered that this was not functioning the way it was supposed to, we had to notify these other groups. But we had to be very careful; if handled badly, this could have given the X group an excuse to "slip" their schedule [i.e., justify not meeting a production schedule], something they have been trying to do. And

after we notified people, there were still precautions to take. Now everyone is dubious about the . . . and they are fearful about accepting it or believing anything we say that is good about it. So we have to spend a good deal of time in meetings reassuring people, trying to get a more relaxed atmosphere. Also we have to get them to give us more time. They usually want immediate results or an excuse they can give top management, but we just want more time and people to bear with us and not panic.

Without the right motions in the right sequence and frequency, the manager who has bad news to announce, a significant deviation that is going to affect the flows of others, can create a panic that will make his job and that of other managers doubly difficult.

Sometimes the number of meetings, telephone calls, and negotiating sessions required to resolve rather small crises is staggering.[6] Minor disagreements over the "goodness" of a particular part can initiate a series of interactions lasting a period of weeks.

For example, one later-stage group announces that the material received from an earlier-stage group is unacceptable. This throws off the work schedule of another manager who insists that the material is acceptable. Various auditing and stabilization experts are called in by both sides to support their positions. Evidence, both relevant and irrelevant, is gathered from other parts of the organization; each such mission also requires prolonged, persuasive contacts. Managers call one another for "aid" and support. Finally a settlement is negotiated.

Knowledge of the Organization

In dealing with a threatened or actual disruption in the flow of work, the manager needs to know the form and behavioral characteristics of the organization. In effect, the manager must know in advance the steps he will take to remedy the problem. Here are some examples of this type of programming:

---

[6] It would be useful for management to log the entire cost of typical cases in order to increase the awareness of the dollars involved.

If we run into problems with supplies of a certain part or component, I have to know exactly where in the company these come from, that is, who controls them, who is responsible for pricing them, and who else may be agitating for them.

On big jobs we can get held up at a number of places. When one of my managers doesn't get the cooperation he needs in the X group, he knows that he should see the supervisor. On the other hand, when this same kind of difficulty crops up in the Y group, he can go directly to the employees who are doing the work. In fact, that is the way of getting the quickest kind of action.

When you want something extra from that fellow, you just insist you have got to have it, and if you push hard enough he gives in, but dealing with the other manager is entirely different; you have to go about it in a very subtle fashion or he gets hurt and becomes uncooperative.

In all these short-term remedial measures the manager must have in mind a clear operational picture of what is occurring. These are short-term correctives that should disappear when his controls indicate that the system has returned to stability. Otherwise, the manager will find that he has taken on new administrative patterns that are permanent drains on his energy. Therefore, the manager has to be aware of what changes he has introduced and the need for continued monitoring during the emergency. Needless to say, many forget this in the excitement of coping with the problem.

LONG-TERM CHANGES

Some of a supervisor's problems cannot be solved by the administrative actions just described. To put this in more quantitative terms, the manager must be concerned not only with the rate of change but with the rate of the rate of change, the second derivative. Where disturbances are accumulating, short-term corrective actions are wasteful, either because they fail to rectify the problem and/or because there are underlying structural problems requiring attention.

The administrator who relies solely on short-term corrective actions (which in another work we have called "conversion") is ignoring one of the most important parts of his job: seeking out and remedying the persisting and compounding problems. These require the introduction of changes in the organizational constraints: the flow of work, the components of jobs, the incumbents of jobs, the structure of authority, the incentives, and even the controls themselves.

We shall endeavor to give an operational description of this change process as an integral part of the manager-leader's day-to-day administrative activities. The analysis lends itself to behavioral quantification and objective validation so that the organization can provide for change within its structure and appraise the success of its members in carrying on these patterns. Rather than a "last straw," when all else has failed, organization change can precede serious crises. Furthermore, administrators can be trained in unambiguous behavioral skills to handle such programs.

Detection of Need for Long-term Change

In the previous section we described administrative actions designed to return the work flows to stable operation. Where such short-term remedies are either wasteful or ineffective, the situation requires the introduction of what can best be called "long-term" or organizational change. What signals the existence of these situations?

Recurring Problems.   These situations repeat in a highly predictable fashion. "Every week I get involved in at least one hassle with the . . . department over schedules." Similarly, problems of unbalanced work load for subordinates, persistently scarce resources, or constant seniority grievances—all may drain the manager's time and energy resources. Each time he invokes emergency measures to change the behavior of an individual or of a number of people associated in a work flow, he commits himself to a difficult task and potentially neglects other parts of his job.

"High-amplitude" Problems. Disturbances that involve major deviations from planned patterns of interaction and work flow are very costly. Taking everyone from their regular work to tackle last-minute rush jobs, crash programs, and task-force investigations devours managerial time as well as disturbs the regular work habits of subordinates. Even though irregular in occurrence, such problems are worth identifying because of their seriousness.

"Spiraling" or "Long-chain" Problems. Figuratively, an initial infection (disturbance) in the organizational system "spreads" to other flows, and these new upsets cause further reaction. Thus, the original difficulty is magnified as many groups become involved. As managers make compensating adjustments to deal with their own problems, these accumulate and begin to create their own backlash of disturbances. Similarly, failure on the part of key managers to take decisive action on critical problems shows up as "long chains." These problems may not be recurring; they just are never solved.

Problem Diagnosis. The manager's monitoring system should include a summarization of his own use of short-term remedial actions. He should know where and for what he spends his scarce time resources. The incidence of such disturbances identifies problems that may require long-term as distinct from "fire-fighting" or short-term managerial actions. In the same fashion, repeated requests for aid can identify internal problems in the work flows of employees. Thus managers at any level in the hierarchy can monitor the intersection points of the flows over which they have jurisdiction as well as some of the internal dynamics of the jobs of managers below them. All, however, represent second derivatives, the rate at which deviations show up, the rate of the rate of change.

There are three sources of such problems. One is internal stresses and strains that have not been solved by previous short-term efforts. Another is externally based problems: for example, another work group whose timing or standards of performance are a source of disturbance. The third is new factors, new equipment, new market forces, or new management controls and structures to which adjustment must be made.

The administrator also needs to be able to identify in his own organization the elements that are most susceptible to breakdown under the pressures of day-to-day organizational life. These are the individuals and jobs receiving the greatest buffeting because of the way in which the structure has evolved. For example, a manager should know that a subordinate in charge of some scarce resource, which is under heavy and incompatible demands from other groups in the organization, is likely to be such a vulnerability. Only an unusually "strong" personality in the position of that service manager will be able to maintain a fairly regular and stable relationship with the rest of the organization. Similarly, where advisory and auditing administrative patterns are combined in the same job, the manager should be able to predict that this may become a structural defect. Where positions that should be part of a single or "unit" work flow are placed under different managers, a heavy drain on the next higher level of management can be anticipated.

Other examples of organizational vulnerability could be cited. However, the significant point is that the manager can be in a position to identify both the problem and its source in the organization. Then he must make a choice: What are the costs of continuing to function with the defect in structure as compared with the costs of introducing a change. The former is the actual losses due to work-flow interruptions plus the drains on managerial time created by the need for constant intervention to deal with the haggling and internecine conflict and to restore work flows. These costs, which are rarely measured faithfully by existing cost accounting systems, have to be compared with the not inconsiderable costs of changing the structure. The latter means not only retraining people but also persuading both those who must approve the change and those who must change that the new pattern is worthwhile. Fearing the recalcitrance and lethargy of the organization, many managers shy away from the attempt to introduce long-term change.

IMPACT ON STAFF CONTROLS

A frequent source of management uncertainty is the evaluation of so-called staff groups who are only indirect contributors to the production process. In most organizations, intricate measures have been evolved by staff managers themselves to justify their costs to the organization. These usually consist of highly questionable self-appraisals of the total savings for which their activities can be held responsible. These "totals" serve to increase the tension between staff and line officials. (See Chapter 13.)

Such measures encourage the staff to compete for credit for innovations, to impose them on the line manager, and to maximize the number of projects, ideas, and proposals they circulate. Many of these innovations are perceived as hampering, hamstringing, and wasting the energies of the manager.

As an alternative means of evaluation, the foregoing analysis suggests that those staff groups responsible for complementing the efforts of the line manager be held to quite different standards. Controls on advisory groups, for example, should measure the rapidity with which the line manager's work-flow patterns are returned to equilibrium and the frequency of disturbance reduced. Minimization of both should be evaluated as representing the "work" of advisory managers in contributing to the introduction of what we have called "long-term" changes. This would include:

1. The ability to develop satisfactory working relationships with managers whom they should be aiding
2. The ability to diagnose real administrative problems (including the continual development of improved data-gathering systems)
3. The ability to propose solutions to these problems

Some of the so-called staff-line problems are the result of a failure to organize on this basis. Staff groups go into action in areas and at times when the supervisor has not agreed that there is a significant deviation. Then his dealing with the staff itself becomes a stressful and time-consuming relationship. In turn, this is partially the result of the failures of traditional administrative management theory in defining the staff role. The advisory staff should be measured by its success in returning deviating systems to equilibrium; this, in turn, would minimize their conflicts with line managers.[7]

It is worth noting that where such staff groups are, in fact, used to aid the manager in restabilizing an erratic work flow, the typical staff-line conflict problem disappears. The latter results from the instabilities introduced by the staff into the manager's flows through its initiations and proposals for change. When the *manager seeks the help of the staff* to solve a pressing problem and he is able to identify the existence and costliness of the problem, the basis for conflict is removed. (The manager must know what organizational resources are available to him for diagnosing second-derivative problems.)

Ideally, the manager has his own "staff." In our recent volume on organization design, we endeavored to define the job of such assistants:

> Because they are concerned with developing programs to expedite the work flow and eliminate stresses both within and between unit work flows that affect the total work-flow system, the specialists inevitably become the specialized assistants of the work-flow systems manager. Their responsibility then is to act for him in their respective areas to improve the operation on the unit work-flow level. It is important to note the word "responsibility." In the usual sense of the word, specialists do not have staff responsibility with advisory or consultative relations to the line, nor do they have the responsibility of line supervisors, one step removed. They are actually *of* the staff of the manager and accountable to him for developing, install-

[7] For a fuller discussion of this problem, see George Strauss and Leonard R. Sayles, *Personnel: The Human Problems of Management,* Prentice-Hall, Inc., Englewood Cliffs, N.J., 1960, pp. 399–417.

ing, and auditing the results of programs in terms of the major objective of removing stress.[8]

MARGINAL ADJUSTMENTS VERSUS CRISES

Good administration involves continual change: marginal shifts here and there to remove sources of instability and deviation, as highlighted by the control system. Most organizations do not function this way; the administrator is not held responsible for introducing change except at very high levels. The result is needlessly high administrative expenses because managerial problems accumulate and are not solved. Eventually, the costs become so heavy that a major crisis is precipitated. Under these circumstances, there is usually a general shake-up and one hears the familiar shibboleths:

A new broom sweeps clean.

People get too comfortable if you don't rock the boat once in a while to shake them up.

These shake-ups are enormously costly. It often takes months, sometimes years, for the members of an organization to regain stable patterns of work that provide efficient ways of achieving coordination.

Such crises are partially the result of failure to comprehend the pattern of managerial activity and transmit it to managers. It is often assumed that detecting the need for change and managing this change are reserved for top management, that the quantity of innovation is proportional to the level in the hierarchy.[9]

Overemphasis on "conversion" or short-term remedies in the

[8] Chapple and Sayles, *op. cit.*, pp. 43–44.

[9] See Robert Dubin, *The World of Work*, Prentice-Hall, Inc., Englewood Cliffs, N.J., 1958, p. 84.

management literature and folkways is also at fault. Nothing could be less appropriate for the complex, dynamic organization.

But the problem is also one of proper monitoring—ensuring that each manager is appraised in terms of his ability to stabilize his flows and introduce change where serious instabilities are present. This requires appropriate detection mechanisms—and rewards—operated by successive levels of management.

It should also be recognized that short-term palliatives can be more attractive than long-term answers. Usually a manager must spend a great deal of time convincing superiors in the organization that a structural or long-term change is necessary, even before he gets an opportunity to engage in the difficult job of establishing the change in the organization. Many managers, or leaders, are kept so busy "putting out fires" that they never have time to find the source of the recurring blazes. In a sense, a rather great capital investment, in terms of time and energy, is necessary to provide a more permanent solution. The manager must take time from his regular activities to engage in lengthy "selling" contacts with superiors and others, plus undertaking the major problems of coping with affected subordinates. Many lack the energy and the ability to do this, and this—*not* the recalcitrance of subordinates and persistence of habit—is the major reason that change is not introduced at an appropriate rate in the organization.

In our field work, we observed many managers who included these long-term changes as part of their jobs. In fact, this was one of the most noteworthy characteristics of good managers. They undertook the long, arduous task of convincing superiors and colleagues to change established practice, where this practice was causing serious problems. They changed the work flows of their groups to eliminate uneven flows (thus creating smoother work loads). They spent a great deal of time doing missionary work and lobbying for new specifications on vital components, new methods of doing certain jobs, introduction of development work into less creative tasks, technical innovations that were not in the approved plans and designs:

At present my people spend a lot of time on the phone giving information to people who find the present system of manuals difficult or unappealing. I am going to start working on a better method of keeping up-dated a system of informing people in order to eliminate so much telephoning.

Our work load has "ups and downs" that make it difficult to maintain the right staff. We spend time letting people know the kind of work we can do for them and getting ourselves known. We take on people for short periods for the same reason.

My subordinates are going to have to develop a totally different kind of relationship with those people who provide them with support or we will continue to have frictions. [The pattern of interaction was inappropriate to the professional status of the support group.] For one thing, they will have to get the . . . to initiate ideas and proposals.

If we can get other projects, this will mean that we can acquire certain new equipment that will prevent our having to negotiate for the use of this equipment in the other department.

At present, the lack of special specifications for our use of this part means that we frequently find ourselves in serious technical difficulties that take up a lot of time. While at present there is little management sentiment in favor of this, I am gradually convincing people that it is important to establish such specifications.

I can identify those regional people who don't believe in taking the time to have their personnel fully trained to service our new equipment. As a result, when the equipment gets into the field, they run into trouble and have to call on us. I have to send out one of my technical people and even occasionally go myself. I need to find some way of incorporating our training activity as a part of their regular activities.

We're going to start adding to our own staff one or two men from the groups we do work for. We'll treat them just like our own people and they'll work side by side. I think that this new staffing procedure will result in more acceptance of us by those departments who haven't understood our work before. In a sense, this is going to be an apprentice program.

All this is contrary to the usual hierarchical conception of an organization in which plans and policies—innovations—are introduced at the top and carried out as they are made more explicit by the lower levels of the organization.

IMPLEMENTATION AND VALIDATION OF CHANGE

The final stage in the monitoring process is the implementation and validation of structural modifications that are introduced by the manager to deal with recurring instabilities. The traditional human relations literature has also concentrated on this problem: gaining acceptance for structural changes. Here one reads about participation and timing, the use of informal leaders, etc. Arensberg, however, again from the point of view of the applied anthropologist, has provided the only clearly operational description of the implementation process that permits programming managerial behavior: [10]

1. First, an increase in managerial initiative to subordinates
2. Opportunity for increased interworker contacts (presumably informal group activity)
3. Next, an increase in redressive contacts or initiations to the manager (who must be prepared to accept these)
4. Rewarding managerial responses to these subordinates' initiations (often omitted because the change period is such a busy one that time is not available for this step)

(Note: In our terminology, steps 2 and 3 both represent compensatory behavior: reactions of the individuals to the stress of changed jobs, managerial contact patterns, etc.)

10 Conrad M. Arensberg and Geoffrey Tootell, "Plant Sociology: Real Discoveries and New Problems," in Mirra Komarovsky (ed.), *Common Frontiers of the Social Sciences,* The Free Press of Glencoe, New York, 1957, p. 316.

The manager cannot afford to assume that a change introduced by him has actually become part of the operating system. We know that human relations systems tend to return to previous equilibrium when pressures that have shifted them away from that comfortable position are removed. Parenthetically, however, it would be a mistake to assume that all changes are imposed on "comfortable" equilibria, although these are the grist for the case writers. In many situations people are under substantial stress and tension; the organization is not providing them with personal satisfactions, and they welcome change. As noted in a recent paper, "Without stress, organizations don't learn." [11] The manager must utilize methods of appraisal to validate that the change has become stabilized, whether initially welcomed or not. Essentially, this means checking to see that the flow, sequence, and coordinating patterns are as planned.

As anthropologists have long observed, ceremonies or *rites de passage* facilitate the acceptance of structural change. By highlighting dramatically the new patterns of behavior that will be required of organizational members and permitting the practice of new roles, outmoded patterns of relationship are inhibited.

ENTROPY AND CHANGE

On the one hand, it can be argued that the "good" manager constantly changes both his own behavior and the parameters of the situation in response to internal and external sources of instability. On the other, it should be noted that the manager in a dynamic environment has no choice if he is to survive or, better, if his part of the organization is to remain "organized." He must introduce well-directed change. The alternative to this constant input of managerial energy is entropy: lack of order, randomness. The entropy increases with time as various pressures distort

[11] Robert Chapman and John Kennedy, "The Background and Implications of the Rand Corporation Systems Research Laboratory Studies," in Albert Rubenstein and Chadwick Haberstroh (eds.), *Some Theories of Organization*, Dorsey Press, Homewood, Ill., 1960, p. 144.

the work patterns. These include the tendency for employees to seek easier ways, to shift responsibility, and for outsiders to gain unreasonable concessions, to impose their controls and their values.

Another way of looking at long-term change is that the manager's job must change as much as the skilled worker or the specialized technician. It is almost a cliché to observe that modern industry makes individual skills obsolete at a frightening pace (e.g., the flight engineer). What has not been realized is the extent to which this is true for administrative skills.

CONCLUSION

We have endeavored to present an operational description of the change process as an integral part of the manager-leader's day-to-day administrative activities. This analysis lends itself to behavioral quantification and objective validation so that the organization can provide for change within its structure and appraise the success of its members in carrying on these patterns. Rather than a "last straw," when all else has failed, change, in the applied anthropologist's view, can precede serious crises. Further, administrators can be trained in terms of unambiguous behavioral skills to carry forward such programs.

In our view, the process of change has consisted of these interrelated sequences of managerial action:

1. Specific organizational and technical checks (of prescribed characteristics and frequency) on the stability of the system under the jurisdiction of the manager
2. Established criteria for evaluating significant deviations from the desired stable state
3. Prescribed administrative patterns of corrective action to bring the system back to equilibrium (short-term change)
4. Appraisals of recurring or continuing instabilities in the system with provision for staff (or specialist) assistance in investigating potential structural sources of organization stress and remedial measures

5. Administrative patterns for implementing long-term organizational structural change
6. Administrative action to validate the change

We have purposely ignored the usual shibboleths about starting at the top of the organization, getting "grass roots" support, etc. In our view of change as part of every manager's job requirement, this pattern is repeated at each level, with adjustments in controls of the processes below. There is no starting or ending point as such; change is an integral and essential part of all organized behavior.

Basic to our view of controls as an administrative activity is the concept of marginal adjustment. In general, the manager does not make *the* decision (or plan) that shapes the future activities of his unit for the foreseeable future. Rather, he constantly makes readjustments in what he and his people are doing as he gains new information, new and unforeseen problems emerge, and the feedback accumulates. A manager cannot afford to think in absolutes, of fixed positions, or the "right way." The world of the organization does not permit this type of absolutist thinking. Administration is an iterative process; the manager must constantly rethink old decisions, remake tacit and explicit agreements with external groups, and adjust the directions he has given to subordinates.

His overall objective does not change, however, and this must be the basis for his monitoring effort. A control system is conceived as the process by which perturbations in the work systems —disturbances and irregularities—are gradually brought under greater control; i.e., the limits of variability are decreased. In essence, this means that the manager seeks techniques and adjustments by which the system becomes more self-maintaining, self-regulating, more nearly a reciprocating work-flow model (in which lateral contacts predominate). His efforts to minimize interventions, i.e., to reduce the leadership component of his administrative actions, are not likely to be blessed with complete success. However, the manager must have this objective in mind, as the goal toward which he is directed, if the proper short- and long-term adjustments are to be made.

The essence of this view of monitoring and controls is not consistent with either the scientific management nor the human relations view of supervision. Both stress the delegation of tasks to individuals and evaluation of their performance. Under the most modern view, the subordinate might set his own objectives and evaluate his own performance, with the superior acting as coach and counselor.

We have stressed assessment of the interrelationship of jobs in work systems. The manager must know the operating characteristics of the *system*. Thus individual subordinates are not free to do their jobs in whatever way is best for them (as long as it is completed). And the manager does not wait to measure the results or outputs. Surveillance mechanisms are in constant use, and subordinates must learn the complex behavioral patterns that will fit their activities into the network of activities of others.

What is the implication of this change process for the growing social concern with the impact of large hierarchical structures on initiative and creativity? It would seem that this type of analysis presents a far different prognosis for the role of the individual than the usual political science view of delegated and strictly delimited authority or the psychologists' emphasis on palliatives to reduce the sting of hierarchical power.

We have observed the actual behavior of managers in large organizations, and we find that their organizational positions give them much leeway in utilizing their personality skills and energies to meet the challenges of constant restabilization requirements and the need to introduce change. The notion that the lower-level manager serves passively as a transmitter of orders from higher-ups and as a feedback mechanism, reporting what is going on below, is just not reality, except where the manager's personality is inadequate to taking the initiative.

Another myth exploded by reality is the neat, reassuring dividing lines between various degrees of authority. In traditional theory, top levels establish policy and lower levels administer and execute. But how realistic is this? A long-time student of management gives us the answer:

> Most businessmen still believe that these [entrepreneurial] decisions are made by "top management." Indeed, practically all textbooks lay down the dictum that "basic policy decisions" are the "prerogative of top management." At most, top management "delegates" certain decisions.
>
> But this reflects yesterday's rather than today's reality, let alone that of tomorrow. It is perfectly true that top management must have the final say, the final response. But the business enterprise of today is no longer an organization in which there are a handful of "bosses" at the top who make all the decisions while the "workers" carry out orders. It is primarily an organization of professionals with highly specialized knowledge exercising autonomous, responsible judgement. And every one of them—whether manager or individual expert contributor—constantly makes truly entrepreneurial decisions which affect the economic characteristics and risks of the entire enterprise. He makes them not only by "delegation from above" but inevitably in the performance of his own job and work.[12]

When the organization is viewed as a complex series of interlocking patterns of human relationships, work-flow patterns, and control patterns, the opportunity for the individual to innovate and shape his own environment becomes apparent. Creativity and innovation are a product of the individual's ability to extract the time and energy from the "fire-fighting" preoccupations of the moment, in order to modify the pressures and stresses on himself and on his subordinates. The hierarchy is no barrier to this; it is, as it has been in every culture, a challenge to the able.

[12] Peter F. Drucker, "Long-range Planning, Challenge to Management Science," *Management Science*, vol. 5, no. 3, p. 242, April, 1959.

12

The Manager and the Decision Process

As we noted at the outset, the manager is usually conceived in static terms: He has a certain amount of authority that permits him to make certain types of decisions, and these decisions must be carried out by subordinates who have the responsibility to follow his instructions. This conception of administration and the manager's role produces the neat organization pyramids with their unquestioned hierarchical characteristics and, in the process, deludes many observers into condemning the monolithic structure.

More realistically, decision making is an organizational process. It is shaped as much by the pattern of interaction of managers as it is by the contemplation and cognitive processes of the individual.

Various special-interest groups converge or intersect at the point at which the decision must be made, namely, the manager. Most of the external groups to which the manager is exposed provide him with the intensely specialized point of view of the expert. But since many, if not most, questions to which he must find solutions are composite generalist problems (e.g., production *and* personnel, product reliability *and* cost, etc.), he cannot rely on only one view, nor does top management want this parochialism to exist.

This convergence at the manager's position is really a dynamic pattern of contacts, not a solitary process. Observation suggests that the manager also accomplishes his objectives by moving about the organization and persuading people with special knowledge and points of view to agree with him against those who seek an alternative objective. Thus, those who design the structure of the organization must arrange for such contacts in the organizational location and job descriptions of those who are supposed to impinge on the thinking of the manager.

Conflict is as good a word as any to describe this process, since the manager-executive-leader finds that the points of view of the various vested-interest groups are by no means mutually compatible.

> The guy responsible for approving the safety features of the equipment raised an awful fuss about that wiring. But I knew there wasn't a chance in a million that someone would get hurt, and if we tried to change it, our scrap bill for the month would bring the accountants down on us like a pack of wolves.

> If we make this improvement, we increase the reliability of the equipment and please the reliability engineers, but we increase the time it takes to make repairs on it, and the group responsible for evaluating that aspect of our work will be on our necks.

We thus prefer not to consider planning and decision making as separate, distinct activities in which the manager engages. They are inextricably bound up in the warp and woof of the interaction pattern, and it is a false abstraction to separate them.

A good example of this is Dean Acheson's description of what he believed to be the naïveté of the then new Secretary of State Dulles' expectations concerning his job:

> He told me that he was not going to work as I had done, but would free himself from involvement with what he referred to as personnel and administrative problems, in order to have more time to think.

I did not comment, but was much struck by the conjunction of ideas. I wondered how it would turn out. For it had been my experience that thought was not of much use without knowledge and guidance, and that who should give me both and how competent they would be must depend on who chose, dealt with, assigned and promoted these people and established the forms of organization within which they worked.[1]

Later in this same essay, Acheson expresses criticism of the view that even the President (Eisenhower at that time) needs more time for isolated contemplation:

This absorption with the Executive as Emerson's "Man Thinking," surrounded by a Cabinet of Rodin statues, bound in an oblivion of thought . . . seemed to me unnatural. Surely thinking is not so difficult, so hard to come by, so solemn as all this.[2]

CONFLICTING SIGNALS AND MANAGERIAL DECISION MAKING

In this not-the-best-of-all-possible worlds, the distinction between *variations* and *deviations* can be obscured by organizational forces as well as by imperfect perception and quantitative skills. The manager cannot be blamed for the organization's use of competing-interest groups who focus on him to fulfill their own missions and win their own rewards. As noted in the preceding chapters, multiple outside originations are directed at the manager by groups that are charged with influencing him and are evaluated on the basis of their ability to do so. They may endeavor to persuade him to devote more of his budget to training or less of it to salary increments, to build more aesthetic appeal into his product or to make it with less costly components. In other words, the manager is evaluated on and can have his job affected by a number of potentially conflicting standards. The de-

[1] Dean Acheson, "Thoughts about Thoughts in High Places," *The New York Times Magazine,* Oct. 11, 1959, p. 20.
[2] *Ibid.,* p. 21.

sign of the organization can be adjusted to increase or decrease the potential success of these standards in wooing and winning his attentiveness.

Thus, at some point, the manager usually has to make some intellectual choices. Each auditing group can claim some direct or indirect means of rewarding or punishing him:

> You have to listen to the budget people; they control the purse strings.

> If your work is not approved by the product test people, you are really in a bad way.

> Personnel has to approve all increments that aren't given at the semiannual evaluation period.

> I happen to know that the boss listens to those guys; if they have it in for you and don't like the way your designs look, they can make it hot for you.

They endeavor simultaneously to persuade him to move this way or that, and many times the "pulls" are mutually contradictory.

Then the manager must react like a computer program to the demands of each group that he take some action. Here the manager must make the decision continually, much as a binary-system choice: Is it a "0" or a "1"? If his appraisal indicates "0," he can stand pat; if, however, a "1" is his interpretation, he must go into action to rectify a potential disturbance to his work-flow system. This, in all our analyses, has been the purpose of monitoring.

An Indeterminate Solution

Essentially, this means that the manager's job program frequently does not prescribe a completely determinant course of action. A number of people act on him through requirements that he initiate contact with them or be accessible to them, and their requests, suggestions, ideas—even orders or demands—are not mutually compatible.

Thus, given a programmed job description, manager X may behave differently from manager Y with the same program, and yet both may act in accordance with the program. It is important to note that this is very different from the usual hasty assumption that two managers do the same job in very different ways. The point of view of this volume is that there are determinable, optimum patterns of managerial action and that the organization process requires that these be maintained.

Is this good or bad? A safe answer is usually that most things are both, and so it may be in this situation. The advantages can most readily be seen in a research or development organization.

The organization wants the work-flow manager to be exposed to the influence of a number of specialists and interest groups. Under prescribed circumstances, he should check with each of these experts by taking the initiative to arrange a meeting. He should also make himself available to them (usually when the experts' checks or audits reveal a departure from a prearranged standard of achievement). These contacts should be so timed and with that degree of frequency and internal pattern as to assure appropriate consideration for the specialty involved.

However, because the final "solution" or project report cannot be envisioned perfectly, the organization expects and must rely upon the manager to make certain *trades*. By this we mean that he must make certain intellectual decisions when a suggestion or request falls outside of what Barnard appropriately has called the "zone of indifference." Here the manager decides—and this is an instance where decision making is, in fact, a crucial element in what happens within the operation—how much of one element he is willing to give up in order to gain more of another.

Usually there is a risk factor involved as well.

A case in point is the situation in which the manager knows that he is risking a project completion date by introducing a further improvement in characteristic Z of his design. Such a failure will create serious instability for him; his immediate manager will begin to act on him with increased frequency and in a way that will involve many tensions. He may have to make special demands on his subordinates for overtime, extra effort, etc.; these will also involve time-consuming, difficult contacts. He must compare these with the potential and much later "reward" of having achieved a significant breakthrough. If he achieves this, presumably he will be in a better position to get assignments and to enjoy relationships with subordinates and other organizational groups that will synchronize more closely with his own personality needs—the usual fruits of higher status.

While there is little point in demonstrating the geometry of the analogy, it is interesting to conceive of the manager as having a certain preference scale for the objectives sought by outsiders through their initiations to him. Let's review a rather simple case:

A group charged with overseeing the safety of equipment produced by manager X wishes him to change the wiring, claiming that it is now unsafe. To make the requisite change will bring him into conflict with the "customer" for whom he is designing this object and who is seeking to minimize his costs. Because of the personality and past experience of manager X, he has a certain personal preference scale or rate of substitution by which he evaluates lower costs in comparison with safety. This relationship could be expressed by an indifference curve, at any point on which he is equally well satisfied. If he feels that there is already a great deal of safety in his designs, the curve indicates that there will have to be a very great improvement in any safety feature for him to be willing to sacrifice any costs. On the contrary, when his costs are already very low, he will be willing to make more expensive adjustments to gain an increase in the safety of the equipment.

As we have said, the exact relationship is a product of such things as the manager's emotional feelings regarding economic variables and safety, the conditioning he has received by past experiences, his liking or disliking of the personnel involved, etc.
At any given time there is a kind of price relationship between

safety and cost. Presumably the manager has adjusted the quantity of safety built into his equipment and related it to costs on the basis of the total organizational rewards and punishments operating at that time. When the company goes on a huge safety campaign, any even slightly unsafe part that a safety man can call to top management's attention brings sharp reprimands and lengthy, unpleasant sessions. Thus manager X will detect that safety has increased in price relative to costs. When cost-saving campaigns are in full tilt, the "price" ratio changes in the other direction.

When Barnard speaks about the "zone of indifference," he is describing the circumstances under which the manager, in response to outside originations, will go into action to make changes. The amount of improvement necessary is a function of the current organizational "price structure" and the manager's personal set of indifference curves.

Where the manager is unwilling to act (i.e., he reads "0"), the outsider must find some way of changing the going "price." This can take the form of bringing new pressures to bear on manager X or convincing him that he will be able to muster support for the change that X had not taken into account in his calculations.

These, in the economist's terminology, "are marginal rates of substitution" or *trades* that the manager is making. Given the total complex of forces on him (many of which are applied in the external flows that we described) he endeavors to adjust the performance of his work-flow system so as to reach the highest level (i.e., equilibrium) possible. He will consider a deviation significant when his direct monitoring or the pressures of an outsider show him that he can make changes and improve his overall position. He stands pat when the changes proposed to him or demanded of him would cause him to hurt his overall position, again given his own preferences (i.e., indifference curves) and the going "price" structure (payoff function) in the organization.

When an organization talks about decentralization or further delegation, it is referring to lowering the hierarchical level at which these trades or marginal rates of substitution take place. Obviously, illegal behavior on the part of the manager can vitiate this forced choice. For example, the manager, by adjusting or "fudging" his records and similar aberrant actions, can "have his cake and eat it too." Here, subterfuge substitutes for a "real-cost" decision.

In today's organizations the number of rules and evaluations (audits) mean that the manager rarely can "win." He cannot live up to all the dicta and please all the specialists who are evaluating his performance.

To the naïve observer, this means tight confinement within the chains of bureaucratic regulation and control. But this conclusion ignores both reality and the systems view of administration. Since the manager is not able to score 100 per cent on the multiple and conflicting standards imposed on him, he makes "trade-offs." Given his assessment of current pressures, he emphasizes one area of evaluation, as represented by one or more pressure groups, at the expense of others.

As one perceptive observer has said, this perpetual indebtedness or guilt keeps the successful manager "on his toes," eversensitive to the winds of change, and the organization gains flexibility in the bargain.[3] Thus another myth of organizational life is destroyed: namely, that checks and balances are inevitably cumbersome and stultifying. By helping to create a system of give and take, they can, in fact, speed up the adaptation to change:

> The appearance of a serious technical problem threatened a manager's tight schedule. Manpower shortages in adjacent departments had caused the personnel department to tighten its surveillance over surplus manpower to ensure that all such personnel was distributed by the central staff and not directly transferred by line managers. Violating established regulation and exceeding his quota of technical personnel, the manager in the trouble-beset department "raided" an adjacent work group to provide manpower to meet the requirements of the schedule.

[3] Andrew G. Frank, "Goal Ambiguity and Conflicting Standards: An Approach to the Study of Organization," *Human Organization*, vol. 17, pp. 8–13, Winter, 1958–1959.

The gradual recognition that rules are not absolute, that standards are not inflexible, and that one must live with the risks of being "in the wrong" guarantees insecurity. For this reason, the modern organization, with its appearance of bureaucratic rigidity and conformity, is anything but the perfect haven for the timid. The manager in the textbook checks his decision against the rules and knows whether he is "right." The manager in the effective organization has no such guarantees; when he tries to use as an excuse for failure that he had been hamstrung in using ingenuity and initiative, he is well on his way to demotion.

Amount of Managerial Authority

A favorite effort in typical management texts is to try to define authority. Various quasi-legal or philosophical concepts are usually brought into the picture, to impress the reader with the profundity of the subject and, more importantly, its worthiness as a professional field of knowledge. Such definitions are of little value to the manager who is seeking the means of operating his organization more effectively, although they look impressive in company policy manuals and training-program brochures.

We can use the type of situation just discussed to illustrate a more *operational* definition, that is, a definition to include the elements that enable one to measure unambiguously the degree of authority.

Question. How much authority is exercised by Mr. Jones, who is a staff expert?

Answer. Look and see. Rather than being an abstract possession or club, authority consists of the ability to make things happen; it can be evaluated by looking at the sequence of events within the organization. Jones has a discussion with manager Smith. Smith then departs from his normal job pattern in order to initiate certain contacts necessary to carry through Jones's ideas. If this sequence reappears with sufficient frequency, we would generalize that Jones has authority. Human relations thus become a clue to the effectiveness of various organizational controls.

Real-cost Principle

As long as economic theory has intruded, we can illustrate the homily "once a finger, then a hand." A crucial element in the theory of "trades" or marginalism as a principle of managerial decision making is the *real-cost principle*. Simply stated, this merely is a plea for the inclusion of all relevant costs in establishing criteria for making economic decisions. Paradoxically, the lower-level line manager is more likely to abide by this principle than is top management.

The manager knows that he is not getting something for nothing when he introduces a fancy record-keeping system or a tighter piece rate. While his boss may be deluded by the consultant or the special pleadings of the advisory group manager into thinking that output soars or costs drop directly and in proportion to the savings represented by the brilliant new idea, the manager knows that there are real costs involved in the installation. He must devote time to it, which means that other parts of his system may go astray and new pressures will be placed on his subordinates; this may result in a greater demand for his personal intervention, if this part of the organization is to continue to function effectively, etc. He may even have to hire an additional employee to handle the work involved in the new program. These must be fully "costed" in his mind before he can decide how to trade on the margin.

Significance of Conflicts of Interest

Many critics of the human relations view of administration have belittled what they interpreted as a naïve and politically dangerous emphasis on harmony and an absence of conflict.[4] Usually the criticism is in terms of "ought" or "ought not"—what the social

4 See particularly the writings of the sociologists Herbert Blumer and Robert Dubin and the economists Clark Kerr and the late Lloyd Fisher.

scientist calls a normative judgment, meaning that it is not science. These critics say that management *should not* (note the normative point) seek to eliminate conflict within the organization. Inevitably, workers and unions have different objectives, and to assume otherwise is damaging to the position of the employee because his interests are lost in the sunny merger of interests. Such an absence of competing-interest groups is also inconsistent with our democratic way of life. One of the important mainstays of this way of life is the competition for the allegiance of individuals, as citizens or employees, by strong interest, pressure, or lobby groups.[5] Thus, organizations that condition people to accept a monolithic as distinct from a pluralistic structure are incompatible with our political beliefs.

Managers in the middle have known for a long time that it was illusory to speak of harmony, unity, or absence of conflict. The concept of the organization as a unified, cohesive, homogeneous entity pitted against its rivals in a struggle for survival or supremacy has been shattered by actually observing the operations of large, complex organizations. The whole is fractionated into parts that compete with one another for relative status, growth, and special perquisites.

CONCLUSION

The implication of this analysis of administrative decision making as an organization process, not essentially as cognition, is in the area of change. If decisions are unsatisfactory, the answer most often lies in shifting the patterns by which various interest groups converge on a given manager. In a sense, decision making is a flow process. There is an observable sequence in which

[5] It is interesting to note the contrast between this point of view and an earlier view of democracy in which each individual participated actively as an individual. The political scientist is now recognizing reality. Society does not represent pure competition, but monopolistic or oligopolistic competition in which freedom is maintained by the interaction of opposed, organized groups.

individuals come together when a problem emerges. Their relative impact is also a function of the type of administrative pattern each exercises, which, in turn, relates to the organizational position of the group or manager. All these must be taken into account in order to shift in some predictable fashion the quality of decision making.

In our system terms, then, decision making is an action process, the very dynamics of "playing" the organization. This means that a successful manager in the contemporary, complex organization is sure-footed in modifying his behavior as he detects shifts in allegiances and pressures among subordinates, in the groups around him, and in external flows. These detections are a product of the manager's actual interactions with others in the organization and his assessment of the interactions of his subordinates, with one another and outside his own unit. Administration involves the delicate balancing or trading of favorable responses from one sector in exchange for (or in risk of) stress or hostility from another source. This balance changes constantly as a result of both internal eruptions and external disturbances; thus the manager must recalculate his appropriate marginal adjustment. As we have often repeated, these "decisions," like those of the economists or the mathematicians, are indeed marginal adjustments rather than the all-or-none decisions envisioned by the student of traditional management theory. A manager does not decide to do something and stick to it, come what may. Just as his detection system gives varying readings on the state of the various relationships he is monitoring, so, too, is there a new "best position" that will modify his original conviction.

Perhaps the best description of decision making as an organization process has been provided by Assistant Secretary of State for International Organizations Harlan Cleveland:

> This increase in the extent to which each individual is personally responsible to others is most noticeable in a large bureaucracy. No one person "decides" anything; each "decision" of any importance is the product of an intricate process of brokerage involving individuals inside and outside the organization who feel some reason to be

affected by the decision, or who have special knowledge to contribute to it. The more varied the organization's constituency, the more outside "veto-groups" will need to be taken into account. But even if no outside consultations were involved, sheer size would produce a complex process of decision. For a large organization is a deliberately created system of tensions into which each individual is expected to bring work-ways, viewpoints, and outside relationships markedly different from those of his colleagues. It is the administrator's task to draw from these disparate forces the elements of wise action from day to day, consistent with the purposes of the organization as a whole.[6]

From the point of view of an outsider, looking "inside" at one point in time, decisions are made by individuals. But insofar as they appear fixed and solely the product of a single mind, appearances are deceiving. In physics, statics is a special case of dynamics, a balance, although often a tenuous one, of the respective forces. Similarly, one can view the resultant of dynamic forces as a decision, but the realist knows that it is a result of many actions and interactions. For some purposes, we may wish to know only the result and be happy with that. But the student of organization should be able to distinguish the process from the result. On occasion, a price is set by individual decision making, but most prices are the resultant of the actions of many decision makers, no one of whom can be said to have made the decision as to what price will prevail.

[6] Harlan Cleveland, "Dinosaurs and Personal Freedom," *The Saturday Review*, Feb. 28, 1959, p. 36.

13

Engineering Managers:
A Case Study[1]

In the preceding chapters, we have provided a kind of skeleton for analyzing administrative activity or managerial work in the modern complex organization. To look realistically alive, the skeleton needs the addition of case materials in which the total configuration is looked at simultaneously. For this case material we have chosen a very large modern company in the chemical industry. It is a highly profitable enterprise, one of the largest and most successful growth companies in its field, with a national reputation for efficiency and modern operation.

One could not pretend that an analysis of a small part of the company represents its total operation. Our mention of the total is only to suggest that we have not purposely chosen a uniquely bad situation. This revelation may seem more important when the reader becomes aware of the rather substantial quantity of

[1] The author would like to express his indebtedness to Ross A. Webber, a Ph.D. candidate in the Graduate School of Business, Columbia University, at the time this book was completed, who investigated the managerial problems described in this chapter and who is also responsible for most of the analysis and a good share of the writing.

waste motion and conflict in the case. Yet, it is our contention that these elements pose the challenge of all managerial work. While it has been relatively easy to rationalize and systematize blue-collar and clerical work, coordination between technical, professional, and managerial personnel remains a challenge.

This challenge will not be taken up as long as management continues to think of these jobs as discrete entities and in terms of who has authority and responsibility for what. As we shall see, these jobs require a sequencing of explicit patterns of behavior which, in turn, are shaped by the types of controls that are operating. In most instances the organization is not conscious of the degree to which activities that "look good" on paper but frustrate the larger goals of the enterprise are encouraged.

Another value of the case will be to reemphasize the shortcomings inherent in discussions of "management." Management is usually viewed as a unity, or at least a homogeneous group with similar, if not identical, interests (as distinct from workers, unions, etc.). Nothing could be further from reality. Inherent in the division of labor in the modern organization are many factors that exercise a divisive influence at the level of manager or technical specialist.

Also, we shall emphasize that those who view the manager's administrative functions as marginal and likely to be eliminated with the advent of computers and management science have their work laid out for them. The jobs we shall analyze involve very extended interaction patterns with difficult problems of timing and sequence. They provide a challenge for the theorist and the practitioner to regulate and systematize the sporadic, the bargaining, the inherently conflicting relationships characteristic of management work.

Thus, we have chosen a case illustrating that the integration of specialized units into an effectively functioning management group is not nearly as simple as most management texts assume. Our example is typical of the division of labor within management and the conflict between putting the divided parts back together again into a whole work process (the goals of the larger organization) and the evolving dynamic demands for greater recognition of individual-group goals (what has been called suboptimization).

Finally, the case illustrates our earlier theses that managerial work is primarily a process and a system of human interaction, rather than of individual cognition, decision making, and creativity. In preceding chapters we have given some conceptual definition of the parts of the process—the operationally distinguishable administrative patterns—but we have not heretofore seen what happens when these must be carried out simultaneously by the same managers.

THE SITUATION

Description of the Division

The ABC Company is a large, nonunion, industrial concern in the chemical industry. A major part of the production operations is carried on at the plant with which we are concerned. Examples will be derived from observations of the relations existing between the chemical manufacturing division and the industrial engineering group servicing it.

The industrial engineering division is officially "staff" to the plant manager; the director of I.E. reports to an assistant plant manager. However, internally, I.E. is organized into areas and groups paralleling the plant manufacturing divisions and departments. An engineer in industrial engineering normally serves one or two department heads. The engineer's superior, an I.E. group leader, gives official staff support to an engineer's proposals to a production department supervisor while "working for" the superintendent of a manufacturing division.

Industrial engineering performs both measurement and methods studies. Measurement work is an elaboration of the work of the time-study man. The industrial engineer is primarily concerned with deriving figures that can be used to relate production (or other control figures) to labor use. This information may be

Parallel Industrial Engineering and Manufacturing Organization

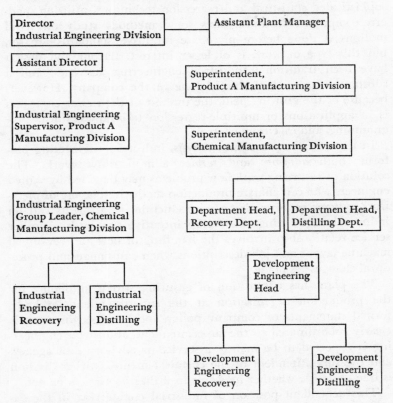

the basis for individual and group incentive standards or for fixed-pay-labor control plans to provide data to management for evaluation purposes. The techniques have expanded from simple observation with a stop watch to work-sampling procedures utilizing IBM card systems and various mathematical correlation techniques with electronic computers. From the point of view of intergroup relations, it is important to note that a major part of the measurement work requires the engineer to be on the floor in the production area.

Methods work for the industrial engineering field covers a

broad range from modern applications of Gilbreth's therbligs to sophisticated statistical and regression techniques utilizing modern computers. In most cases some methods study on hand motions is done before piece-rate incentive standards are set, but this type of work is of lesser interest. Layout and design have been traditional industrial engineering activities, and a substantial amount of this is done in the company. However, because of the growing field, the interest of the newer engineers is in applications of multiple-regression techniques, linear programming, and inventory control.

In terms of the preceding analysis, industrial engineering performs both *advisory* and *service* administrative work. The solution of recurring work-flow problems may be aided by skilled engineers who can analyze production methods. The use of piecework systems requires that the production departments call on industrial engineering to develop incentive standards. Another service relationship involves the handling of new and revamped machine layout and job descriptions when equipment and procedural changes are made.

The plant has a tradition of ensuring strong autonomy for the production organization at the superintendent level. In formal statements of company policy, industrial engineering is clearly subordinated to the superintendent. Industrial engineering is expected to be mainly a service or advisory staff agency, and the superintendent of the chemical manufacturing division is free to decide whether he wants to utilize its services or not.

This dependent position of industrial engineering in the designed formal structure is complemented by a system of budget hour accounting. The assistant plant manager gives a limited number of hours directly to the division, but each I.E. supervisor annually must negotiate an hour budget with his opposite production department superintendent. In our case, the real bargaining takes place between the chemical manufacturing plant superintendent and the industrial engineering group leader. Even with an approved budget, the group leader is supposed to request hours from the superintendent whenever he wants to work on a specific problem.

However, other administrative patterns are present as well. Insofar as engineers develop data that are used to evaluate the performance of other managers (in terms of the productivity of their departments), they are involved in *auditing*. The reference to work on the newer management science techniques, such as linear programming, suggests that at least some engineers seek *innovation* components for their jobs, in which they can work on advanced problems quite aside from the immediate demands of production personnel.

Clearly these jobs contain a variety of administrative patterns, and we shall explore the problems of integrating them into day-to-day working relationships in later sections of the case study.

THE SEARCH FOR WORK

In Chapter 5 we noted that service relationships are often neither comfortable nor easy to maintain. Further, we saw that many "advisers" do not wait to be asked. They initiate the contacts with those who are supposed to call on them. Before an industrial engineering manager can put his people to work on new activities and techniques, he finds it useful to have identified an existing production "problem" that needs solving. Thus, rather than waiting to be called on, industrial engineering spends substantial time in searching for problems on which it can obtain assignments. The division has authorization for a general account, research and development, to which time is charged when trying to develop ideas to present to production supervision. However, these funds are quite limited, and more informal search approaches must be used.

In his work in the production department, the engineer tries to become intimately familiar with what appear to be difficulties. Although he may not be asked to work on these problems specifically, they help him to direct his thinking toward the underlying or less apparent conditions. It is then up to the engineer to establish a case for his prospective study, indicating his estimate of the scope of the problem and potential savings.

Approval is required from both I.E. supervision and the chemical plant superintendent.

One of the advantages of a centralized industrial engineering division is the constant interchange of ideas and information that takes place among the engineers. Engineers learn about projects being conducted by other production departments that might, in the future, affect the production departments to which they are assigned. This type of information is of value to the production supervisor in protecting the position of his department. Whenever an I.E. brings information of this kind to the attention of a department head, the supervisor almost always approves the engineer's suggestion that he look into the possible implications of the change.

For example, in the ABC Company, the paper mill had customarily recovered its own waste paper for reprocessing into lower grades of paper. It came to the attention of the industrial engineering "servicing" the recovery department that the paper mill was considering a proposal to purchase only new raw pulp and to send all scrap to be burned. This would amount to a substantial quantity of scrap. Since the recovery department operated the burner, and capacity was limited, this information was valuable to recovery supervision. They readily agreed to the I.E.'s suggestion that he look into the entire long-term capacity problem of the burner. This assignment would never have gone to I.E. if the information about the plans of the paper mill had reached recovery through other channels.

Frequently, although the idea for an assignment has originated with an industrial engineer, he recognizes that the nature of the job or the personality of the department head is such that chances for approval and success will be enhanced if the production man feels it was his idea. This leads to the familiar phenomenon of "planting" the idea with a department head. Often, both know whose idea it is, but the fiction ensures cooperation. Actual authorization requires approval by the superintendent, and this little ruse makes it more likely that the department head will be a political ally in future discussions with the superintendent.

As we have already hinted, industrial engineering has auditing relationships. Some of these arise from rather irregular special assignments from top management to undertake a large evaluation project.[2] From our present point of view, the most important implication of this source of assignments is the privileged information position it gives to I.E. in comparison with production people. In fact, an engineer sometimes is doing a study for plant management that requires investigation in a production department, and the superintendent knows nothing about the assignment.

Here is one rather unusual example. The company was committed to assisting a local charitable organization serving the blind and handicapped. There was a policy that work that could be performed by the charitable organization at costs competitive with those resulting from internal processing should, where possible, be contracted out. Industrial engineering was asked to evaluate some of the costs of sorting reprocessed materials in the recovery department. The engineer servicing recovery learned of this and was able to go to the department head and obtain an assignment for a complete restudy of sorting costs. The department head was concerned because he had several older women sorters who were unsuitable for other types of work.

In Chapter 5, we suggested that most new assignments involve the manager's ability to engage in trading relationships with other managers in the organization for whom he may perform some assignment. In the case of industrial engineering, we can see how extensive and time-consuming is this activity; this is often ignored as a component of managerial work. Clearly, such assignments are not automatically made on the basis of abstract descriptions of a department's functions or skills. They arise out of the sophisticated interactions of managers who are seeking to strengthen and enlarge the scope of their activities. They do this because such additional work is intellectually rewarding in

[2] Since these are attractive and enhance prestige, there is a great deal of competition among departments within the company to secure such assignments. Often the topic is such that any one of several groups could insist that its expertise justified its receiving the work; therefore a high level of political activity is associated with the decision.

terms of new challenges, and economically rewarding in terms of greater department size and importance.

It may appear that the only criterion used in expanding the industrial engineering work load is the one of "more." That is misleading. Because of certain internal factors, the engineer seeks certain kinds of assignments that will provide him with greater rewards in terms of the unique controls operating on him.

There is an increasing trend toward professionalization and use of advanced mathematical techniques in industrial engineering. The division has an active research group which conducts courses in new techniques. In addition, a substantial portion of the engineers are pursuing graduate Statistics and Industrial Management master's programs in the evening sessions of a local university. Finally, the newly hired graduate-degree I.E.'s are anxious to utilize sophisticated methods. This natural tendency to use modern techniques is reinforced by the rewards given to those engineers who are successful in applying them to production problems. These engineers are invited to give talks on their work at meetings of other I.E. groups and to all the I.E. supervisors. In addition, promotions within I.E. in recent years have gone to those people who have had significant success in applying some of the more esoteric techniques. Given these pressures, the engineer searches until he finds a problem that might lend itself to his methods and again tries to sell the project to production supervision.

THE PROCESSING OF WORK

In earlier chapters, we endeavored to propose a view of managerial or administrative work that we believe is closer to the reality of the modern organization than traditional views of leadership. Substantial stress was placed on lateral relationships and the need for greater recognition and definition of a variety of administrative interaction patterns. These concepts and descriptions could not do full justice to the complexity of the managerial task.

Now, we shall follow the industrial engineering group in their day-to-day relationship with the departments with which they must coordinate in order to do their work. These coordinations are prescribed by the division of labor in the managerial structure imposed by earlier top-management decisions. But unlike the more circumscribed, purely leadership patterns, these work activities require more initiative, negotiation, and elaborate sequencing of interaction.

Work with Chemical Manufacturing Division Superintendent

The superintendent of the chemical manufacturing division has a strong personality. He is in his late forties and started in the division as a development engineer.[3] His education as a chemical engineer and experience as a development engineer have strengthened his interest in the technical aspects of all proposals, and he exercises close supervision over innovative and capital investment recommendations.[4] Since most innovative ideas that are eventually adopted originate with the division's own develop-

[3] As distinct from the methods-layout-management engineering activities of the industrial engineers, the development engineers are concerned with technical problems arising in maintenance and production. These are typically chemical engineering problems.

[4] Although the superintendent also tries to exercise close supervision over most production aspects of division operations, the technology of the work processes is such that it is not possible for him to exert much direct influence on work-flow operations. Most of the production installations contain continuous-chemical-processing equipment. Since the departments are spread out over a wide area and decisions require rapid answers, the work-flow relationships among departments must be carried on by the department heads themselves when operational problems arise. In many cases, the foremen must consult with other departments and reach decisions. For example, a recurring operational decision in the manufacturing process is the relative quantities of recovered scrap material, new raw material, and solvents to be used by the acetate department. The decision can be reached only by rapid switching-center-type contacts between the acetate department, the distilling department, and recovery because of the continuous nature of the processing equipment, the technical nature of the information exchanged, and the required "feel" for how things are going.

ment engineers, the superintendent encourages them to talk with him about ideas and demands it when he learns of problem areas.

In addition, the promotion ladder to chemical plant supervisory ranks is through the development engineer position. Accordingly, the superintendent is anxious to give these people as much experience as possible. He encourages (almost indoctrinates) them to work on their own without calling for advisory assistance.

To a significant extent, industrial engineering is management engineering and provides good experience for a future manager. The superintendent is aware of this and wants his development engineers to gain some of this training by performing their own work of this type.

For all these reasons, the chemical plant superintendent is opposed to any extension of industrial engineering activities beyond the relatively routine service work that they have to perform to maintain incentive plans. He discourages what he calls "idle speculation on my time and budget." His intimidation of department heads discourages them from going to him for approval of I.E. projects that they would like to see performed. The superintendent's well-maintained technical expertise subjects department heads to unpleasant grilling when they propose study programs to him.[5]

His attitudes also discourage development engineers from collaborating with the industrial engineers. Thus, many of the calculations of the development engineers use highly unrealistic time and labor estimates. At the same time, the industrial engineers recognize that they are making laborious efforts to obtain and compute technical and procedural information that the development engineers have at their finger tips, because of their close relationships with department heads.

Because of this failure to include adequate interaction with one another in the work-process sequence, the industrial engineers endeavored to improve coordination. Rather than just trying to secure information from the development engineers, a

[5] In a sense, the superintendent places himself in a stabilization relationship with his subordinates on matters concerning the use of I.E. personnel.

calculated effort was made to educate the development engineers regarding the services that industrial engineering could perform for them.

Industrial engineering began to send the development engineers copies of assignment progress reports in order to let them know what industrial engineering was doing. Industrial engineering wanted to receive reports on development engineering projects in return but was never successful. The only improvement in the work flow was that development engineers could be induced to answer specific questions posed to them in the course of an I.E. project. Even this took substantial effort to attain. But the development engineers could never be induced to seek aid from or to volunteer information that might be of value to I.E.

The amount of interaction initiated by the development engineers increased somewhat but a system of mutual exchange of information, without specific request and without specific purpose, was never achieved. It was a great achievement, in fact, for industrial engineering ever to develop a situation in which development engineers answer most questions put to them.

The most characteristic means utilized by I.E. to attempt to overcome problems in these relationships is to "improve communications." Emphasis is on elaborate reports of project findings and salesmanship. This is influenced by the active part assumed by the I.E. supervisor in this phase of an assignment. He listens to, revises, and approves all presentations before he and the engineer give the report to the chemical manufacturing division superintendent. In the classic sales tradition, the presentation is large, formal, and presumably impressive. The emphasis is on "completed staff work" covering every alternative and requiring only management's signature for implementation.[6] Essentially, this means that assignments are overworked, overpolished, and diluted. There is such effort to impress the superintendent with the caliber and completeness of I.E. work and to eliminate the possibility of embarrassing questions that emphasis tends to be on selling the solution rather than solving the problem. Formal

[6] See William H. Newman and Charles E. Summer, Jr., *The Process of Management*, Prentice-Hall, Inc., Englewood Cliffs, N.J., 1961, pp. 61–63.

charts and graphs are excellent shields behind which to hide when making a presentation. They protect the speaker. By avoiding introduction of questions, the engineer minimizes the danger of being asked something for which he has no answer.

Work Relationship with Production Department Foremen

The foreman and assistant foremen all have come up from the ranks in the same department.[7] The function of the foreman consists most simply in getting men on the right jobs at the right time. The recovery department has many types of equipment and a large number of miscellaneous hand operations. All these activities are not performed simultaneously, and it is the responsibility of the foreman to assign the men as necessary in order to meet the schedule for each shift. The closeness and accessibility of development engineers and higher supervision relieve them of concern about technological aspects of the equipment.

There is no question that one of the most fertile sources of problem identification is the foremen. In any discussion with them, they mention explicit problem conditions. However, the individual foreman is not inclined to request I.E. assistance on methods problems because of his limited knowledge regarding their functions and lack of reciprocal interactions with industrial engineering. A major part of the foremen's experience with I.E. has been as unwilling subjects of time studies for incentive pay plans (when they were still hourly paid operators).[8]

With the exception of questions on incentive standards, foremen seldom initiate interaction with an industrial engineer. On the other hand, virtually every completed assignment by an engineer results in some action by foremen. In many cases this means new forms and calculations for incentive performance of a

[7] Promotional opportunities are limited but policy has been to draw on these people for assistant department heads and department heads. In many cases, personnel conditions are so fluid that assistant foremen often split their weeks, part on hourly operator work and part as salaried foremen.

[8] See William F. Whyte et al., *Money and Motivation*, Harper & Row, Publishers, Incorporated, New York, 1955, pp. 11–39.

crew. Most of the foremen see little reason for having group incentive standards and intensely dislike making the necessary calculations. Except for a few initial questions, nothing in the operational job requirements of the foremen makes it necessary to call in industrial engineering unless new standards are required. The foremen try to avoid the engineers as much as possible.

Because of familiarity and physical proximity, foremen naturally go to the development engineer or department head when they have problems or ideas. This is also related to the nature of their jobs and their production goals. For the most part, they are concerned with short-term operational matters that demand solutions relatively quickly. When it is necessary to have I.E. do service work (setting a temporary standard), this is an operational matter and the foreman consults an engineer. However, he is not really aware of the I.E.'s availability for advisory problem solving, i.e., methods work, and even if he were, the formal procedure for requesting I.E. services of this nature discourages involvement for a short-term problem.

Finally, we should observe that the goals of the foreman in solving his problems are quite different from the industrial engineer's. The foreman is mainly interested in getting out production while maintaining stability among his personnel and equilibrium in his relationships. His interest in problem solving is directed mainly toward ensuring the equilibrium he desires. On the other hand, the industrial engineer is busy looking for problems that are not apparent, in the hope of applying his various techniques to modify existing conditions. It is an oversimplification to say that the foremen are short-sighted whereas the engineers are looking ahead. It is more meaningful to say that the foremen see no real need for industrial engineering assistance in meeting their goals as stated by their job definitions and as rewarded by production management.

Work Relationships with the Division Cost Engineer

The division cost engineer performs mainly accounting functions. He is located in the division office and plays a key role in many projects, since he is the primary source of cost information for engineers and supervisors. For evaluation and promotion, he is under the supervision of the controller's division; this gives him important authority in handling cost data. As a representative of the chemical manufacturing division superintendent, he gathers information from production departments. However, as a member of the controller's division, he is able to decide what information is confidential and what can be divulged.[9] He is in a position to favor certain individuals with information at the expense of others.

Once again, information is an important consideration in the processing of administrative work. As accountant to all departments in the chemical manufacturing division, the cost engineer is the source of the most complete data on costs of various subunits. This information is invaluable to anyone interested in problem areas and in making preliminary evaluations of possible solutions to problems already identified. The difficulty is that the cost engineer is extremely reluctant to divulge any of his data. He will not even describe what type of information he has in his records, and it is difficult to learn for what specific problems he is developing new information.

When cost information is requested from him, the cost engineer points to a controller's division procedure and says that a written request must be submitted to his supervisor. This handicap is not insurmountable, but I.E. often finds it difficult to describe in detailed terms the type of cost data desired.

There are, of course, some good reasons for security in dealing with cost data. However, the cost engineer appears to go beyond these security requirements. From his point of view, this is sensible. Involvement with I.E. activities would be time-consuming and perhaps upset the equilibrium of his department. Since most of his work involves an auditing relationship, he is used to initiating to others, particularly production department heads, and has little experience with responding to requests from others (except

9 The company has a number of key chemical operations that are not protected by patents, and so the concern has historically depended on secrecy to protect its interests.

his superiors). Although many of the work activities of I.E. could be facilitated if the cost engineer could be included in the sequence, there are no controls operating on him to motivate such inclusion. Job descriptions fail to include operational information on the pattern of interaction required to perform administrative work, and therefore his personal decision to be excluded stands uncontested.

THE MONITORING OF WORK

The actual patterns of coordination that are evolved and the effectiveness with which work is performed are also functions of the control system utilized. Let us endeavor to see what measures are used (and how obtained) by industrial engineering management itself in regulating the activities of its personnel. In so doing, we can observe the interrelationship between the measures and the kind of work to be accomplished.

It would appear that I.E. management is not sure whether it intends to monitor the caliber of industrial engineering work, I.E.'s use of budget hours, how I.E. obtains assignments, or how production departments are managed. In some ways, we shall see that bits and pieces of all these intentions are found in the actual monitoring techniques. However, no unifying purpose or philosophy has been consciously developed.

Historically, the major criterion has been the "cost savings" indicated on job-completion reports. Engineers who reported sizable savings were rewarded by being invited to make presentations to staff and higher line management. Cost savings attributed to an engineer in a preceding period were the major factor in awarding periodic merit wage increases.

However, most managers now recognize that these savings are not a clear indication of industrial engineering contributions to the company. They contain many ambiguities.

1. In reports of measurement assignments, the cost savings are less an indication of the engineer's contribution than a summation of all

the methods and personnel changes instituted by the production department since the last measurement study. Although I.E. probably makes some contribution to these total savings, it has been strongly resented by line management that industrial engineering final reports claim the total savings as a result of I.E. efforts.

2. Cost-savings reports are too discrete. Even if the figures were an indication of I.E.'s contribution, they are not formulated frequently enough to serve in monitoring how industrial engineering is performing its task in any particular time period. Many measurement reports are made only every three to four years. There is no measure of what I.E.'s efforts have produced in interim periods.

3. Finally, cost-savings reports (especially on methods work) are speculative. Industrial engineering makes its report when a project has been accepted by line management but before action has been taken. The savings are based on expected cost reductions and the engineer gets credit for his estimate. There is no systematic procedure to determine if the savings are actually realized. This is obvious encouragement to maximize the estimate of savings and to ignore matters of financial prudence regarding capital investment.

This effort to measure "cost savings" effected by the department is really a management-by-result technique. Not only does it encourage destructive competitiveness between divisions; it also motivates excessive time wastage on exaggerating the figures and shifting responsibilities.

It ignores the crucial problems of how to direct the energies of the division and its managers to areas requiring attention: techniques for deciding what to do and where to do it—what we have called short-term remedial actions. Because of both the shortcomings of the "result" measures and the need to do something in terms of directing efforts, I.E. management has improvised certain other monitoring devices.

Amount of Potential Work Obtained

The orientation of industrial engineering management toward selling services and obtaining assignments has already been mentioned. Monitoring these activities is very subjective because traditional theory and stated company policy do not recognize a need for them. However, ensuring existence and expanding jurisdiction are common to all dynamic groups within an organization, and substantial effort is devoted to this by I.E. supervision.

One obvious technique is frequent meetings of all I.E. supervisors to discuss what assignments have been obtained. This shows a particular supervisor how his group compares with others in obtaining projects, and it serves as an incentive to get assignments, because the division director takes part in the sessions. There are no objective criteria as to what constitutes satisfactory levels of obtaining assignments. However, most supervisors renege on reporting all assignments during fruitful weeks in order to have at least one or two to announce at subsequent meetings. (This withholding raises a question of the usefulness of the meetings as a monitoring device.)

Most supervisors scan production department capital-expenditure requests to see if there are projects in which I.E. is not involved. This procedure has some usefulness in indicating possible areas where I.E. should redirect selling efforts. However, the expenditure request appears somewhat late in the game, and projects listed usually have already been the subject of substantial effort by production engineers in the design stage. Industrial engineering, in effect, would be trying to climb aboard at later stages; this is resented by production technical people.

Certain arithmetical techniques are also utilized. Department budget reports and incentive-plan figures are examined to detect changes in trends or exceptional weeks. The supervisor uses these figures to determine whether significant organizational or technical changes have been instituted, which are reflected in modified hourly worker earnings. If such is the case, the supervisor has considerable procedural backing to demand a measurement assignment for I.E. to revise the labor-control or work-measurement plan. In terms of obtaining more service work, i.e., measurement assignments, this has been a useful technique. It serves no purpose in increasing methods assignments (advisory work), however, because the figures come out after the fact. The change already has been made, and there is no place for industrial engineering to intervene.[10]

The operational acceptance of I.E. measurement work mentioned earlier, coupled with the above monitoring techniques, probably ensures a sufficient volume of measurement assignments. The desire for methods projects varies with the inclination of the supervisor. Those with primarily measurement experience are less energetic in looking for methods work. However, the whole trend of industrial engineering as a discipline is toward mathematical techniques. This encourages a search for methods-type work, although systematic efforts are difficult with the monitoring techniques available to the supervisor. He tends to depend on his own subjective judgment of whether his group is getting "enough" such assignments or whether they will have to sell their services more vigorously.

Caliber of Work Done

There is no question that the paper "cost savings" discussesd earlier are still the major criteria in evaluating performance. They have the merit at least of focusing on what is supposedly being saved in the production department. However, awareness of the limitations of this approach and growing professionalization, with emphasis on techniques, have caused some substitution of a rather vague judgment of the *sophistication* of projects. Some engineers have been rewarded for costly assignments that produced negligible savings because of the ingenuity and sophistication of their work. Evaluation by this criterion demands knowledge of developments and acquaintance with applications. The division attempts to ensure this by encouraging the pursuit of post-graduate training and by supporting a research and develop-

---

10 There is some similar difficulty with measurement work also. If the technological changes are not obvious, it is difficult for I.E. to point them out to justify a study without first investigating the situation. The production department (and the workers) can maintain that no changes have been made, the operators have increased their productivity, and there is no justification for resetting standards.

ment group within industrial engineering. This group is charged with keeping abreast of outside academic and industrial developments and conducting training programs in new techniques for supervisors and engineers.

Monitoring the performance of measurement work utilizes arithmetical and statistical measures to a large extent. The engineer's performance in setting piece-rate incentive standards is evaluated by comparing the operator's earnings with what the engineer expected. The dubious assumption here is that the standard is "good" if earnings are around the engineer's expectations (say 125 per cent of the base rate). Many observers have pointed out that this is fallacious because employees' earnings may be highly controlled and bear little resemblance to what they "should" be able to do.[11] The engineer is critically evaluated if workers' earnings are much higher or lower than he predicted.[12]

In an effort to overcome the "discrete" limitations of measurement-assignment reports of cost savings, I.E. keeps trend charts of labor use in the production departments so as to detect significant statistical changes that might be attributed to I.E. work.[13] This procedure suffers from the same limitation as do all the techniques of measuring savings. It is impossible to relate realistically specific I.E. activities with observed cost developments within a certain time period.

No real effort is made to monitor I.E. utilization of time. A weekly report of hours devoted to different assignments, miscellaneous, and personal activities is required from each engineer, but the validity of these figures is low. One supervisor went so far as to conduct a secret sampling study on his subordinates to see if they were working or talking and so on. However, with

[11] See Whyte et al., *op. cit.*, pp. 20–28.

[12] The engineer is aware of this, and he tends to peg his standard where he thinks operators will work, not at the so-called "correct" level.

[13] From time to time the I.E. supervisor sent some of these trend/savings reports to the chemical plant superintendent. The latter finally vigorously objected to I.E. "auditing" his production departments in this manner. He felt it was up to the production department to maintain these records if they wanted them. It was not up to I.E. to make such reports without being specifically requested to do so.

jobs requiring contemplation and discussion in addition to "working," a sampling study is virtually useless for determining efficiency or effectiveness.

Because of the absence of other suitable criteria, substantial weight is given to number of assignments completed, for purposes of awarding merit wage increases. It matters little how long or how big the assignments were; "credit" is given for the number of jobs completed.

Monitoring of Production Departments

Industrial engineering managers have endeavored to add auditing patterns to their administrative functions. They do this by looking at weekly incentive-earnings reports and budget reports. Many I.E. supervisors believe that they are helping production supervisors by bringing problems to their attention that they might otherwise miss. Most fail to note that this auditing activity interferes with other aspects of their relationship with production.

Since industrial engineering has no policy mandate from plant management to engage in this kind of activity, I.E. has only limited knowledge of precisely how individual production departments should fit into company progress. Consequently, I.E. uses its own standards of evaluating production performance. These criteria are subjective and unique for each I.E. supervisor.

INTRODUCTION OF STRUCTURAL CHANGE

In Chapter 11 we argued that successful monitoring systems provide detection of and methods for coping with recurring problems. These problems consume substantial quantities of administrative time, and they are not solved by short-term palliatives. Good management seeks to impose changes in the structure to eliminate the source of the problem rather than coping with the symptoms.

In the company we are studying, the industrial engineering

division had been divided into two fairly autonomous groups. Since incentive systems were very popular with management the measurement section was consulted frequently and filled many job requests. The particular engineer serving a production area was accepted as a working member of the production department. Because this presented many opportunities for interaction, the measurement engineer would be consulted on subjects outside his service assignment. Often he would perform these small advisory jobs rather than refer them to the methods section. The methods group was not so fortunate. Lacking any regular interaction with the production departments, they were received as outsiders. As outsiders, they were less likely to be called, even when problems arose that top management would have assumed would require their expertise. Clearly, abstract job descriptions and departmental "charters" do not determine who does what as much as do evolving patterns of work relationships.

The difficulties experienced by the methods section were suddenly aggravated by an external change. The company instituted a new budget hour charging system, partially as a response to an economic recession. With charges for all "staff" activities now clearly allocated to departmental budgets, department heads were motivated to reduce further their utilization of methods activities. After all, they had their own development engineers as well as the services of measurement engineers who represented no variable costs.

Thus, the relative disadvantage of the methods section as compared with the measurement section had increased. Internal pressures built up to gain greater equality of utilization, and more and more of I.E. management's time was devoted to "selling" activities as a means of stabilizing their internal work arrangements. It was at last decided to deal with these problems by a structural change, which, in effect, brought the formal procedures more in line with existing practices.

The methods and measurement sections were combined into one division, organized along the lines of the existing measurement service groups. The engineer assigned to a particular department was supposed to perform both types of engineering.

The purpose was to take advantage of the close relationship existing between the measurement section and production departments.

Dynamic Shifts in Administrative Patterns

While I.E. was endeavoring to adjust its structure to facilitate a close working relationship with production departments (to increase the volume of its advisory activity and reduce the administrative difficulties and effort involved in justifying its activities), it was also making other structural changes. These were designed to have a very different effect. Because of the frustrations associated with both service and advisory patterns, where the group has to be asked by another manager to perform work, I.E. sought administrative patterns whereby it could be more dominant, less deferential, and enjoy more prestige.

Thus, changes were made that would increase the relative quantity of innovation, stabilization, and auditing relationships in its work load. In these, I.E. could take the initiative and rely less on selling itself and being called in by production.

One of the most important steps in this direction was to place greater emphasis on operations research and more sophisticated mathematical techniques of analysis. Here I.E. was to devote itself to advanced developments that might not have any immediate applicability to production groups. In addition to this innovation relationship, operations-research techniques also provide new evaluation techniques for top management that can set standards for production groups. They also give I.E. the opportunity of using new mathematical formulations to solve production problems that the chemical manufacturing division had not recognized as an internal difficulty; that is, I.E. is assuming stabilization functions. Here I.E. wants to take the initiative in identifying the problem, solving it, and inducing production to carry out the requisite changes. There was a struggle between a group in the controller's division called Management Systems Development and I.E. over who should have jurisdiction over operations research and design of a new electronic data-processing system. The specialized knowledge required put this type of work out of reach of the staff engineers attached directly to production. As a consequence, both M.S.D. and I.E. desired plant management to assign to it exclusive responsibility in these areas.

Another means of implementing these new relationships has been efforts to insulate the division from the rest of the organization. This is a common organizational phenomenon: the growing sense of self-identification among constituent groups endeavoring to strengthen the boundaries that separate them from outsiders.[14]

The most important decision here was to increase the number of managerial positions and promotional opportunities within the I.E. division. This was part of an effort to encourage people to make a career in the division. It took the form of increasing the ratio of managers to nonmanagers and the establishment of a parallel promotional ladder that permitted engineers to advance in pay and status without accepting supervisory responsibilities.[15] (We have called these maneuvers "professionalization" in Chapter 7.)

Unlike professional employees reported on by some other observers,[16] most nonsupervisory I.E.'s have been definitely company- and management-oriented. The I.E. division has historically served as a company-wide training area for newly graduated engineers. Employment in the division has given these people wide access to valuable experiences. The normal term of service in the department used to be three years, after which the engineers generally moved into a production area either in a line capacity or in a staff engineering position directly attached to the

---

[14] This is also a problem for every large organization because, in the process of separatism, the goals of the small group tend to diverge from the whole and members lose sight of the needs of the total system.

[15] There were some unintended consequences of these structural changes. There were now more supervisors than there was work for them to do. This encouraged rather disadvantageous closer supervision of engineers, and it increased the amount of auditing of production department performance conducted by I.E. The increased external and internal monitoring absorbed the excessive administrative time created by the increase in the number of managers.

[16] See David G. Moore and Richard Renck, "The Professional Employee in Industry," *Journal of Business*, January, 1955, p. 60.

line. The path of promotion was definitely up the line hierarchy, and few desired to stay in technical work.[17]

Industrial engineering supervision began to push career opportunities within the division by modifying the promotion schedule as indicated above and by changing hiring policy. Increased emphasis was put on hiring engineers with graduate Business, I.E., and Statistics degrees. These engineers are impressed with the opportunities for utilization of their college training and for advancement within industrial engineering. In addition, promotions out of the division into production departments have been sharply curtailed so that, since initiation of the changed policies, engineers have been in the division an average of almost seven years versus three years as it was in the past.

The staff management organized training programs to augment the knowledge of older engineers and to keep the newer people up to date. Emphasis is increasingly on development of specialized expertise and working knowledge of sophisticated techniques. Engineers without graduate degrees are encouraged to attend evening sessions at a local university.

Concurrent with all these developments has been increased emphasis on methods work and minimization of measurement jobs. In part, this is a reflection of growing awareness of the faults and naïve assumptions of piece-rate incentive plans. It is also a result of the desire to avoid work of relatively low status and concentrate on subjects of higher prestige, such as operations research.

Changes in Engineer Evaluation

Further to implement these efforts to recast the administrative patterns of the division, I.E. management placed greater emphasis on internal criteria in monitoring the work of its own members. Rather than evaluating an engineer in terms of what production management thinks of his contribution to it or some quantification of savings for which he is "responsible," I.E. management

[17] A small minority always remained in I.E. and advanced up the staff supervisory ladder.

stresses performance in the quality of engineering reports and oral presentations. Thus, ingenuity, new techniques, and mathematical sophistication get the rewards, particularly promotions.

IMPACT ON THE INDIVIDUAL ENGINEER

Life is not quite so simple as it might appear for the individual engineer who still must live in both worlds, his own I.E. division and a production group. He tends to evaluate himself, in part, on his success in getting work and keeping busy. As we have seen, this search for assignment is an indispensable part of the total work process. His most acute awareness of lack of success in getting assignments occurs when he has no work or when he consciously has to stretch existing jobs because he has nothing else on which to start. This is not an uncommon situation. For this reason, attempts by the engineer to obtain work tend to be fitful: a push when jobs are needed and neglect when he has a small backlog.

Above this minimum indication of having work or not, the individual engineer's monitoring of obtained assignments is also subjective. In line with his desire to be more vital to the production department, the engineer is less concerned with number of jobs than with a vague evaluation of the number of times production supervisors go to him with problems and how often they respond to his suggestions. The engineer makes a great effort to encourage initiation by production supervisors by acquainting himself with department operations and making himself indispensable in certain areas.

An example is the case of a fairly junior industrial engineer who, without being requested, made a complete study of the future production volume trends, space requirements, and labor implications for a new product treatment area. The engineer charged his hours to another assignment in the same department. The study was a type usually made by a production department development engineer, but none had been made in this instance.

When the industrial engineer produced the study, he in effect made himself an "expert" on the new area. Subsequently, the department head consulted him on this area because he was a known source of information. In short, the efforts of the individual engineer are designed to break down the outside advisory relationship, minimize the selling function, and increase his indispensability to the department head.

The engineer finds himself in a very ambiguous position in evaluating his own performance because of uncertainty about goals. Historically, the engineers have hoped for shifts into production departments while at the same time being dependent on I.E. supervision for merit pay increases (and for recommendations for advancement into production departments). Therefore, the individual has been uncertain whether to evaluate his actions in terms of pleasing production management or his I.E. superiors.

The common answer was to adopt the "cost-savings" criterion used by I.E. supervision for evaluation and try to sell this to production management as an indication of industrial engineering's contribution. Obviously, on some jobs, reported cost savings indicated the engineer's efforts, but in most instances it led to resentment toward industrial engineering on the part of production people. Engineers have attempted to avoid this situation by emphasizing cost savings to I.E. superiors but minimizing it with production managers.[18]

In terms of measurement work, the individual engineer evaluates his efforts on whether the operators' earnings are at the level predicted and on complaints from workers.[19]

---

[18] In some cases, the engineer does not even add cost savings to the assignment report until after production supervision has seen it but does so before final approval by I.E. superiors.

[19] These are related. We saw earlier that staff management evaluates the engineer's setting standards in terms of the operators' earning what the company expects, on the assumption that the standard is right if this happens. On the other hand, the individual engineer predicts that earnings will be at the expected level because he picks a standard at which the operators are willing to work. Normal complaints from workers are expected, but the volume and persistence are an indication of how well the standard reflects their conception of a fair day's work.

The engineer shows the inherent conflict in his dual sets of relationships by wanting both more and less contact with his I.E. base. The engineer often desires greater backing by higher I.E. management to force acceptance of his proposals for production areas. Although he likes freedom in his technical work, he often appreciates support of his efforts by I.E. management's giving him leverage in negotiations with production departments. In contrast, the engineer is also vaguely aware that I.E. management hinders his efforts to minimize his sense of being an outsider and his attempts to integrate himself into the production work flows. He therefore wants to increase his autonomy in all respects.

In many cases, the engineer tries to minimize contact between line supervisors and his I.E. superiors. If communication is necessary, he wants to be the sole link between I.E. and production management. This is particularly true in final presentations and proposals where the influence of I.E. supervision is most felt. The presence at a meeting of an I.E. supervisor (who earns appreciably more than production supervisors) can lead to an adverse interpretation of staff proposals.

There is similar tension regarding divisional restructuring as it affects his long-range personal goals. The orientation toward integrating into production department operations is partially derived from a desire for eventual promotion into production supervisory ranks. However, increased emphasis on I.E. as a career area coupled with concurrent changes in personnel policies make the future confusing to the newer engineers. Perhaps their first inclination, derived from recent educational experiences, is to pursue the innovational relationship recently formulated by I.E. management. However, the realities of the job process and a desire to get things done make them sympathetic to a closer advisory-service relationship to production.

The new engineer has a rather naïve belief in the traditional concept of staff. He believes that he will be called upon because of his superior training and knowledge. The I.E. management makes him aware that this is not quite the case, and he is encouraged to sell himself and his assignments. Armed with his arsenal of techniques, he goes forth to find problems and offer his services to production supervision. However, our young knight soon recognizes that, in attempting to perform these functions, he cannot behave entirely in the way implied by I.E. management's call for selling. Geographic, social, and administrative factors emphasize the separation of I.E. from production. The stress on selling reinforces this by emphasizing that the engineer is an outsider trying to get in. The industrial engineer becomes aware that he must break down this handicap of being a "stranger" to production people. This is necessary for two reasons:

1. Engaging in selling activity requires something to sell. Normally, this is an idea based upon observed working conditions.
2. It is usually not possible to maintain a significant level of projects through search and selling only.

Realizing the limitations of scanning budget requests as is done by I.E. supervisors, the engineer tries to get closer to production operations. By monitoring department communications, the engineer can often learn of department projects in their incipiency where he is better able to approach production supervision with ideas for I.E.'s role of assistance. At this early stage, the engineer's offer of aid is more plausible than at a later stage, since I.E. actually may know more than the production department, because of past experience. The difficulties of obtaining this information have already been discussed.

Mere physical presence in the production department becomes vital to the most important means of monitoring: observation of activities in the department. Lengthy measurement studies generally offer excellent opportunities to pick up methods assignments because the engineer stays in the department to observe activities for long periods of time. He begins to see where problems exist, and he observes on what projects production department people are working. He can develop ideas and offer services based on problem-stimulated ideas rather than simply on knowledge of techniques. By observing department projects, he can estimate what the production department thinks it should do for itself and for what it wants to ask I.E.'s cooperation. These observations may help the staff to direct its selling to those areas where it can increase its chance of being called.

Complicating the engineer's job is the large number of distinctive patterns he is supposed to maintain, some of which are in conflict:

1. He provides services for the department head, e.g., computing differences in labor costs between baling scrap in plastic and storing it loose in metal boxes.
2. He audits foreman performance for the I.E. supervisor, e.g., when he checks on excess hours charged to a particular crew.[20]
3. He maintains stabilization functions, e.g., imposes a maximum hour limit on an incentive plan in a specific foreman's jurisdiction.[21]

[20] The I.E. supervisor, partly as a result of lack of job duties resulting from division reorganization, spends a great deal of time in his office checking budget figures and pay-plan performance. Whenever he has a question, he notifies an engineer to call the production department and find out what happened. In this event, the I.E. is forced to initiate with a department head an interaction that is obviously questioning the manager's activities. This has an adverse influence on the sentiments of the department head toward the engineer making the inquiry.

The ambitious engineer makes every attempt to anticipate these questions from his supervisor and to answer them without calling the production department involved. He does this for two reasons: first, because the supervisor controls advancement and a ready answer is impressive, and second, simply to avoid initiating interaction and causing an unpleasant situation with the department head.

[21] Here, in greater detail, is a picture of how this operates: I.E. sets maximum hour limits for which crews can be paid and then must approve the department head's special wage payment letter that is necessary to pay any *excess* hours. At least one crew exceeds the hour limits almost every week. The strains this puts on relations between the department head and I.E. should be obvious. This is the only interaction that *must* be initiated by the department head to get I.E.'s action, and it is just the reverse of the relationship implied in the traditional theory of advisory staff. Actually, an industrial engineer normally appears on the scene without request and signs the letter without questioning it. He runs a risk of criticism from his I.E. supervisor,

4. He provides service for production foremen, e.g., sets a temporary incentive rate on a changed job.
5. As an adviser, he develops new layout to reduce excessive labor costs for materials movement for the department head.
6. For I.E. management, he is expected to get away from day-to-day production problems to evolve new, sophisticated statistical scheduling techniques, e.g., as innovation relationship requires.

CONCLUSION

In establishing the industrial engineering division, it was clear that management did not think through the implications of combining these administrative patterns. Certain jobs were assigned to I.E. quite early and others were acquired over time, either by design or by accident. Now the question was whether the organization structure and existing controls permitted and encouraged the I.E. to conduct the work expected of them.

It is usually taken for granted that an engineer is a problem solver, thinking up new answers, new ideas, for existing difficulties. But problem solving, like the decision making discussed in Chapter 12, is not an act of creation conducted in isolation.

The effectiveness of I.E.'s contribution depends upon its ability to develop regular sequences of interaction with a number of managers within the chemical plant as well as in its own division. A free information flow among various levels, peers, and colleagues is crucial. However, we have seen that access to information is severely hindered by the relationships between industrial engineering and the production department, development engineers, and the cost engineer. Access to production department files is limited, the development engineers are reticent to consult industrial engineering or offer information because of the superintendent's influence, and emphasis in the use of data gath-

---

who closely checks the weekly recovery department budget report. However, the engineer is not interested in forcing interaction with the department head on this matter. He wants initiation by production supervision on other problems to which he can respond with services.

ered by the cost engineer is on control and evaluation rather than spurring investigation and innovation. When the I.E. has been given a specific problem that is of some concern to production management, the engineer can overcome these difficulties by dint of interactional energy and hard work. However, it is not so clear-cut when the problems are not apparent and the interest of the I.E. group is in searching for problems. All these various factors in I.E.'s relationships make it difficult to achieve the level of familiarity and commitment implicit in this kind of technical management effort.

Scientific practitioners maintain that creativity, as with most human enterprise, prospers most in a friendly atmosphere of cooperation. This friendly atmosphere is apparently related to a need to free individuals from pressure for uniformity in ideas and to take advantage of sympathetic "resonance" from contemporaries. One student commented that the greatest boon to the innovator is an intellectual collaborator.[22] In our case, the resonance from production personnel that is available to an industrial engineer is very limited. The desire to maintain an air of knowledgeable superiority severely hampers any discussion of innovative ideas with line production managers in the initial stage of consideration. Ideas within I.E. have normally hardened into proposals before they are discussed with a department head.

Valuable innovative effort at the production level depends on constantly receiving information of various kinds to act as a stimulus to encourage and direct thinking. If such information is withheld, the creative process is hampered at one of its most crucial stages, the discovery of a problem.

[22] "In particular, we are impressed by the peculiarly resonant relationship that successful innovators, at least, set up with individuals in their social environment. Similarly, although the means to which people resort in defeating themselves are devious and subtle, we suspect that potentially significant innovators are often stunted through lack of a friend to play the resonating role, and through dependence upon an environment only too willing to exert a dampening influence." Harold D. Lasswell, "The Social Setting of Creativity," in Harold Anderson (ed.), *Creativity and Its Cultivation*, Harper & Row, Publishers, Incorporated, New York, 1959, p. 216.

Conflicts in Controls Operating on Various Groups

The foremen are primarily concerned with maintaining equilibrium and stability in the work situation while meeting very short-term production quotas. They work with I.E. when measurement work helps them to do this, but they have less interest in the longer-term aspects of I.E. methods work.

The department head is also concerned with production but his primary area of evaluation is costs. Certainly his point of view is longer-range than that of the foremen, and he is interested in innovative change. However, the heaviest pressure he feels is still on costs and relatively short-term costs at that. He is not rewarded so much for long-term down trends in cost as he is for not exceeding weekly budgets. Industrial engineering has a major part in setting these budgets, and so his aims in having a loose budget clash with I.E.'s aims in showing "paper" savings by cutting the budget as much as possible.

The superintendent has a greater interest in long-term costs and innovation but he is concerned with using the engineers on his own staff. He maintains that this is cheaper and that he gets better work and trains his future supervisory personnel at the same time. His desire to control all new proposals and promote origination of ideas from within the chemical plant division conflicts with I.E.'s expansionist aims in the methods field.

We have pointed out the desires of both I.E. management and the newer engineers to broaden the application of sophisticated techniques and to increase the power of their division to initiate changes for production supervision. We have observed that this has resulted in an emphasis on *selling* industrial engineering skills. In many cases, the engineer with his repertoire of techniques simply tries to find a problem to which he can apply his expertise. A Nobel physicist, Hans Bethe of Cornell, has commented that the use of computers has led to a tendency to think only about *how* to *solve* problems instead of *analyzing* the problems themselves.

In our case, it is possible that too much emphasis is being placed on the techniques instead of the problems. The I.E. management aggravates this tendency by concentrating monitoring on the needs of the I.E. division as a professional discipline. There is still much lip service to the concept that industrial engineering is a service organization, but the operating emphasis has subtly been shifted away from service to the production department and its often mundane problems. The focus is on developing a discipline and serving the company as a catalyst and innovative force in instituting change and formulating control systems for production.

If a man wants to sell something, he naturally wraps up his product in the biggest and prettiest package. Job proposals by I.E. are sometimes sold by pure salesmanship but not without some poor by-products. Application of high-powered techniques to inappropriate situations has led to disappointing consequences that aggravate the difficulty of obtaining future jobs.

However, the primary fallacy of an emphasis on selling and image making is that it may bear little relevance to the needs of the entire work organization. "Completed staff work" and the introduction of a specialized department point of view as a dominant philosophy tend to substitute small-group decision making for more careful determination and investigation of alternatives. Realistically, in any human organization there is need for selling in order to secure consideration of legitimate alternatives. However, there is a tendency for salesmanship to become the dominant behavioral pattern to satisfy small-group goals. Any such group has a limited outlook, since it works from a circumscribed frame of reference.

From the preceding discussion, we see that the so-called rational man of economic and statistical theory makes optimal choices in a highly specific and clearly defined environment. The most prominent aspects of this environment are awareness of problems, presence of alternatives, and a value system as a criterion in decision making. However, our study indicates that knowledge of the existence of problems and subsequent investigation of alternatives are not simple individual processes but are greatly circumscribed by elements of the organization.

The absence of time consideration is one of the most remarkable limitations in the traditional concepts of rational decision making. Our own observations and those of others indicate that organization decision making is fundamentally a political process. It is inherent in the nature of political realities that the play of conflict, interests, and accommodation takes time. In the same way, the process of search is time-consuming.

The crucial weakness involving time in this organization was the lack of coordination of interests. We have seen that the impetus to a production department to search for alternatives begins when a problem is recognized or a condition is felt to be unsatisfactory. On the other hand, I.E. is continually initiating interaction on unrecognized problems—an earlier stage in the time sequence. Thus not only is the engineer searching for problems when the production department can see no need to do this; he is also engaging in the first step in the creative and decision-making process at a different phase point in the recurring behavioral cycle of consolidation, equilibrium, and change.

Because of the difficulty of completely integrating group goals, bargaining normally depends on the relative strengths of interacting subunits. In reaching decisions through this political process, we have obviously moved a long way from a "rational" choice of the best alternative.

Most of the engineers in our case would say that the observed difficulties between themselves and production personnel were mainly the result of the superintendent's personality and attitude. They would feel that the situation could be improved by changing personnel and/or by having plant management give staff more authority and define its responsibilities more clearly. Some academic observers have shown how personal communications affect an organization and the innovative process.[23] They demonstrate that communication is impaired when demands of the job bring together people who have incompatible conceptions of each other's role in the organization. Drawing on traditional psychology, the engineers tend to oversimplify by im-

[23] Harriet O. Ronken and Paul R. Lawrence, *Administering Changes,* Harvard University, Graduate School of Business Administration, Boston, 1952, pp. 287–320.

plying that the superintendent has a personal frame of reference, a conception of himself and his relationship to the job, that colors what he hears and sees. Under this hypothesis, communication will be facilitated when someone is able to recognize and accept a frame of reference other than his own.

This explanation and emphasis on the difficulty of communication between different personalities are too narrow. As we have seen, technological, structural, and experience influences affect the superintendent's attitude. Simple redefinitions of authority and hierarchical structure are also inadequate, because they neglect the total system of interaction required to complete managerial work. In fact, the entire case illustrates the clash between the requirements for effective administrative patterns under a systems concept of work and the traditional managerial myths and practices associated with industrial management principles and a simplistic human relations theory.

chapter

14

Summary:
The Systems Concept
of Managerial Behavior

It has become fashionable to distinguish alternative styles of administration, giving to the manager the choice of being democrat or autocrat or something in between. The import of the preceding chapters has been that the manager does not have this choice open to him.

Given the division of labor characteristic of modern public and private organizations, the number of special interests and viewpoints represented in diverse groups whose efforts must be coordinated, the inevitable conflicts and incompatibilities among various control measures, and the dynamic shifts in structure and pressures, the manager cannot pick and choose his "style" with impunity. His managerial behavior is a function of the organization of work and the controls operating upon him (rewards and punishments). He must adopt a variety of administrative patterns to fit the varying requirements of the interface: where his job meets others. Successful stabilization contacts require modes of action and reaction different from those of work-flow relationships, to cite just one example.

Superimposed on these day-to-day administrative patterns is the requirement that the manager evolve an adequate control mechanism to assess the functioning of his subpart of the total organization. As a manager, he must assess his direct subordinates' responsiveness to his initiations, just as he must check the behavioral pattern of his lateral relationships. For the most part, the manager operates on a contingency basis, trying to detect where the system of human relations may break down. Insofar as his control measures enable him to identify the problems, he seeks through remedial changes to return the system to equilibrium. This requires changes in his behavior and efforts to change the behavior of others. Failing here and in situations where such deviations occur with significant frequency, the manager seeks to introduce structural change.

Such structural changes necessitate new patterns of behavior on his part as well as of others at the interface. Such innovations require large investments of managerial time and energy. However, the manager, regardless of his level, must be aware that he is part of an *open,* not a *closed,* system. Both internal and external disturbances are likely to require change, and the manager must accept this as an integral part of his job. Many times the pressures for a change build up via subordinates. A good deal of research confirms the generalization that the manager must be prepared to accept initiations from "below" and then seek to convince higher organization levels if changes are to be made.

The balancing of initiations to subordinates with responsiveness to their demands is just one example of the reciprocal and dynamic characteristics of the manager's job. This brings us to a restatement of what we mean by a systems concept of management.

According to the traditional human relations and management theory, the manager is an order giver and receiver. He tells subordinates what to do (delegates part of the responsibilities he has been assigned) and then checks to see whether the results are adequate and communicates this to his superiors. If he is given authority equal to these responsibilities, problems can stem only from wayward subordinates or breakdowns in communication.

In contrast, a systems concept emphasizes that managerial assignments do not have these neat, clearly defined boundaries; rather, the modern manager is placed in a network of mutually dependent relationships. All the strands of the net are not alike; some impose one pattern of initiation and response upon him, some impose very different tempos and rhythms. Furthermore, the tensions and stresses of the net change constantly as the manager seeks to improve his own capacity for obtaining rewards and as others seek to change the structure to be more compatible with their interests. Further dynamism is imposed by the essential instability in the reward-punishment area, analogous to a field of force that tends to shift the direction of the entire network of relationships, first in one way, then another. At one point in time, schedules are all important; saving cash becomes crucial at another; and maximum innovative power takes precedence at another point in time.

Successful managers recognize these dynamics and seek to shift their own behavior, both as a means of detecting changes in the system and responding to the changes that are identified. Rather than becoming frustrated by rules that are always changing, where one is not automatically given the resources needed to do a job (the dimensions of which are in flux), the sophisticated manager recognizes these as hallmarks of the world in which he must live.

He concentrates on marginal adjustments rather than all-or-none responses to pressures and initiations. He trades more attention to this part of his job for a slight diminution in some other aspect. But, importantly, he does not give up the less critical area entirely. For example, in the process of dealing with a work-flow crisis, he still maintains certain essential leadership relationships.

The one enduring objective is the effort to build and maintain a predictable, reciprocating system of relationships, the behavioral patterns of which stay within reasonable physical limits. But this is seeking a moving equilibrium, since the parameters of the system (the division of labor and the controls) are evolving and changing. Thus the manager endeavors to introduce regularity in a world that will never allow him to achieve the ideal. That is the inherent challenge, the essential nature of managerial positions. The manager does not primarily seek to solve a problem once and for all or to achieve a single objective. Rather he endeavors to compensate and improvise, constantly to readjust his behavior, marginally, in response to the ever-changing environment about him. While seeking stability, holding deviations to a minimum, he can approximate the ideal only by constant change.

Thus iterations, dynamic relationships rather than compartmentalized jobs, are basic characteristics. Continuity of flows are the objective, tying together the independent parts of the total operation that have been fractionated by the need for specialists, departments, and organizational checks and balances. There are not the neat beginnings and ends, the sharp demarcation lines between what is inside and what is outside, between what is past, what is present, and what is future that are associated with essentially legalistic, static models of human groups.

Only managers who can deal with uncertainty, with ambiguity, and with battles that are never won but only fought well can hope to succeed. The success must be measured by managers' managers in terms of the ability to maintain the system as an on-going organization rather than to achieve some abstract "victories."

Many managers assume positions of executive responsibility with a topsy-turvy view of their world. They have been taught that, in a "good" organization, a manager spends his time making key decisions, planning, and "motivating" subordinates. When they find their jobs quite different from the ideal, they are likely to blame the petty frictional elements and bide their time, waiting for the kind of job that will have the anticipated heroic proportions.

But the essence of management is not of heroic proportions.

Rather, most managerial behavior is mundane—and frustrating. As we have seen, it involves endless negotiations, trades, and bargaining; meticulous assessment of the state of the organization system; and redirection of one's own and one's subordinates' activities in the light of the information derived from monitoring.

This is the normal state of affairs, not the abnormal or unusual. The price of specialization, multiple experts, and hierarchies is the unworkability of traditional management theories and practices with their neat equating of authority and responsibility and unitary direction. But because organizational behavior is not predicted nor mirrored by the organization chart, one need not despair. The challenge of fulfilling these positions is not a modest one. Enormous personality energy is required to interact in as diverse and multiple roles as those encompassed by the typical executive position. These are not dehumanized, rote conformists who fill the work-a-day world of the large organization.

Too often we have thought of managers as being almost classical entrepreneurs, seeking to maximize some accounting-like profit. But maximization is not a realistic concept in a system such as we have described, where the manager seeks some kind of viable *balance* in the controls to which he responds, in his position vis-à-vis a number of competing sources of both reward and punishment.

Neil Chamberlain has put the argument most succinctly:

> Maximization is logically defensible in a static system, with each moment of time isolated from the time stream. It is logically indefensible in a system in which time runs on without providing any discrete intervals within which there is some reason for maximization.[1]

Further, as Chamberlain notes, maximization is impossible without some common denominator into which all pressures and incentives can be factored. It is fallacious to think that one can add or subtract such diverse "satisfactions" as peace of mind,

[1] Neil Chamberlain, *A General Theory of Economic Process,* Harper & Row, Publishers, Incorporated, New York, 1955, p. 70.

possibility of promotion, salary bonuses, fear of criticism, and the desire to retaliate upon a rival department.

Just as our systems model refutes the apparent incompatibility between change and stability, so too have our observations revealed the association of competition and cooperation. Here, again, our findings have been preceded by Chamberlain's theory. He notes that, as long as there is a scarcity problem, resources have to be allocated, and cooperation depends on a "competitive resolution of the scarcity problem."[2]

Somewhat naïvely we have often restricted our notion of competition to union and management or management and the new employee, bargaining over the terms of a contract. We have long since discovered that bargaining between union and management is a continual process.[3] So too are the relationships among departments both competitive and cooperative. Terms of trade are established and modified continually within the boundaries of the organization. Bargaining is thus a common process made necessary by the fact that within the organization there are many "teams" in the fray; each does not win by the same sets of measures, nor are there enough resources (capital, space, maintenance facilities) to satisfy all equally. One manager inevitably gains at the expense of another.

Some of the characteristics of the systems model that distinguish it from the legalistic model of administrative action may be summarized as follows:

♦ Many styles of administration rather than just one
♦ Monitoring techniques rather than concentration on results
♦ Structural changes introduced by all levels of supervision: an open system
♦ Absence of compartmentalized responsibilities
♦ Mutual dependence and shifting boundaries between groups and activities
♦ Multiple and often incompatible objectives

[2] *Ibid.*, p. 78.
[3] James W. Kuhn, *Bargaining in Grievance Settlement*, Columbia University Press, New York, 1961.

- Emphasis on marginal adjustments, not maximization and fixed decisions; equilibrium and adaptation
- Negotiations and trades, reciprocal action rather than just orders and reports

Unfortunately several generations of business students have been impressed with a distinction between the formal and the informal organization. Traditional human relations doctrine makes this distinction between the way the organization is supposed to function and the results of real people interacting with one another. But there is only one organizational process or system. When management shifts its attention from legal forms of responsibility and authority to the patterns of relationship necessary to accomplish work, there will be no need to refer to false dichotomies. Work output and efficiency are the product of a *system* of relationship, not of individual assignments and motivation.

For the most part, management theory and management principles stress abstract categories and entities rather than *process*. They are usually concerned with the nature of authority and its preservation (when there are multiple hierarchies and staff specialists). Many are purely logical: Planning and setting objectives should come first. Much is static description: The functions performed by typical controllers are surveyed and listed.

As a result management principles fail to deal with the dynamic problems of human systems in action. For example, it is easy to state legalistically that staff advisers should not have authority because, lacking it, they will not destroy the principle of unitary command. But, as we have seen in Chapter 6, the actual conduct of an advisory relationship—the pattern and sequence of contacts and their qualitative characteristics—involve complex and subtle behavioral requirements. In fact, a whole series of interrelationships must synchronize:

- The primary flow of initiations is from work-flow managers to advisory managers *after* monitoring identifies recurring problems or higher-level managers or auditing groups applying pressure.

◆ Advisory managers strictly limit their initiations to both subordinates and superiors of work-flow managers.

◆ In responding to initiations from work-flow-manager subordinates, advisory managers must not reduce the balance of such initiations to the work-flow manager himself.

◆ Limits must be placed on the total number of advisory managers who interact with work-flow managers.

In the absence of these behavioral patterns, we can predict organizational consequences that vitiate the usefulness of these positions:

◆ Reduced initiations from work-flow managers to advisory managers and those that continue are more restrained, guarded, and less effective in communicating real problems.

◆ Advisory contacts are virtually eliminated as part of the total monitoring system of work-flow managers.

◆ Work-flow managers are uneasy about their leadership position vis-à-vis subordinates.

◆ Conflicts over "multiple bosses" must be arbitrated at increasingly higher levels.

Similarly, leadership must be conceived in process terms. It is not simply a matter of diagnosing morale problems, utilizing small-group conference methods, or obtaining loyalty. Rather, leadership involves a total system extending from ongoing measures of job behavior and reciprocities (that identify the need for intervention and the adequacy of the superior-subordinate relationship) to "signals" that structural change and/or the assistance of outside experts is necessary. Leadership behavior must be seen in the total context of managerial action. The manager's relationship with outside auditing and stabilization groups, for example, has direct ramifications for his dealings with subordinates. In turn, subordinates who are engaged in service relationships require a different order of leadership responsiveness than those in simpler work-flow positions.

A process-systems view will assist the firm in avoiding what a colleague has aptly called the "dispatcher theory" of management. As often practiced, this involves dealing with new responsibilities, neglected tasks, and broken rules by naïve additive methods—usually the creation of a new organizational position. If rules are continually broken or something is not being done, a new man is added. Little thought is given to the total complex of relationships that the new position (and the proliferation of others like it) makes necessary or to solving the problem by modifying existing roles or controls.

As in the dispatcher theory, a typical managerial response to the identification of a "problem" is a legalistic search for who is the guilty partly and what rules were violated. A systems approach encourages exploring the organizational sources of the problem and seeks behavioral modifications.

Traditional views of managerial behavior tend to retain their vigor after the organizations in which they were conceived have disappeared. This is not a result of cultural lag only, the hold of the past on the present; it is also attributable to two major interrelated themes in American and Western European political thinking. On the one hand, we think of unitary leadership such that each member of an institution has one and only one superior from whom he accepts initiations and to whom he owes responsiveness. Related to this is the value placed on consensus and an abhorrence of dissent and enduring conflicts of interest.

The modern organization violates both tenets, although we rarely openly admit it. Production and sales do not have completely compatible interests, and the organization-chart manager is usually only one among many sources of power and initiation to which the alert subordinate responds. Bargaining, negotiation, trade-offs, temporary alliances, and revised and reversed decisions are the by-products of complex organizations and are far removed in practice from the simple monolithic pyramids of traditional theory.

Index